THOUGHT'S WILDERNESS

THOUGHT'S WILDERNESS

Romanticism and the Apprehension of Nature

Greg Ellermann

Stanford University Press
Stanford, California

STANFORD UNIVERSITY PRESS
Stanford, California

Printed in the United States of America on acid-free, archival-quality paper

ISBN 9781503628489 (cloth)
ISBN 9781503633018 (electronic)

Library of Congress Control Number: 2021052379

Library of Congress Cataloging-in-Publication Data available upon request.

Cover painting: Johan Christian Dahl, *Cloud Study over Flat Landscape*, 1837. Wikimedia Commons
Cover design: Rob Ehle
Typeset by Newgen North America in 10/14 Minion Pro

for Naomi

Table of Contents

Figures

Acknowledgments

I began thinking my way toward the topic and claims of this book during graduate school. In those years and ever since, William Galperin and Colin Jager have been the very best of mentors. I thank them for their enormous generosity and for the inspiration of their critical writing. They will recognize more than a few of their own thoughts in the pages that follow. I am deeply grateful to Margaret Ronda for many years now of support, intellectual engagement, and enthusiasm about this project. Thanks to my former colleague Jonathan Sachs for good advice and warm hospitality, and for believing in this work.

I want to thank Nathan Brown for responding to several portions of this book, for discussing some of the central problems with me, and for the sustaining force of his philosophical friendship. I appreciate immensely the friends who commented on various chapters, which I know are better for all the care and time that they gave. Thanks to Sean Barry, John Savarese, and Jensen Suther for their thoughtful feedback. In addition, I am indebted to all those who expressed interest in, invited me to talk about, or otherwise encouraged my research, including Ron Blumer, Leslie Brisman, Peter Conroy, Marcie Frank, Josh Gang, Lauren Gillingham, Jonathan Kramnick, Tim Kreiner, Jed Lewinsohn, Katja Lindskog, Anne McCarthy, Tobias Menely, Muffie Meyer, Cynthia Mitchell, Julie Murray, Joe North, Christine Paglialunga, Brian Rejack, Michele Speitz, Anne Terrill, Alan Vardy, and Chris Washington. Thanks, too, to the remarkable human beings who came to the rescue in the spring of 2020, at the beginning of this project's final phase and so much else: Zack

Barnett-Howell, Andy Bruns, Morgan Day Frank, Maggie Deli, Tasha Eccles, Ben Glaser, Alanna Hickey, Priyasha Mukhopadhyay, Melissa Winders, and Shirley Wong.

I sincerely appreciate those who took part in the seminars and conferences where I first presented some of this work, including two seminars on "Anthropocene Historicism" at the American Comparative Literature Association and the North American Society for the Study of Romanticism; conferences on "Expanded Poetics: Romantic, Modernist, Contemporary" in Montreal and on "Form" in Dubrovnik; and a seminar on "The Knowledge of Art" again at the ACLA. Thanks, too, to the participants in several recent reading groups—on the *Grundrisse*; on Weber, Adorno, and social theory; on Heidegger; and on Fichte—who have kept my faith in intellectual exchange alive. I am also happy to express my gratitude to the Keats-Shelley Association of America for their recognition and support, and to Erica Wetter and the two anonymous readers at Stanford University Press for their pivotal roles in the development of this book.

I feel lucky to belong to an amazing community of friends and family in Montreal—a constant in my life for twenty years, even though I (and some others) no longer live there. Thanks especially to JJ and Handy Levine, Dylan and Zoë Cousineau, David Barclay, Eleni Castro, Tim Castro, François Dansereau, Heather Hayes, Claire Hurtig, Evan Miller, Rochelle Ross, and Cee Strauss. Thanks to Laura Fisher and Ali Qadeer for their love and friendship over the long term. I am always grateful to David Hensley and Ivana Djordjevic for their generosity and for many convivial evenings, including at and around the Cinémathèque.

My family has been a source of abundant love and care. Thanks to my parents, Marti and Ray Ellermann, for absolutely everything, but especially for believing that this book was worthwhile and for taking on my struggles and successes as their own. Thanks to Jon, Kate, and Xavier Ellermann for their love and many kindnesses, and to Jon (again) for sharing with me his knowledge of the world. Thanks also go to some very old friends, now effectively family: Russell Barnhart, Oliver Edsforth, and Asher Lack. I am so grateful to Norman Levine and Penny Cousineau-Levine for their deep affection and their ongoing interest in my work.

I know that I cannot adequately express the depth of my love for those two beautiful souls who have been closest to me while I was completing this book: Abraham Levine-Ellermann and Naomi Levine. Thanks to Abe for taking me on daily (at least) walks in the park, for (sometimes) napping when I needed to write, and for the astonishing beauty and charm of his presence. This book is for Naomi, whose love and intelligence have shaped every word. Her incisive responses to the manuscript, her impeccable sense of prose style, and her faith in the face of my own doubts have made it what it is.

An earlier and substantially different version of chapter 3 appeared in *Essays in Romanticism* 23.1 (2016). An earlier and substantially different version of a portion of chapter 6 appeared in *European Romantic Review* 29.3 (2018). My thanks to Liverpool University Press and to Taylor & Francis for permission to republish.

THOUGHT'S WILDERNESS

Introduction

Like many romantics, Percy Shelley was drawn to wilderness. The language of wild nature recurs in his poetry in often surprising ways. For Shelley, wilderness is not a tangled wood or a craggy mountain face. It is nature in flight from consciousness: a manifold of evanescent forms. In *Prometheus Unbound* (1819), he writes of a "swift cloud that wings the wide air's wildernesses."[1] Meanwhile, in the famous "Ode" (also 1819), he hails the "wild West Wind . . . breath of Autumn's being." Such images of "unseen presence" are not only images of the natural world.[2] They also evoke a state of consciousness, a poetic or aesthetic state, in which wilderness might be perceived. In a phrase borrowed from Shelley, I call this "thought's wilderness"—a relation of mind to nature, yet a relation without mastery or control.[3]

Titled after Shelley's words, this book shows how romantic writing circumvents the domination of nature that is essential to modern capitalism. Moving between the poetry and philosophy of the period, I find an attunement to nature's ephemeral, ungraspable forms: clouds of vapor, a trace of ruin, deep silence, and the "world-surrounding ether."[4] For the writers featured here, including Immanuel Kant, G. W. F. Hegel, Mary Wollstonecraft, William Wordsworth, and Percy Shelley, nature is fleetingly sensed but never finally grasped. This book describes how nature's vanishing—its vulnerability and its flight from apprehension—becomes a philosophical and political problem. Of course, the romantics still try to present nature aesthetically. They do so by developing what I term a poetics of wilderness—a poetics that is attentive to fleeting presence and that seeks to let things be.[5] Trying to imagine what ultimately eludes capture, the romantics recognize the complicity between conceptual and economic domination; they see how thought itself becomes a technology for control. This insight, I argue, motivates romantic efforts to think past capitalist instrumentality and its devastation of the world.

Thought's Wilderness is not a social or an environmental history.[6] Yet it does examine the interconnected histories of romantic studies and Marxist critical theory: at the conjuncture of these intellectual formations, I identify new methodological possibilities for the study of romantic nature. This book renarrates the history of romantic studies by pursuing unexpected affiliations between the field-defining scholarship of M. H. Abrams, Paul de Man, and Geoffrey Hartman and the critical theory of Max Horkheimer, Alfred Sohn-Rethel, and Theodor Adorno. In doing so, it foregrounds the political implications of familiar literary critical statements about nature and the imagination—often cited now as expressions of naive quietism. This book contests the prevailing historicist and ecocritical consensus by arguing that the dialectic of nature and imagination is, in fact, an inherently political matter.

My claim is that revisiting debates about nature around 1960 can give us a fresh vantage on nature around 1800—and today. While recent ecological thinking rejects distinctions between social and natural processes, human and nonhuman things, I maintain that a concept of nature is analytically and politically indispensable. Since the 1980s, in romantic studies and the broader environmental humanities, "nature" has been regarded with consistent skepticism.[7] There are, however, compelling reasons to preserve such a concept. For one, as Dalia Nassar observes, none of the proposed alternatives—Bruno Latour suggests "the Parliament of Things," while Timothy Morton offers "being-with" and "coexistence"—have real philosophical benefits.[8] Concepts like coexistence, she argues, do "not tell us anything other than that things stand next to one another. *What* they are, *how* they stand next to one another, and *what their relations are* remain unclear."[9] The things themselves get lost in "'the constant flux.'"[10] This impulse toward homogeneity has profound political implications. In Rei Terada's assessment, the contemporary theory of ecology and objects— premised on such claims as "'Everything in the universe gets to access everything else'"—is, at its core, "an epistemology of sparkly universal colonialism."[11] Despite the now-familiar charge that "nature" simplifies or abstracts, it is "ecology" that reduces all things to abstract equivalence. The concept of nature, on the other hand, allows thinking to begin with difference, or nonidentity.[12] And only thus can thinking "juxtapos[e]," as Andreas Malm remarks, "relations and laws of motion internal to *capitalist* society" with "relations and laws of motion internal to *nature*."[13] Without a concept of nature, thought's limits are the limits of the world that capitalism has made.

To think nature's nonidentity means developing new forms of thought—forms that might suspend or interrupt the pursuit of mastery. In the philosophy of romantic idealism, the notion of apprehension presents just such a possibility. On one hand, apprehensive consciousness grasps or appropriates nature. It seems to bear out Adorno's claim that "our knowledge of nature is . . . preformed by the demand that we *dominate* nature."[14] On the other hand, as the romantics suggest, apprehension may be *re*formed, in the name of a less demanding relation to the world. This ambivalence persists, I shall argue, in the romantics' frequent recourse to the term.

In Kant's *Critique of Pure Reason* (1781/87), for example—interpreted since Hegel's earliest writings as a theory of appropriative consciousness—apprehension is a central concept: a synthetic activity of the mind required for the cognition of nature. As Kant explains it, if "every intuition contains a manifold," then "in order for this manifold to become unity of intuition . . . it must first be gone through and gathered together. This act I call the *synthesis of apprehension*."[15] Significantly, this picture of mental activity is also a picture of labor. It draws out the sense of physical grasping latent in the word *apprehension* itself.[16] Kant's language of "going through and gathering together" evokes, perhaps, a solitary reaper in a field. For an early critic, J. G. Schlosser, Kant's philosophy is better described as a "manufacturing industry for the production of mere forms."[17] These images, Kant's and Schlosser's alike, suggest an intimacy between consciousness and economic life, between intellectual and manual work—both of which take nature as an object.

The romantics see the apprehensive mind as distinctly modern, insofar as it both reflects and participates in the capitalist mastery of nature.[18] According to Friedrich Hölderlin, modern consciousness entails an "original separation of the most tight unity of object and subject," a separation that "injur[es] the nature" of "being."[19] It is essentially alienated, then, marked by division from the world. "We, with nature, are fallen," he says, "and what once, one can believe, was one, now struggles against itself, and mastery and servitude alternate on both sides."[20] The distance from nature that Hölderlin depicts is an instrument of manipulation and control.[21] It promises freedom—from determination as much as from want or need—yet it cannot make good on its promise. As Shelley explains, in the course of a similar discussion, "Man, having enslaved the elements, remains himself a slave," condemned to labor for the profit of a few.[22] This discourse of mastery and servitude, *Herrschaft* and *Knechtschaft*, is not just metaphoric. It connotes the advancing technical control of nature, as well as the separation that makes it possible. It evokes too the plantation slavery that Susan Buck-Morss, after C. L. R. James and Eric Williams, characterizes as "a quintessentially modern institution of capitalist exploitation."[23] This association is no accident, as others have observed: capitalism defines the unwaged—primarily lower-class women and the enslaved—as a "natural resource" (Silvia Federici) or as "living *ore*" (Achille Mbembe) from which value can be extracted without limit.[24] In sum, the romantic theory of consciousness and nature involves the whole of modern social life.

There is no returning to simple unity with nature; history's path cannot be traveled in reverse. But in the thought of nature's nonidentity, romanticism holds out a hope of something else: a poetic form of apprehension. While never entirely separable from appropriative consciousness, or from the laws of commerce that condition it, poetic apprehension suggests—if only in fleeting moments—that the mastery of nature need not run its course.[25] The romantic poetics of wilderness, developed in various ways from this thought, reminds us that another relation to the world is possible.

This book's argument proceeds in three stages. In the first chapter, I examine the connections between romanticism and Marxist critical theory. Reading the canonical romantic criticism of Abrams, de Man, and Hartman alongside contemporary work by Horkheimer, Sohn-Rethel, and Adorno, I bring out the crucial, and often overlooked, political-economic dimension of those mid-twentieth-century narratives about romanticism that still inform literary studies. I propose that the well-known scholarly debate about the apocalyptic imagination intersects with the critical theorists' investigation of capitalist abstraction and the domination of nature. Both the romanticists and the critical theorists, I contend, rely on a notion of apprehensive consciousness. Thus, this first chapter establishes the methodological coordinates for the book, outlining an interpretation of romanticism responsive to the reality of conceptual and economic abstraction. This distinguishes my approach to consciousness and nature from the critique of ideology pursued by the new historicism. As the chapter ends, I look to Wordsworth, the poet at the heart of midcentury romanticist debate. Juxtaposing the famous "marriage of mind and nature" with the critical theory of "real abstraction," I find in Wordsworth's poetry a glimpse of nature at the threshold of apprehension.

The next two chapters are philosophical, and together they demonstrate how the romantics themselves conceived the relations among consciousness, nature, and social life. I focus on Kant and Hegel, the two most influential European philosophers of the period, both of whom sound out the limits of apprehensive consciousness. For Kant, whom I discuss in chapter 2, it is natural history—in its catastrophic and evolutionary forms—that the mind can never quite grasp. For Hegel, whom I discuss in chapter 3, apprehensive consciousness turns against itself: in seeking freedom from nature by dominating it, the modern (Kantian) subject reveals its dependence on the world. Hegel insists that this dialectic of consciousness corresponds to an economic reality—to the abstract exchange value and the exploitation of nature that characterize early industrial capitalism. These philosophers do not just anticipate Marxist critical theory, which likewise sees modernity as a process of violent abstraction. They also show, in ways that historicism has still to account for, that romanticism is its own "critical consciousness."[26]

The final three chapters move from the philosophical to the aesthetic, examining the poetics of wilderness as practiced by Wollstonecraft, Wordsworth, and Shelley. Chapter 4 addresses Wollstonecraft's theory of poetic language, elaborated in the Scandinavian *Letters* (1796) and in the essay "On Poetry" (1797). According to Wollstonecraft, the figure of anthropomorphism is a memorial to violence—to the appropriative humanization of nature. Challenging poetic and aesthetic convention, including the generalities of the picturesque, Wollstonecraft's own experiments in figure record a ruinous history of nature in commerce. In chapters 5 and 6, I turn to Wordsworth and Shelley, who both call on poetry to interrupt the pursuit of mastery. Chapter 5 reads the famous lyric "There was a Boy" (1798)—later included in *The Prelude* (1805/50)—to show how Wordsworth portrays ephemeral appearance as a gift or an "accidental revelation" of nature. Chapter 6 attends to metaphor in *Queen Mab* (1813), and it aligns the poem's figures of spirit with the ethereal atmospheres of natural philosophy. I suggest that Shelley's ethereal poetics expresses a hope for reconciliation with nature. The book concludes by returning to *Prometheus Unbound*, where Shelley invokes "common love" as another way of being in and with—but not quite having—the world.

If, as I am arguing, the concept of nature remains vital, romanticism is uniquely able to show us why. I offer here what might be described as a defense of romanticism—both as a literary and philosophical movement *and* as a field of study singularly attentive to the poetics of nature. At a time when the future of romanticism looks less and less certain, *Thought's Wilderness* insists on the importance of thinking romantic nature again.

1 Romanticism and Real Abstraction

Romantic studies has recently seen a renewed interest in the politics of aesthetic form. This new political formalism differs from its predecessors in its ambivalence toward the project of ideology critique and in its insistence on the truth content of art. No thinker has had a greater influence on these developments than Theodor Adorno.[1] In many ways, the current fascination with Adorno and his collaborators in critical theory is unsurprising.[2] Writing and reading in a moment defined by multiple and intersecting crises—professional, economic, environmental—romanticists have found in Adorno an ally. In language that echoes the poets and philosophers of the early nineteenth century, who are frequent points of reference for him, Adorno speaks incisively, and often movingly, about capitalism's domination of nature and the critical or utopian possibilities latent in aesthetic forms.[3] For romanticists, Adorno appears to anticipate our present-day concerns, while affirming the politics and aesthetics of the romantic era.

I share the intuition of powerful affinities between Adornian critical theory and romanticism. In this chapter, I offer, in precise historical and theoretical terms, a new account of their commonalities. Rather than start from anticipations of critical theory in romantic-era writing, I begin with the conjuncture of two major midcentury intellectual formations: the critical theory of Max Horkheimer, Herbert Marcuse, Alfred Sohn-Rethel, and Adorno, among others; and the great flourishing of academic romanticism in the work of M. H. Abrams, Paul de Man, and Geoffrey Hartman.[4] My aim is not primarily to establish direct lines of influence between these projects, though such lines do exist. Rather, I read these bodies of work together, with an eye to their shared intellectual and political horizons.

This allows me to demonstrate a few things. First, I propose that a certain romanticism does inform critical theory, insofar as the latter asks questions about consciousness and the mastery of nature that recur in the foundational works of romantic studies. The romantic vision underpinning Horkheimer and Adorno's narrative of instrumental reason is remarkably like that of Abrams and Hartman. Common romantic-era influences are not the only explanation for their shared vision. My suggestion is that romantic studies as we know it developed in response to some of the same intellectual and political exigencies that motivate critical theory.

Further, I show that reading critical theory and romantic criticism together illuminates the crucial political-economic aspect of a story about romanticism that continues to inform literary studies. To the extent that the romantic critique of modernity must be understood in political-economic terms, it remains undertheorized. By attending to the thought of Adorno and Sohn-Rethel—particularly to the notion of "real abstraction"—I aim to give new depth and unity to the classic problems of romantic criticism: the critique of modernity and of what Shelley called the "calculating principle," the relationship between imagination and nature, the structure of the poetic image.[5] Such matters are never purely aesthetic, nor should they be dismissed as ideological distractions; my method is not that of the new historicism.[6] As I demonstrate, these seemingly discrete features of romanticism (as influentially outlined by the critics of the mid-twentieth century) speak to a single, abiding concern: the mastery of nature in the era of early industrial capitalism.

Romanticism at the Midcentury

I begin by considering some points of contact between the critical theorists and their romanticist contemporaries. My focus is a remarkable set of texts, published largely in the 1950s and '60s, that emerged from two very different intellectual circles. The best known of these include Horkheimer and Adorno's *Dialectic of Enlightenment* (written in the mid-1940s but not published widely until 1969), Abrams's *The Mirror and the Lamp* (1953), Hartman's *Wordsworth's Poetry*, and Marcuse's *One-Dimensional Man* (both 1964). To arrange these works in a single chronological list is already to make a claim for their relationship, for their participation in a shared "spirit of the age," as Abrams defined romanticism itself in a 1963 essay. There are closer connections too. As a professor at Cornell (starting in 1960) and at Johns Hopkins (starting in 1968), de Man served as an important conduit for the ideas of Walter Benjamin, Adorno, and Peter Szondi, all thinkers associated with the tradition of critical theory.[7] Hartman, who also taught at Cornell in the mid-'60s (where he became close friends with de Man), would engage throughout his later career with the thought of Benjamin and Adorno.[8] Looking further back to the 1950s, de Man's affiliations with the French journal *Critique* and with interpreters of Hegel such as Jean Wahl and Jean Hyppolite should also be understood as important elements in the story of romantic studies. In these years, de Man would compose one of his earliest major essays: a critique of Martin Heidegger's interpretations of Friedrich Hölderlin that anticipates, in often strikingly similar terms, Adorno's work on the same topic.[9] Throughout it all, Abrams was based at Cornell, where he spent his entire academic career beginning in 1945.

To tell this story as I do is not to deny the enormous differences among these thinkers; even describing this generation of critics as involved in a shared project will provoke skepticism in some. Abrams, in particular, was openly hostile to the deconstructive turn taken by romantic studies in the 1970s.[10] Nevertheless, I submit that these scholars collectively generated an image of romanticism, which, in many ways, is still ours. This is an image of poetics and politics, to be sure, but its greatest originality in US academia was its insistence on the philosophical stakes of romantic literary writing. Of course, as we know now and as I will affirm throughout this book, none of these elements can be separated: in romanticism, poetry is politics is thinking. But it is hard to overstate the "peculiar power" of Abrams's early work, published as it was in a moment still marked by F. R. Leavis's negative judgments about the romantics.[11] Alongside more stylistically oriented critics such as Earl Wasserman and Walter Jackson Bate, Abrams wrote against the lingering antiromanticism of the academy. In so doing, he raised, with unprecedented conceptual precision, the question of consciousness in its complex relation to nature.

To the present day, romantic studies is defined by Abrams's articulation of this question, which began in his study of "metaphors of mind" in *The Mirror and the Lamp* and continued in his classic 1957 essay on the figure of "the correspondent breeze": an "air-in-motion" pervading the romantic lyric that is "not only a property of the landscape, but also a vehicle for radical changes in the poet's mind."[12] By the 1960s, Abrams's account of the "marriage of mind and nature" had become a critical touchstone.[13] Accordingly, in *The Visionary Company*, Abrams's student Harold Bloom could present "the dialectic of nature and imagination" as the starting point for all romantic writing.[14] Yet for some readers Abrams's insistence on a relatively unproblematic approach to these "conjugal metaphors" had begun to look, at best, naive.[15] As Hartman wrote in *Wordsworth's Poetry*, it was a sense of the more "deeply paradoxical character of Wordsworth's dealings with nature" that linked his work to related investigations by de Man and Bloom.[16]

In what follows, I reanimate these various positions by returning to the moment in which they were first staked out. I am not, however, telling the story of deconstruction or the rise of "theory" in the US academy.[17] My focus in this chapter is an earlier phase in the history of romantic studies, when the field's affinities with Adornian critical theory were arguably most significant.[18] Or, to frame it another way, this chapter concerns the work of the romanticists before they have fully absorbed the lessons of structuralism.[19] Attentive readers will see that I am primarily engaged with books and essays written before 1970 or '71. The romantic criticism of the midcentury is shaped by what de Man would later describe as "the thematic vocabulary of consciousness and of temporality that was current at the time."[20] It is this vocabulary, I suggest, that allowed the problem of nature, in its relation to imagination and to social life, to emerge with unmatched clarity. The outmoded methodology at which de Man gestures is, of course, phenomenology. Others have traced the influence of philosophers such as Edmund Husserl, Heidegger, and Jean-Paul Sartre on the development of romantic studies.[21] I stress that de Man's and Hartman's work in the 1960s should be seen, in part, as a critique of phenomenological approaches to consciousness—a critique exactly contemporary to similar investigations being undertaken by Adorno. This major, and often overlooked, area of overlap between romantic studies and critical theory will be a concern in the next section.

Before returning to the question of nature and imagination, let me offer a brief overview of critical theory as it developed after the Second World War. Having spent the war years in exile, mostly in New York and California, Horkheimer and Adorno returned home to Frankfurt in 1949. (Neither Marcuse nor Sohn-Rethel, who had escaped to the US and to England respectively, returned to Germany at this point.)[22] Back at the University of Frankfurt, Horkheimer and Adorno continued their long-standing collaboration as co-directors of the Institute for Social Research and as lecturers in philosophy and sociology. Much of the work done at and around the Institute was sociological, including important studies of social-scientific method; positivism and the status of facts; mass psychology; and rationalization.[23] Nevertheless, Adorno's present-day readers tend to focus on his contributions to aesthetics, composed at the same time and often in dialogue with the sociological research: "On Lyric Poetry and Society" (1957–58), "Parataxis: On Hölderlin's Late Poetry" (1963–65), and *Aesthetic Theory* (1961–69; published posthumously in 1970) have all been influential.[24]

These writings offer a uniquely significant appraisal of the romantic and postromantic tradition. They also bear out Robert Kaufman's claim that "fundamental aspects of a Left 'critical aesthetics'" can be traced back to romanticism.[25] In *Aesthetic Theory*, for example, romanticism plays a central role. Here, Adorno argues that in capitalist modernity art loses all self-evidence as a category: it seeks "to pull itself free from its own concept as from a shackle."[26] Since at least the mid-nineteenth century, all true art has expressed an unfulfilled "longing for the new."[27] Faced with an intolerable reality that it can neither transcend nor affirm, "Art must turn against itself, in opposition to its own concept, and thus become uncertain of itself right into its innermost fiber."[28] In the context of such statements, Adorno's appeals to late romantics such as Baudelaire and Mallarmé are not surprising; these poets have often been recognized for their struggles with aesthetic norms. Yet throughout *Aesthetic Theory* and elsewhere, Adorno shows an interest in the range of romantic art. He looks to Goethe, Hölderlin, Beethoven, Shelley, Keats, Schubert, Heine, Hugo, and Poe, among others, as exemplary aesthetic cases.[29] The redefinition of the artwork as a work of "self-negation" appears to be, as Espen Hammer has it, "mainly a late romantic achievement."[30]

Still, it must be acknowledged that Adorno's comments on romanticism are ambivalent. In his 1958–59 lectures on aesthetics, romantic art is described as a "worldview art" in which, as in Wagner's operas, the idea or "intention" of the work cannot be harmonized with its "actual material content."[31] In *Aesthetic Theory*, Schiller and Hegel are charged with the "repression" of natural beauty and with a "subjective usurpation [of nature] that degrades what is not subordinate to the subject . . . to mere material."[32] Such claims are not so different from those pursued by Adorno's romanticist contemporaries, for whom romantic poetry is concerned with nature as apprehended (sometimes violently) by "verbal figures and structures of consciousness."[33] Adorno too remarks on "the violence that the artwork—a pure artifact—inflicts on nature."[34] At the same time, he insists that art is singularly capable of communicating on nature's behalf. In what follows, I shall argue that the literary critical problematic of nature and imagination develops from a shared sense of "nature's wounds."[35]

For now, I simply suggest that the question of Adorno's romanticism is also that of nature's status in his thought. Consider, again, Adorno's account of the artwork. In *Aesthetic Theory*, he notes that nature and art, as objects of aesthetic experience, tend to evoke one another.[36] This points to a more intimate relation at the level of aesthetic form. For Adorno, form is not an abstract category, because it is bound up with the "material content" of the work.[37] As he famously puts it, form is "sedimented content."[38] To describe aesthetic form as "sedimented content" is to recall the artwork's social and intellectual situation—a situation that the work often indicates only by withdrawing from it. The phrase also speaks to a process of historical transformation, whereby the purposive or contentful features of an object become, over time, pure formal ornamentation. In his lectures, Adorno explains that "with the everyday objects we use, the ornamentations are usually rudiments or residues of necessities from earlier phases of production that have survived."[39] "The ornament," he observes, "is the scar that appeared on a vase at the point where it could not be made at the potter's wheel without such an interruption."[40] Sedimented content includes even those acts of making that give form to the work's materials—to stone, light, sound, and so on. In the complex relations among form, content, and material, Adorno sees nature surviving in art.[41]

Adorno insists that all art preserves a memory or trace of nature. These traces are most legible in works "divested of the subject's intentions"[42]—works that present, without directly mimicking, nature in its muteness and indeterminate beauty. Significantly, Adorno takes Goethe's "Wanderer's Night Song" (1780) and Beethoven's *Kreutzer Sonata* (1803) as examples. About Goethe's lyric he writes, "Through its language the poem imitates what is unutterable in the language of nature. No more should be meant by the ideal of form and content coinciding in a poem, if the ideal itself is to be more than a hollow praise."[43] If romantic art is dominated by an idea (Wagner), and if it subsumes nature under spirit (Schiller and Hegel), it also expresses at the level of form a longing for release—a wish to cast off subjective intent and to listen as nature speaks (Goethe and Beethoven). As we are beginning to see, for Adorno, romanticism is its own "critical consciousness."[44]

Still, the subjection of nature in art cannot simply be undone. Art has no history apart from the progressive mastery of the material. It belongs to a long history of culture as the artifactual and technical remaking of nature. As

Adorno describes it, "The course of this progress, which plowed under everything that did not accommodate to identity with spirit, was also a course of devastation."[45] Only despite itself does art promise an end to mastery. There are no firm distinctions to be drawn between bad and good, or violent and nonviolent, art; all artifacts leave the scars of their making. But even in capitalist modernity some artworks "hold fast to the idea of reconciliation with nature": they "have consistently felt the urge," Adorno writes, "as if in need of a breath of fresh air, to step outside of themselves."[46] In their efforts to give autonomy to the material, or to suspend the subject's imposition on its others, these works seek to let nature speak. Art is thus a product of violence against nature as well as a promise of its end. In the experience of aesthetic form, Adorno tells us, we encounter nature as a "raw material" and as the hope of reconciliation.[47] I have already suggested that similar thoughts can be found in the romantic criticism of the midcentury. I turn directly now to the notion of a "dialectic of nature and imagination," showing how this influential formulation in romantic studies intersects with Adorno's aesthetics.

Nature, Imagination, Intentionality

Since *The Mirror and the Lamp*, no issue has been so important to romantic studies as the relation of mind to nature. Moreover, there has never been a moment in the history of the field when this was not a political concern.[48] When Abrams explains that "the mind is imaged by romantic poets as projecting life, physiognomy, and passion into the universe," he also notes, in the language of midcentury humanism, that this vision of the imaginative mind responds to a deeply felt need: it is "an attempt to overcome the sense of man's alienation from the world by healing the cleavage between subject and object, between the vital, purposeful, value-full world of private experience and the dead postulated world of extension, quantity, and motion."[49] The oppositions structuring Abrams's claim—mind and nature, subject and object, life and death, value and fact, quality and quantity—define the critical discourse of the period. So too does a sense of romanticism as the poetic and philosophical response to these separations. A few years later, Abrams writes about the figure of the correspondent breeze that "the moving air lent itself preeminently to the aim of tying man back into the environment."[50] Through its most distinctive metaphors, romantic poetry strives for reunification with nature; it is a kind of therapy for alienated beings.

There are obvious shortcomings in such an account. For one, Abrams often returns nature to the status of metaphor. No "emblem of the free Romantic spirit" can bridge the gap between subject and object.[51] All the same, Abrams's account is significant for its insistence on the politics of nature and consciousness. To imagine nature, or to know it poetically, is to challenge the dominant modes of knowledge in the period: the mechanistic and the utilitarian, in Abrams's lexicon. If romanticism attends to "the life of things" in all their particularity, it does so against the grain of an epistemic modernity, according to which nature (now a "world of extension, quantity, and motion") can only show us the basic equivalence and even exchangeability of material things.

Abrams's humanistic narrative is informed by a very particular diagnosis of modernity. Associated with such influential, and profoundly different, thinkers as Max Weber and Carl Schmitt, the diagnosis pivots on notions of disenchantment and rationalization.[52] We could describe it as a theory of enlightenment, in Horkheimer and Adorno's sense: "The mind," they write, "conquering superstition, is to rule over disenchanted nature. Knowledge, which is power, knows no limits, either in its enslavement of creation or in its deference to worldly masters."[53] For Horkheimer and Adorno, as for Abrams, nature is disenchanted and made knowable by reduction to "abstract quantities."[54] Moreover, knowledge is power, because such conceptual abstraction is inseparable from the technical and economic domination it enables; a "world of extension, quantity, and motion" is a precondition for the "unmitigated exercise of the calculating faculty," as Shelley describes it.[55] Now, I am not claiming that midcentury romantic criticism offers anything like a sufficient political-economic analysis. Rather, I am observing the affiliations between romantic studies and critical theory, including a shared sense of modernity's fundamental coordinates. I suggest that the history of modernity underpinning romantic criticism is already, however conceptually thin, a history of capitalism and its mastery of nature. Thus, the dialectic of nature and imagination is a fundamentally political problem. In recalling this, we move closer to the political-economic thinking of the romantics themselves.

We have seen how, in Abrams, the relationship between nature and imagination is conceived as essentially harmonious. All the same, there is a hierarchy latent in this apparent harmony. As Abrams writes, in an important study of book VI in Wordsworth's *Prelude*, "Man's infinite hopes can never be matched by the world as it is and man as he is, for these exhibit a discrepancy no less than that between his 'hopes that pointed to the clouds' and the finite height of the

Alpine pass."[56] There is consolation, he continues, only in the realization that human hope is limitless; this is "the measure of man's dignity and greatness."[57] Following the familiar logic of the sublime, Abrams converts a loss into a gain: the poet may be thwarted in his desires, but nature's failure to give fulfillment lets him look forward to "a marriage between subject and object, mind and nature, which creates a new world out of the old world of sense."[58] In this account, imagination always emerges as the dominant term. Despite its conciliatory, even "healing" intent, Abrams's humanist sublime subordinates nature to consciousness. In Adorno's apt assessment, "the 'dignity' that is native only to humans, and which gives them a superior status in relation to everything else," degrades nature to the level of "mere material."[59]

Abrams's contemporaries were quick to observe these tensions. Bloom, for one, would conclude that the romantics were "not poets of nature" at all but prophets and "hero[es] of the imagination."[60] Equally attuned to the conflicts implicit in Abrams's account, Hartman and de Man offer more nuanced pictures of the poetic mind in its relation to nature. While Hartman concurs that the romantics are not "fundamentally nature poets," the adverb points to an enormous difference from Bloom.[61] Indeed, the great drama of Hartman's Wordsworth book lies in its awareness of the poet's efforts to stay true to nature, despite the autonomy of his mind; "the secret behind his fidelity" is the ethical and political core of the analysis.[62] Here I see romantic studies drawing surprisingly near to critical theory. I thus reconstruct, in some detail, Hartman's theory of imagination, going on to address its connections to de Man's 1960 study "The Intentional Structure of the Romantic Image." As I have noted, Hartman's and de Man's earlier work responds to phenomenological currents in mid-twentieth-century thought. Centered on the notion of "intentionality," the romanticists' critique of phenomenology parallels, in many ways, Adorno's—according to which "phenomenology only radicalizes the tendency to domination (Herrschaft) that underlies all forms of philosophical idealism."[63] In light of these connections, I read the romantic criticism of the midcentury—only somewhat against the grain—as an ethical and political project motivated by the possibility of a nonviolent relation to nature.

Like Abrams's, Hartman's account of the Wordsworthian imagination turns on book VI of The Prelude. Departing, only slightly at first, from the work of his soon-to-be colleague, Hartman argues that Wordsworth's "disappointment" on crossing the Simplon Pass is "a prophetic instance of that blindness to the external world which is the tragic, pervasive, and necessary condition of the mature poet."[64] Hartman's term for such blindness is "imagination." In the 1850 *Prelude* (the version Hartman relies on), Wordsworth recalls the awakening of this mental power in the moment of realizing he has unknowingly "*crossed the Alps*":

> Imagination—here the Power so called
> Through sad incompetence of human speech,
> That awful Power rose from the mind's abyss
> Like an unfathered vapour that enwraps,
> At once, some lonely traveler. I was lost;
> Halted without an effort to break through;
> But to my conscious soul I now can say–
> "I recognise thy glory."[65]

From these well-known verses, Hartman adduces the fundamental workings of imagination. Seemingly tied to an experience of external nature, the imagination reveals itself to be an autonomous power. Indeed, it manifests itself "like an unfathered vapour" only after the poet has crossed the Alps. The crossing's belated impact loosens, or even gives the lie to, the bond between nature and consciousness. In Wordsworth's language, the "glory" of imagination is also its "strength / Of usurpation" (599–600); when we are fully in its grasp, "the light of sense / Goes out" (600–601). Despite the usual associations with intuition or visuality, imagination in Hartman strives to be free of the sensible world.

Thus, the "shock" of imagination is radically disorienting: the poet seeks to commune with nature, but the result is nature's annihilation from his consciousness.[66] The triumph of imagination, with its "awful power," is inseparable from loss, and the self-assertion of consciousness takes place at the expense of nature. In Hartman's often-theological vocabulary, such a violent "'conversion' or 'turning' of the mind" is a kind of apocalypse; the imagination, he famously writes, is "*consciousness of self raised to apocalyptic pitch*."[67] Later, he explains that the imagination is "apocalyptic" insofar as it is driven by "an inner necessity to cast out nature."[68] The process of its sublime self-revelation demands an end of the given world. When Wordsworth sees in a mountain chasm the "Characters of the great Apocalypse" (VI.638), his imagination may be returning from out of itself, but only to affirm its power to make the world anew. "I sometimes use 'apocalyptic,'" Hartman writes, "to characterize any strong desire to cast out nature and to achieve an unmediated contact with the principle of things."[69] According to the movements of consciousness described by

Hartman, this "principle of things" appears to be the imagination. Extending into and then recoiling back from nature, imagination seeks reunion with itself.

In many ways, then, Hartman recapitulates Abrams's argument in a privative mode. Insisting too on the transcendence of nature by imagination, Hartman draws out the loss, even the violence implicit in this relation. This is made especially clear in a now-classic passage from *Wordsworth's Poetry*:

> Imagination, we are usually told, vitalizes and animates. Especially the Romantic Imagination. Yet here it stands closer to death than life, at least in its immediate effect. The poet is isolated and immobilized by it; it obscures rather than reveals nature; the light of the senses goes out. Only in its secondary action does it vitalize and animate, and even then not nature but a soul that realizes its individual greatness, a greatness independent of sense and circumstance. A tertiary effect does finally reach nature, when the soul assured of inner or independent sources of strength goes out from and of itself.[70]

Here, Hartman delineates the three-part movement he sees as definitive of the "romantic imagination." From a condition of immobility or obscurity, prompted by an encounter with nature, the poet's mind awakens to its "greatness independent of sense." Consciousness comes alive and feels its own power in recognizing its freedom from nature. Finally, in a kind of pleasing confusion, the poet overlays the mind's inner greatness onto nature itself. The given world is remade in the mind's image. This trajectory of imagination recalls the moments of the sublime in Kant's philosophy.[71] From a violent disjuncture between imaginative "apprehension" and "comprehension"; to its resolution by an indeterminate idea of reason; to a final misattribution of the sublime to nature instead of the mind—each aspect of Kant's discussion finds an analogue in Hartman's thought.[72] These theories of the imagination correlate, while enforcing the hierarchy between, consciousness and nature. It is thus Wordsworth's ethical and political task, Hartman adds—uniquely among his critical contemporaries—to defer or even defuse imaginative apocalypse. "To stay with nature" against its usurping by imagination "became . . . a moral act: a fidelity beyond what nature itself seemed to urge."[73] With this final claim, Hartman echoes Adorno's theory of the artwork. The poem's "developing structure is an expressive reaction," he notes, to the violence of imagination as well as the precarious, but ongoing, life of nature.[74]

Looking further back, we find a different notion of imagination in Hartman's work. In "Romanticism and Anti-self-consciousness" (1962), for example, imagination is redemptive; it is the power of mind by which we might transcend our self-reflective and self-alienated subjectivity.[75] Romantic imagination, according to this earlier and wider-ranging account, promises to reunite us with nature. So how does the imagination of *Wordsworth's Poetry* acquire such annihilating force? In answering this question, I follow the lead of Tilottama Rajan and Marc Redfield, both of whom read the major midcentury statements on imagination alongside related work in phenomenology.[76] Rajan and Redfield observe that the younger de Man played a pivotal role in introducing phenomenological concepts to US literary studies. By 1962, Redfield notes, "Hartman may be writing consciously with and against de Man."[77] But even before 1960, Hartman had demonstrated a close and ambivalent relation to the phenomenological tradition. His first book, *The Unmediated Vision* (1954), characterizes Wordsworth's imagination as "eidetic," using a term borrowed from Husserl and the psychologist E. R. Jaensch to capture the poet's "immense power for visual retention."[78] Such an intensity of vision allows Wordsworth to make contact with essences, Hartman says, and it grounds his "views on the forming of the imagination through the direct agency of Nature."[79]

Here Hartman also registers some discomfort with phenomenology's central thesis: the "intentionality" of consciousness, or the notion, in Husserl's phrase, "that every consciousness is 'consciousness-of.'"[80] In brief, Husserl argues that to be conscious is to be conscious of something and therefore to be in relation to it. Consciousness is constitutively intentional, insofar as it "can mean the objective essences in the stream of our consciousness."[81] Significantly, this is an argument, not about the existence of objects, but about the basic structure of thinking. So, when Hartman writes in *The Unmediated Vision* that "*Wordsworth's understanding is characterized by the general absence of the will to attain relational knowledge*," he invokes some similar ideas.[82] Unlike his philosophical precursors, he is wary of consciousness's relational or intentional structure. Even in this early work, the moment of passivity in Wordsworth's imaginings takes on an ethical significance.[83]

By reading Hartman's imagination as intentional, we begin to understand the metamorphoses of the concept. To draw out its political significance, I turn to de Man, whose critique of phenomenology Hartman had certainly absorbed by the time of *Wordsworth's Poetry*. A sympathetic reader of Hartman's first book before he knew its author, the younger de Man also defines consciousness (and language) as intentional in Husserl's sense. At the same time, de Man's work of the 1950s and '60s pursues something like an "immanent critique" of phenomenology; it takes up phenomenological positions in search of their contradictions and limits. Like Adorno, whose study of phenomenology was directly contemporary to his own, de Man looks to Hegel for assistance.[84] Writing in the wake of the new French Hegelianism, which followed on Hyppolite's groundbreaking 1939 translation of the *Phenomenology of Spirit*, de Man insists that the intentionality of consciousness is synonymous with its capacity to negate, or to determine the immediately given. In Hegel's iconic phrase, a refrain throughout the midcentury, "This is the tremendous power of the negative; it is the energy of thought, of the pure 'I.'" Famously, this is the power of "death" itself.[85] In chapter 3 of this book, I explore Hegel's own view of the relationship between nature and consciousness. For now, I remain within the horizons of the midcentury Hegel revival. In so doing, I show that de Man's earlier work, rarely read as concerned with the natural world, has major implications for our understanding of nature in romantic studies.

My focus is "The Intentional Structure of the Romantic Image" (1960), which locates in romanticism a profound and nearly forgotten reckoning with the intentionality of consciousness and language.[86] At this stage of de Man's career, the latter terms overlap: the poetic image is the linguistic form that imagination takes. Therefore, when romanticism demands that poetry should be like nature *and* be ever more metaphorical, consciousness is directly implicated in this problem of language. Citing Hölderlin's impossible vision of words growing "like flowers" (from "Bread and Wine" [1801]), de Man argues that the romantic "image is defined by nostalgia for the natural object, expanding to become nostalgia for the origin of this object."[87] Because figurative language, especially, never "achiev[es] the absolute identity with itself that exists in the natural object," a deep longing, and therefore a lack, must define romantic writing and consciousness. For de Man, lack is a necessary corollary of intentionality; as Rajan explains, "Images, as intentional structures, are conscious *of* something which they are not and therefore define themselves as a lack."[88] Therefore, by drawing out the romantic image's intentional structure, de Man bears witness to a gap or void between consciousness and the world, and in the depths of consciousness itself.

Within a few years, de Man's analysis would change; by 1967, he had more or less rejected the notion that poetic consciousness intends toward anything.[89] In 1960, however, nature is still central to the analysis. Elaborating on

Hölderlin's simile, de Man writes, "This type of imagery is grounded in the intrinsic ontological primacy of the natural object. Poetic language seems to originate in the desire to draw closer and closer to the ontological status of the object, and its growth and development are determined by this inclination. We saw that this movement is essentially paradoxical and condemned in advance to failure. There can be flowers that 'are' and poetic words that 'originate,' but no poetic words that 'originate' as if they 'were.'"[90] De Man distinguishes between the growth of a poem and the growth of a plant. Because, he observes, poems and plants develop so differently, any organicist theory of language begins and ends in error. Even before Abrams, whose discussion of "vegetable genius" in *The Mirror and the Lamp* may be in the background, organicist poetics had been regarded as quintessentially romantic.[91] De Man appears to suggest that this error never belonged to romanticism at all, only to its inheritors. Thus, he argues that, for the poets of the later nineteenth century like Mallarmé, the confusion of poem and plant is particularly intense. It recurs, not as an aspiration to rejoin "matter and consciousness," but as an expression of exhaustion and even rage: "For most of them . . . the priority of nature is experienced as a feeling of failure and sterility, but nevertheless asserted."[92]

So far, my overview of what de Man calls "the post-romantic predicament" has focused on one side of the problem: poetic language.[93] It is worth recalling that the essay also addresses the nature of the plant, apart from its apprehension by consciousness or language. A few pages earlier, de Man observes, "The natural object, safe in its immediate being, seems to have no beginning and no end. Its permanence is carried by the stability of its being, whereas a beginning implies a negation of permanence, the discontinuity of a death in which an entity relinquishes its specificity and leaves it behind, like an empty shell. Entities engendered by consciousness originate in this fashion, but for natural entities like the flower, the process is entirely different. They originate out of a being which does not differ from them in essence but contains the totality of their individual manifestations within itself."[94] Specifying the various forms of origin, de Man attributes to the plant a permanence or stability foreign to the order of consciousness. Each flower, he writes, is an immediate instance of the concept of a flower; it cannot help but become what it is. The life of nature, given the chance, immediately realizes itself. Poems, on the other hand—as intentional artifacts—originate differently. Like all products of consciousness, poems depend on what de Man terms "a negation of permanence, the discontinuity of a death in which an entity relinquishes its specificity." In other words, for nature to become an object for reflection (as the romantic image requires), consciousness must bring out the universality hidden in specific things. This task is accomplished by the power of the negative, consciousness's capacity to determine things by what they are not. Engaged in the ongoing process of determination and mediation, consciousness is severed from natural immediacy. Nature is thereby, in the Hegelian lexicon, "put to death." As de Man explains in his 1960 dissertation, for Hegel, "death" is "the destruction of a natural consciousness by a higher form of self-awareness."[95]

As I have said, the midcentury French Hegel is de Man's primary point of reference.[96] At the same time, in a deeply allusive manner, he hews closely to Hegel's own writings. In the *Phenomenology*'s chapter "Observing Reason," which is explicitly cited in de Man's dissertation, Hegel writes that "the plant . . . does not attain to a *being-for-self* but merely touches the boundary-line of individuality."[97] It appears to display the form of "immediate being," or "absolute identity," that, according to de Man, the romantic image tries and fails to achieve. This is not only a point of antiquarian interest. In his dissertation, de Man explains precisely what is at stake:

> We develop by dominating our natural anxiety and alienation and by transforming it in the awareness and the knowledge of otherness. The conviction that this knowledge enters the individual mind by the interiorisation of nature, which one penetrates by the observation of its temporal and spatial dimensions, can be found in Hegel's *Philosophy of Nature*. . . . The identification of the natural with the animal world as representative of unmediated being, and the ambiguous function of unmediated being, which acts as a goal and a dynamic principle, but nevertheless constitutes the substance which must constantly be negated—all these are familiar themes to the readers of Hegel and his commentators.[98]

To reiterate, intentionality entails a gap between consciousness and nature. But this is not to say that they have no relation. Rather, when de Man insists on consciousness's negation of the objects toward which it intends, he is drawing out the violence latent in the "interiorisation" or "penetrat[ion]" of nature by consciousness. If, in Hegel, death is a figure for the transcendence via negation of unmediated being—pivotal to the mind's development and to the beginning of any poem—it is also something more. Thus, the postromantic rage at the natural world expresses a basic "tendency to domination" that, for de Man as for Adorno, defines intentional consciousness.

This explains why, in the final pages of his essay, de Man seeks in romanticism "a fundamentally new kind of relationship between nature and consciousness."[99] Unsurprisingly, perhaps, de Man has no interest in what he terms a "primitivist" or "naturalistic" aesthetics. Rather, by pointing to passages from Hölderlin's 1801 "Homecoming" and (again) book VI of *The Prelude*, he speculates about a poetry of imagination that might suspend or circumvent intentionality altogether. Crucially, he adds, such a poetry does not exist. In romanticism, there are only hints at "a possibility for consciousness to exist entirely by and for itself, independently of all relationship with the outside world, without being moved by an intent aimed at a part of this world."[100] Finding in *The Prelude*'s apostrophe to imagination something very different from Hartman, de Man reads the "unfathered vapour" as the anticipatory trace of an intentionless mind.

It is not quite the case, however, that the essay ends with the dream of "an internalized supernature" or "an autotelic, world-transcending imagination."[101] Ultimately, de Man finds in romanticism a movement toward something else, which he terms the "celestial": "another nature" signaled only by the images of air, light, and ether that suffuse romantic verse.[102] Insofar as they are referential, these images still intend. At the same time, they seemingly prefigure an end of intention—unachievable as that may be. Such romantic images reduce intention's impact to a minimum. Thus, the poet's ether is "an entity that could still, if one wishes, be called 'nature,' but could no longer be equated with matter, objects, earth, stones, or flowers."[103] Instead, this is nature in flight from apprehension, and it is only ever fleetingly present. The poems that depict it dissolve in contradiction as figurative language struggles, or refuses, to follow that which cannot be grasped. We might read its "disclosure" in verse as a form of "recessive action"—or, in Anne-Lise François's terms, as "a self-canceling revelation [that] permits a release from the ethical imperative to act."[104] But we should also look to Adorno, who similarly sees Hölderlin's verse as "gently suspend[ing] the traditional logic of synthesis."[105] Through the singularity of the poet's rhetoric, he says, "the subject's intention . . . is ceded to language along with the legislating subject" itself.[106] Without intention and without the power to legislate, there is no way to act—at least as we now conceive it. In Hölderlin, Adorno observes, the nonviolent suspension of intent is a "protest" against "the domination of nature."[107] This is not so different from what de Man imagines. We should also recall Adorno's notion of the artwork, which, as we have seen, resonates with Hartman's. To let the materials speak, to hear the voice of nature and of language—for Adorno, this is Hölderlin's poetic task. I am arguing that, in de Man's "Intentional Structure," a similar desire can be felt.

Thus, in de Man's critique of phenomenology, we discover a (latent) political theory of romantic consciousness. In concluding this section, I suggest that it exerted a profound influence on Hartman's changing view of the imagination. In *Wordsworth's Poetry*, we recall, the imagination at its most violent—its most apocalyptic—seeks a new immediacy, which can be achieved only by casting out or negating the natural world. The poet's journey—what Hartman terms, in a decidedly Hegelian mode, "the negative way"—moves, primarily, toward the end of the given world.[108] Similarly, for de Man, negation and loss, as much as transcendence, define consciousness as know it, while "unmediated being" is "the substance which must constantly be negated."[109] Such claims could equally describe Hartman's negative way. In these defining texts of romantic studies, the violence of imagination often appears inevitable—whether it is directly addressed (as in Hartman and de Man) or present as a structural feature of the argument (as in Abrams). Nevertheless, as I have shown, there are countervailing tendencies in all these critics' work. It is these to which I return over the course of this book.

Of course, one might say that to speak about negation as violent is to misconstrue a metaphoric description of consciousness's most basic procedure. In what follows, I demonstrate that the links between consciousness and action, between imaginative and actual violence, are not so unfounded. It is true that they are underdeveloped in Abrams, Hartman, and de Man. Hartman himself seemed to acknowledge this in his 1971 "Retrospect" on *Wordsworth's Poetry*: "I did not neglect the historical milieu, but neither did I offer it as an explanation. In a strange way the violence in France as well as the slower trauma of industrialization coincided with Wordsworth's inner sense of irreparable change: they foreboded a cosmic wounding of Nature—of natural rhythms, of organic growth—which reinforced his fear of an apocalyptic rate of change and nature-loss. The last ten years have made us more sensitive to Wordsworth's anxiety for nature. Apocalypse is not habitable."[110] In the next section, I offer a conceptual account of "the historical milieu" that I believe elucidates the "strange" coincidence between apocalyptic imagination and the trauma of industrialization. I am not, however, giving more or better context for romantic poetry and philosophy. Nor am I performing another historicist critique of the romantic ideology. My sense is that, to understand the connections at which Hartman gestures, we need more theory. So, I turn once more to the critical theorists, whose account of social abstraction is a focal point in the remainder of this chapter.

Real Abstraction and the Labor of Apprehension

The story of modernity in critical theory is a story about abstraction. As described above, this narrative derives from early twentieth-century social thought and shapes much of intellectual and cultural production in the decades following. Romanticists will know the story best from Horkheimer and Adorno's *Dialectic of Enlightenment*, which characterizes "bourgeois society" as "ruled by equivalence. It makes dissimilar things comparable by reducing them to abstract quantities."[111] Famously, for Horkheimer and Adorno, enlightenment thought is defined by its reduction of all things to abstract identity; in the compulsive pursuit of disenchantment, it takes on the status of a new social mythology. The irrationality of this rationalizing process, which begins in early modernity, becomes glaringly obvious in the "totalitarian" politics of the twentieth century.[112] It is not my intention to rehearse this well-known argument, though it has clear antecedents in romanticism.[113] In this section, I am focused on the status of nature in the critical theory of social abstraction. Many have remarked that *Dialectic of Enlightenment*, in its attention to the domination of nature, anticipates later environmentalist thinking.[114] I share this reading of Horkheimer and Adorno's "philosophical fragments," where, as we will see, abstraction is identified as a precondition for the mastery of nature in modernity. Attending to a few key moments in *Dialectic of Enlightenment*, I also rely on a less familiar source: Sohn-Rethel's theory of "real abstraction." Despite his close personal connections to Benjamin and Adorno, Sohn-Rethel has had little influence on romantic studies (or on literary studies at all).[115] Nevertheless, his writings on intellectual and manual labor, among the last contributions of critical theory in its Marxist phase, remain essential for their analysis of abstraction as an economic category.[116] They offer a useful counterpoint, then, to the *Dialectic*'s deeply submerged economic analysis. Drawing on Sohn-Rethel's thought, I propose that a notion of abstraction as "social synthesis"—the medium of thought and economic activity alike—significantly extends the account of nature and consciousness offered earlier in this chapter.

Stylistically, *Dialectic of Enlightenment* tends toward the aphoristic, and it can be hard to discern the underlying logic of the book. I do not aim at a full accounting here, but I do think that the concept of "exchange society"—briefly discussed in the first chapter, "The Concept of Enlightenment," and central to Sohn-Rethel's work—structures the analysis.[117] Drawing on Marx's notion of exchange value, the concept of exchange society is epistemological as much as it is political and economic.[118] It aligns the abstract identity of enlightenment thought with the equivalence of things as repositories of value. As Horkheimer and Adorno put it early in the book, "The identity of everything with everything is bought at the cost that nothing can at the same time be identical to itself."[119] In other words, the quantification of reality that defines enlightenment thinking mirrors the quantification of reality that defines economic exchange relations; in both cases, the quantitative "identity of everything with everything" supplants the qualitative identity of things. By characterizing enlightenment as "universal mediation"—in thought *and* in value—Horkheimer and Adorno are aligned not only with Abrams's humanist narrative of modernity but also with Shelley's *Defence of Poetry*, which describes how language itself is evacuated of singularity in the face of the "calculating principle."[120] Tracing these affiliations should remind us that, in the *Dialectic* and elsewhere, "enlightenment" is a political-economic category.

For me, the most significant, as well as the most romantic, point made in "The Concept of Enlightenment" is that the analogy between modes of "abstract quantity" is closer to an identity. If abstraction is "the instrument of enlightenment," this is not only because it enables the rational schematization of nature.[121] As I observed earlier, Horkheimer and Adorno see disenchantment as a precondition for the economic appropriation of nature. The distancing of the subject from the object world in which it was formerly embedded is a requirement of modern philosophy and industry. "In thought," they explain, "human beings distance themselves from nature in order to arrange it in such a way that it can be mastered. Like the material tool . . . the concept is the idea-tool which fits into things at the very point from which one can take hold of them."[122] Therefore, in exchange society, conceptuality is essentially instrumental. A kind of "idea-tool," abstract thinking is a technology for the mastery of nature, which, according to Horkheimer and Adorno, grounds all other types of exploitation. In a striking dialectical formulation, they add that "reason itself has become merely an aid to the all-encompassing economic apparatus . . . *as calamitous as the precisely calculated operations of material production, the results of which for human beings escape all calculation.*"[123] Again, Shelley anticipates the argument: "Our calculations have outrun conception," he writes, "and man, having enslaved the elements, remains himself a slave."[124] Whether described in terms of instrumental rationality or the calculating principle, such a turn—from "precisely calculated operations" of production to incalculable calamity—exemplifies the tendency toward crisis that has defined capitalism since the start.

Horkheimer and Adorno's claims are central to the entire tradition of critical theory. In *One-Dimensional Man* (1964), for instance—a bestseller throughout the later '60s and a major influence on the student movement in the US and Europe—Marcuse argues that, "as a technological universe, advanced industrial society is a *political* universe, the latest stage in the realization of a specific historical *project*—namely, the experience, transformation, and organization of nature as the mere stuff of domination."[125] Similarly, in *The Concept of Nature in Marx* (1962), Alfred Schmidt bleakly concludes, "Today, when men's technical possibilities have outstripped the dreams of the old Utopians many times over, it appears rather that these possibilities, negatively realized, have changed into forces of destruction . . . [in] a grim parody of the transformation intended by Marx, in which Subject and Object are not reconciled, but annihilated."[126] Such formulations are unthinkable without *Dialectic of Enlightenment*. They also show us critical theory at its most romantic.

Nevertheless, the *Dialectic* is limited in many respects. Despite its insights into the complicity of thought and value in exchange society, the book cannot entirely account for its key terms. As Moishe Postone has argued, the *Dialectic*, along with the other major works of critical theory in the 1940s, lacks "a conception of the specific character of labor in capitalism."[127] Without that, the book cannot explain the notion of value on which it depends, and it reverts to an ahistorical sense of the "process of human interaction with nature."[128] Thus, the notorious reading of the *Odyssey* as a bourgeois epic: without a theory of the historical metamorphoses of value, there is no distinguishing the archaic Greek economy from modern state capitalism. I would add that the *Dialectic*'s account of abstract thinking is equally underdeveloped.

So, I turn to Sohn-Rethel, whose treatment of social abstraction builds on Horkheimer and Adorno's.[129] Importantly for the story I am telling, Sohn-Rethel points to romanticism as the moment when the exchange abstraction finds its greatest philosophical reflection. In making this claim, Sohn-Rethel is not pursuing a critique of romantic ideology. In fact, his theory of real abstraction is significant precisely because it is not a theory of ideology.[130] To frame it in literary critical terms, Sohn-Rethel's method of analysis differs from that of the new historicism, according to which the aesthetic and the philosophical are "idealizations" of a repressed history recoverable only by the critic.[131] Sohn-Rethel shows us how to read the dialectic of nature and imagination in terms of its political-economic determinates, without at the same time denying its reality.

Consider the basic elements of his theory. As I have said, Sohn-Rethel describes abstraction as a process of "social synthesis," grounded in the unifying movements of exchange value.[132] In the words of Jamila Mascat, abstraction is "a *mode of social production*," with an impact on every facet of human and natural life.[133] Its effects are no less real than its causes. The theory of real abstraction demonstrates a richer sense of historical causation than many literary critical accounts of ideology. As Sohn-Rethel explains, in a 1973 essay, "the social process of commodity exchange" must be understood as "a spatio-temporal reality in history which has of itself abstractive force."[134] His analysis begins with the "value abstraction," which initially makes possible the comparison and exchange of qualitatively distinct commodities. This abstraction arises from the economic practices of real historical people, but it goes on to generate a "category of value" that "exists in their minds" without actually "spring[ing] from their minds."[135] Starting, as we have seen, with the deduction of a single "ideal abstraction springing from a real abstraction," the essay proceeds to derive the basic categories of modern thought (pure quantity, abstract space and time, substance, and so on) from the various moments of the exchange relation.[136] If Sohn-Rethel's central claim is that the form of value determines the forms of thought, he is also insistent that thought intervenes in and reshapes the process of valorization. To put it simply, thought is determined by value, *and* value is determined by thought.

This model of reciprocal causation has particular importance for the understanding of nature. In fact, it confirms that the revolutions in the idea of nature during the modern era had economic causes and consequences. As Sohn-Rethel remarks, commodity circulation is inseparable from an ideal of "*abstract movement through abstract (and continuous) time and space of abstract substances which thereby suffer no material change and allow for none but quantitative differentiation.*"[137] Therefore, in its modern form as a mathematized "object world"— the same world described by Shelley, Horkheimer and Adorno, and Abrams— nature is reconceived according to the demands of valorization. Sohn-Rethel does acknowledge that abstraction enabled unprecedented advances in the understanding of nature. He even observes, against Horkheimer and Adorno's sometimes blunt assessments of the enlightenment, that there is no necessary "parallelism between science and the economy. . . . The development of science follows its own independent principles."[138] At the same time, he insists that the "knowledge of nature must have this form in order to suit the requirements of capitalist production."[139] In sum, the value abstraction is the ground of abstract thinking, which makes possible the accelerating development of the productive forces and the intensifying exploitation of nature.[140]

So, while published in the 1970s, Sohn-Rethel's work on real abstraction points back to the earlier *Dialectic* (the argument of which Sohn-Rethel probably helped shape).[141] At the same time, it looks ahead to Carolyn Merchant's essential *The Death of Nature* (1980), a socialist-feminist history of science that begins with the rationalization of common and uncultivated lands in early modern Europe.[142] Merchant shows how the capitalist mastery of nature, which she also links to abstract conceptualization, led to new forms of direct domination over women, whose economic and cultural status changed radically, and not always for the better, in modernity. Merchant reminds us that domination, or *Herrschaft*, is not just a metaphor and that, as a source of extractable value, nature includes many human beings.[143] This, too, could be characterized as a romantic argument; thus, in chapter 4 of this book, I turn to Mary Wollstonecraft, who contends that the ruinous humanization of nature is inseparable from a dehumanizing "commerce" in raw materials and bodies.

For now, I focus on a different connection between romanticism and Sohn-Rethel's critical theory: a shared engagement with Kant. This will lead me back to the debates about nature and imagination from which I began. In an intriguing departure from standard Marxist histories of philosophy, Sohn-Rethel points to Kant, and not to Hegel, as the greatest exemplar of abstract thinking. His book-length study *Intellectual and Manual Labour* (1970) pivots on the claim that Kant's "transcendental synthesis" is the philosophical expression of the social synthesis enacted by exchange:

> Kant was right in his belief that the basic constituents of our form of cognition are preformed and issue from a prior origin, but he was wrong in attributing this preformation to the mind itself engaged in the phantasmagorical performance of "transcendental synthesis *a priori*," locatable neither in time nor in place. In a purely formal way Kant's transcendental subject shows features of striking likeness to the exchange abstraction in its distillation as money: first

of all in its "originally synthetic" character but also in its unique oneness, for the multiplicity of existing currencies cannot undo the essential oneness of their monetary function.[144]

In proposing that Kant's "synthetic unity of apperception" depends on the evolution of the money form, Sohn-Rethel begins to deduce the economic conditions of the critical philosophy. Again, this is not to treat Kant's transcendental idealism as an idealization, in the new historicist sense of the term. In undertaking what Sohn-Rethel characterizes as "a critical liquidation of Kant's enquiry," we do not "discar[d] it."[145] Rather, the interpretive method latent in Sohn-Rethel's work shows us that Kant's philosophy is the epistemology of modern exchange relations. Once more, this is not a method of "negative allegory" or "denied positivism" but a method that, in Sohn-Rethel's words, "lends reality to the Kantian speculation."[146] To be clear, Sohn-Rethel sees Kant's philosophy as determined by the value-form, *and* he insists that the valorization process is determined by intellectual work. This dual claim is the meaning of real abstraction. Admittedly, Kant strives to separate intellectual activity from the economic sphere; in the *Critique of Pure Reason*, subjectivity is defined by its freedom from empirical conditions. But for Sohn-Rethel, this simply demonstrates that "the unyielding dualism of this philosophy is surely a more faithful reflection of the realities of capitalism" than Hegel's speculative logic.[147] Only a philosophy of alienation from the world can convey the alienation that defines the world.

Sohn-Rethel's portrait of Kant is powerfully ambivalent. He is the greatest modern philosopher, *and* he flees from the enabling conditions of his thought. He struggles against a transcendental solipsism, *and* he is the hero in a farce: "Any odd individual doing intellectual work of universal style can rise to the comic-opera confrontation of Man face to face with Nature, to the tune of traditional epistemology."[148] In this last remark, especially, I hear echoes of mid-century romantic criticism. For Hartman, as we know, Wordsworth's apocalyptic imagination, in its confrontation with the natural world, mirrors the Kantian sublime. In Abrams, too, Kant is a central character, an inspiration and an antagonist. Drawing on Kant's famous notion of a "Copernican revolution in epistemology," Abrams defines romanticism as the aesthetic response to "the general concept that the perceiving mind discovers what it has itself partly made."[149] I am struck by these images of labor, or making, though I do not think Abrams means for them to be read in quite the way that I read them.

Nevertheless, he does register, in the activity of the mind, a trace of the labor process. Likewise, in Kant's own writings, "apprehension"—or the synthesis of the sensory manifold—recalls, at the level of the word, a history of labor as the manipulation of nature. Perhaps Hartman's sense of a coincidence between imagination and industry is not so surprising. Reading the dialectic of nature and imagination in light of a theory of real abstraction, we see that consciousness finds in nature "what it has itself partly made," because thought is determined by value, and because value depends (in part) on the mastery of human and natural life. Under capitalism, these relations are inherently destructive— or better, apocalyptic. In their own way, I have argued, the poetry and criticism of romantic nature already tell us something like this.

Conclusion: The Poet's Politics

This book outlines a romantic poetics of wilderness that circumvents the domination of nature. Inspired by Marxist critical theory, as well as by humanist and phenomenological criticism, I find in romanticism itself a persistent questioning of the relation between conceptual and economic mastery. This is not to elide the enormous historical differences between the romantic moment, the mid-twentieth century, and today. Nor do I claim that the romantics have a fully articulated critique of capitalism in Marxist terms. Nevertheless, at the end of an eighteenth-century liberal tradition, before the emergence of a communist alternative, the romantics do possess a profound insight into the modern capitalist form of life as it comes into being. Indeed, in the decades before the triumph of industrialization, and in the nascence of a working-class consciousness, the mastery of nature takes on heightened visibility. It is this, I propose, that explains romantic nature's affective and critical force.[150]

In the spirit of these remarks, I look once more to Wordsworth, who is central to the debates about romantic nature I have discussed. In book VIII of *The Excursion* (1814), Wordsworth undertakes an extended and explicit consideration of England's new economy. Despite the profound influence of Edmund Burke's *Reflections on the Revolution in France* (1790), the poem does not quite long for the days of chivalry. Here, in his second great epic, Wordsworth is torn between admiration of industry and a sense of absolute ruin. In light of *Dialectic of Enlightenment*, the inseparability of progress and destruction presented by the poem should be newly legible. At times, Wordsworth's language even suggests Adorno's, as when the Wanderer speaks of "an Intellectual mastery exercised / O'er the blind Elements; a purpose given, / A Perseverance fed; almost a soul / Imparted—to brute Matter."[151] Recall, these are statements of praise; Wordsworth knows that history is not reversible. Yet he does recognize a profound disequilibrium in the operations of the machine. Thus, the Wanderer "hope[s] that time may come / When strengthened, yet not dazzled, by the might / Of this dominion over Nature gained, / Men of all lands shall exercise the same / In due proportion to their Country's need" (VIII.211–15). This is emphatically not the time of Wordsworth's poem. Without the countervailing force of "the Moral law" (218)—in the absence of the Christian ethic that, it bears mentioning, underpins Marx's doctrine of right—industry violently overturns the long-standing conditions for human and natural flourishing, in pursuit of a false idea of wealth.[152] As the Wanderer exclaims, enraged by the thought of a family condemned to factory labor, "Economists will tell you that the State / Thrives by the forfeiture—unfeeling thought, / And false as monstrous!" (285–87). The Excursion's supposed conservatism gives moral and analytical precision to its critique.

In language that continues to recall the critical theorists, the poem also addresses the appropriation of nature in early industrial capitalism. Describing one of many new factory towns, the Wanderer sees the light of "the punctual stars" (160) usurped by the "unnatural light" (169) of the factory. The stars are a synecdochic reminder of nature's manifold cycles—of "earth's diurnal course," as Wordsworth famously describes it.[153] But the interchange of night and day, punctuated by the stars, is supplanted by the homogeneous time of industry.[154] Thus, in The Excursion, something like Sohn-Rethel's deduction of abstract time from relations of labor and exchange plays itself out on the level of the poetic image. In fact, book VIII of the poem insistently represents the subsumption of all temporal measures, human and natural, under the abstract time of industry: "at the appointed hour a Bell is heard . . . A local summons to unceasing toil! / Disgorged are now the Ministers of day; / And, as they issue from the illumined Pile, / A fresh Band meets them, at the crowded door" (172, 175–78). Today, these lines might evoke a film of workers leaving a factory. Here, however, there is no end of "toil" in sight, because the time of valorization never ceases. Like a "dizzy whee[l]" (180) of bodies, workers leave and "a fresh band" replaces them. Parodying nature's course, the cycle appears unending. This is not the case, though, for the individual worker, whose capacity to go on living is eventually exhausted (299–337). The exhaustion of human life that the poem presents is mirrored by the exhaustion of nature. Thus, the Wanderer ominously intones, "behold, / Through strong temptation of those gainful Arts, / Such outrage done to Nature as compels / The indignant Power to justify herself; / Yea to avenge her violated rights / For England's bane" (153–58). We understand neither the worker compelled to labor (303–4) nor the natural world depleted of vital force when abstract time and value are reduced to ideology. These abstractions are decidedly real in their causes and effects. Intriguingly, Wordsworth also traces reciprocal relations between the abstractions of industry and the abstract thinking of the philosopher. Like the critical theorists, Wordsworth understands how the seemingly "calm abstractions" of philosophy (230) can function as idea-tools for the mastery of nature. "How insecure, how baseless in itself," he writes, "is that Philosophy, whose sway is framed / For mere material instruments" (225–27). Apart from the moral law, and in the name of wealth, reason becomes an instrument of nature's intensifying exploitation.

If *The Excursion* thus outlines a critique of economic abstraction, centered on the apprehension of nature, *The Prelude* offers us a glimpse of what escapes. In book VI, directly after the apostrophe to imagination, Wordsworth recalls a night of strange confusion. Planning to spend the night in Gravedona, on the shores of Lake Como, the young Wordsworth and his traveling companion begin their next day's journey after only an hour of sleep has passed—"by report misled / Of those Italian Clocks that speak the time / In fashion different from ours," the poet explains.[155] Thus, the two travelers leave town in the darkness and are soon "lost, bewildered among woods immense" (VI.631). The episode allegorizes the limits of clock time. Yet the inner time of the poet's mind is equally unsettled. As Sohn-Rethel might have it, the abstract time of the social synthesis almost seems not to hold. Only a few lines after Wordsworth shows us imagination at its most violent, determined to remake or cast out nature, he discovers that "the tyranny of mind" has limits.[156] In the hallucinatory depiction of the night that follows, I see an instance of the romantic poetics of wilderness:

> The cry of unknown birds,
> The mountains, more by darkness visible
> And their own size, than any outward light,
> The breathless wilderness of clouds, the clock
> That told with unintelligible voice
> The widely-parted hours, the noise of streams
> And sometimes rustling motions nigh at hand
> Which did not leave us free from personal fear,

And lastly the withdrawing Moon, that set
Before us while she still was high in heaven,
These were our food, and such a summer's night
Did to that pair of golden days succeed.
(644–55)

These lines are not addressed by Abrams, Hartman, or de Man; the canonical treatments of imagination stop just before this night piece. Yet in this moment, Wordsworth's poem discloses the "celestial" nature that, according to de Man, is sensed only in flight from intentional consciousness. These images of darkness and light, stillness and motion, silence and "unintelligible" eloquence, depict nature at the threshold of apprehension—vanishing as it comes into view. Despite the undercurrent of fear, the scene falls short of the sublime. If the apocalyptic imagination arises out of a struggle with nature, these lines describe something else: a nonviolent disposition toward the world. In fact, the "breathless wilderness of clouds" gently suspends the progress of consciousness. To adapt Adorno's terms, the poet's "bewildered" silence before the night sky permits language to imitate the unutterable. Immersed in an experience of indeterminate perception and duration, Wordsworth glimpses the possibility of another relation to nature.

2　Kant's Remaining Time

The previous chapter showed how romantic studies and critical theory in the mid-twentieth century both came to rely on a notion of apprehensive consciousness. This view of the mind in relation to nature is often identified with the philosophy of Immanuel Kant—the philosophy that arguably inaugurated romanticism itself. In his epochal *Critique of Pure Reason* (1781/87), Kant contends that a coherent theory of nature first demands an inquiry into the cognitive powers that make experience possible. According to many interpreters in the early nineteenth century and beyond, Kant thereby subordinates nature to a law-giving consciousness.[1] Hegel, for instance, in *Faith and Knowledge* (1802), presents Kant as reducing all "objective determinateness" to "man's own perspective and projection."[2] The first *Critique* in particular implies that "the world is in itself falling to pieces, and only gets objective coherence and support, substantiality, multiplicity, even actuality and possibility, through the good offices of human self-consciousness and intellect."[3] In other words, according to Hegel, Kant assumes that nature is incomplete, even meaningless, apart from its manipulation by the mind.[4] In chapter 3, I pursue further this political account of Kantian cognition; for Hegel, I shall argue, the domination of nature by consciousness is a real condition of possibility for modern social life.[5]

Here I approach Kant's philosophy from a different angle. I complicate Hegel's influential line of thinking by considering Kant's concept of time. Famously, time as the "form of inner sense" (A33/B49) is fundamental to the account of consciousness offered in the first and third *Critiques*. Reading the

Critiques alongside Kant's works on natural history, I attend to a planetary, or even cosmological, time irreducible to the forms of intuition. While Kant insists that philosophy inhabit "the human standpoint" (A26/B42), he also recognizes a temporality that exceeds the bounds of inner sense: a natural-historical time that cannot be attributed to the transcendental subject. This "remaining time," which endures with or without finite things, recurs in Kant's reflections on natural history, and it unsettles stories about his inattention or hostility to wild nature.[6]

I begin with the first *Critique*, reconsidering the "Transcendental Aesthetic" in light of an earlier work, the *Physical Geography* (1759–78). By attending to this significant, if underappreciated, text, I outline some of the natural-historical problems that condition Kant's concept of time. Rather than present Kant as simply subordinating nature to consciousness, I show how nature's changeability motivates his articulation of the transcendental philosophy. This is not to say that Kant gives up on natural history. In the first *Critique*'s "Antinomy of Pure Reason" and in the *Critique of Judgment* (1790), he seeks to accommodate the study of natural history to the strictures of transcendental idealism. Here, however, Kant's thinking leads him to the limits of the transcendental. Reflecting on the world's beginning and on the character of organic life, Kant's natural history upsets the notion of time it presupposes. Such tensions powerfully animate his later works, which reveal a fascination with geological upheaval. For the late Kant, always attuned to catastrophe, the time that remains for us, as inhabitants of the earth, may be more fleeting than we had thought; every moment could be the last, he observes. In the notebooks collected as the *Opus postumum* (1796–1803), Kant dwells on the threat of natural disaster, and he wonders how much time remains for humanity.

This is the final revision to Kant's theory of time, and it raises again the question of nature's relation to consciousness. Supposed, as we have seen, to reduce nature to the raw material of knowledge, Kant turns to nature's upheavals to figure the limits of apprehension. Accordingly, the remaining time discounted by the first *Critique*'s "Antinomy of Pure Reason" reasserts itself in the form of these upheavals—strictly inconceivable yet impossible to ignore. In many ways, Kant's natural history makes only the slightest difference; it leaves the transcendental claims of the first *Critique* basically untouched. All the same, in these writings Kant limns, however indeterminately, a nature at the threshold of apprehension. This, I contend, is his major contribution to the romantic poetics of wilderness.[7]

The History of the Atmosphere

In this section, I ask what motivates Kant's transcendental idealist theory of time. I consider, in other words, how time becomes a form of intuition, a property of consciousness rather than a property of nature. There are many ways to tell this story. I proceed from a central issue in Kant's earlier thinking: the relationship between continuity and change, or the "*lex continui in natura*," the Leibnizean principle that nature "makes no leap."[8] For Kant in the 1750s and beyond, the continuity of nature could be guaranteed by a "world spirit," or an ether, underlying all changes in space and time.[9] In the course of Kant's study of natural history, however, the relations between the continuity of nature and the changes that make up its history appear increasingly problematic. Kant thus elaborates a transcendental idealism, in which time as "*pure intuition*" is "the principle of the laws of continuity in the changes of the universe."[10] Separating time from natural history, Kant locates nature's continuity in the form of our presentations rather than in an imperceptible substrate. Of course, he does not stop thinking about natural history—nor does he abandon the idea of an ether—but his investigation of the earth's ancient past does take on a fundamentally different cast. Later in the chapter, I explain how natural history reconstitutes itself after the turn to transcendental philosophy.

First, let me give an overview of Kant's argument for the transcendental ideality of time, which, as I have said, is essential to his theory of consciousness.[11] Opening up the "Transcendental Doctrine of Elements," the *Critique of Pure Reason*'s major division, the "Transcendental Aesthetic" develops that notion of time so crucial to Kant's philosophical project. Briefly, the chapter isolates the basic conditions for any intuition of an object. It is concerned, not with sensation (*aisthesis*) in itself, but rather with what Kant calls "the *form* of appearance": the principles, or rules, that determine "sensible intuitions generally" (A20/B34). Accordingly, the "Transcendental Aesthetic" offers "a science of all principles of a priori sensibility" (A21/B35)—of the ordering forms that govern the mind's receptive capacity. These principles, the "two pure forms of sensible intuition" (A22/B36), are space and time.

As formal conditions for intuition, space and time cannot be considered properties of the natural world. Neither are they categories of the understanding, rooted in the spontaneity of thought rather than the mind's capacity to receive. Again, space and time are principles of sensibility, conditions for the possibility of appearance prior to imaginative synthesis and to conceptual unification by the powers of judgment and understanding.[12] Thus, Kant explains, space must be understood as "the mere form of all appearances of outer senses" (A26/B42). The external world is presented to us spatially, but this is a fact of consciousness, not of things in themselves. Time, on the other hand, is "the form of inner sense, i.e., of the intuiting we do of ourselves and of our inner state" (A33/B49). But it conditions more than our psychological states. Though the "Transcendental Aesthetic" addresses space first, time is the more far-reaching of the two.[13] As Kant argues, in an important passage, "Time is the formal a priori condition of all appearances generally. Space is the pure form of all outer appearances; as such it is limited . . . to just outer appearances. But all presentations, whether or not they have outer things as their objects, do yet in themselves, as determinations of the mind, belong to our inner state; and this inner state is subject to the formal condition of inner intuition, and hence to the condition of time" (A34/B50). So, while space conditions "outer things," time is a condition of outer appearances and inner states alike. It is comparatively unlimited in its ordering of the sensory manifold. Because all our presentations (as presentations) must be subject to the principle, or rule, of inner intuition, time determines everything. Yet, as Kant famously insists, "in itself, i.e., apart from the subject, time is nothing" (A35/B51). Nothing is outside of time, but time is only a form of intuition. In Kant's formulation, it is empirically real but transcendentally ideal.

These claims, now familiar, provoked powerful resistance in Kant's contemporaries. In a well-known letter written in response to Kant's *Inaugural Dissertation* (1770)—which offers an early version of these arguments about the ideality of time—J. H. Lambert appeals to the change of earthly bodies as proof of time's reality. "Existing things," he writes, "that do not have absolute duration are temporally ordered, in so far as they begin, continue, change, cease, and so on. Since I cannot deny reality to changes . . . I also cannot say that time . . . is only a helpful device for human representation."[14] Because change is real and because nothing that exists endures, time itself must be absolutely real. Time remains, Lambert argues, before and beyond any finite thing.

This melancholic thought, so evocative of the romantic aesthetics of ruin, returns in the "Transcendental Aesthetic." "Against [my] theory" of time, says Kant, "I have heard men of insight raise quite unanimously an objection. . . . The objection is the following. Changes are actual. . . . Now changes are possible only in time. Therefore time is something actual" (A36–37/B53). Kant claims at once to "concede the whole argument. Time is indeed something actual, viz., the actual form of inner intuition" (A37/B54). Still, to cite changes in nature as proof of absolute time is to assume too much. While particular things may change—and experience shows us that they do—time itself does not. As a form of intuition, time is independent of any object. If transcendental philosophy seeks the conditions of possible experience, it cannot include among these the concept of change, which relies on "the perception of some existent and of the succession of its determinations" (A41/B58). Lambert's reasoning can only lead us into error. "Reflect," Kant continues, "on the absurdities in which we . . . become entangled" at the thought of absolute time: neither substance nor accident, it "must be something existent," and it "must moreover remain even if all existing things are annulled" (B70–71). Conceiving time as absolute—as the existent that remains beyond all existents—means transgressing the laws of logic.[15]

There are many ways to understand Kant's philosophical motivations here.[16] I read the transcendental ideality of time—the basis of the first *Critique*'s entire doctrine of nature—as a response to problems of continuity and change. More specifically, I see Kant thinking through challenges to continuity identified by his own study of nature's history—including the immensity of cosmological time and what Iain Hamilton Grant describes as "the evident catastrophism of nature's timescape."[17] Lambert's letter is not the only source for Kant's thinking about change, and earlier writings such as the *Universal Natural History and Theory of the Heavens* (1755) and the essays on the Lisbon earthquake (1756) had already posed the question of nature's changeability.[18] In the 1750s, Kant suggests that a universal ether guarantees the continuity of the natural world. In his transcendental philosophy, Kant takes a different approach: he separates time from nature's changes and redefines it as "the principle of the laws of continuity in the changes of the universe." Recall, things change, but time itself does not; it is the "continuous quantity" underlying all appearances.[19] The argument is crucial for Kant's grounding of the physical sciences.[20] Yet the separation of time from history and change also generates a contradiction: between transcendental idealism and natural history.[21] Resolving this contradiction, I argue, is the task of the *Critique of Judgment*.

Before looking at the third *Critique*, let us turn to Kant's *Physical Geography* to examine in greater detail how his idealism about time develops in response to the study of natural history. Published in 1802, the *Physical Geography* was assembled from several sets of lecture notes and a 1759 "dictation text" used in Kant's popular geography course. Though Kant lectured regularly on geography, anthropology, and natural history from 1756 to 1796, the book contains no material written by Kant after the 1770s.[22] This locates the *Physical Geography* on the cusp of the transcendental—a position made clearest by its methodological "Introduction" from 1775. The book's later parts, dated to the 1750s, belong to the "precritical" period of Kant's thought. During this phase of his career, Kant conceives nature, in Andrew Cooper's terms, as "a single and continuous causal chain," in which "matter spontaneously adopts systematic form due to the dynamic interaction of attractive and repulsive forces."[23] Unfolding in space and time, natural history is real, but it is not the ultimate ground of things. The phenomenal world, Kant says, develops from an underlying substance variously described in terms of a world spirit, monads, and an ether.[24] In the *Physical Geography*, Kant uses these principles to construct a "history of the atmosphere," the subtle matter that permeates the natural world.[25]

Despite the material continuity that the ether affords, the *Physical Geography* exhibits a clear sense of its own limitations. In fact, its "Introduction" is one of Kant's most searching reflections on the method of natural history. Here Kant treats continuity not only as a law of nature but also as an epistemic ideal. Looking ahead to the first *Critique*, the *Physical Geography*'s "Introduction" asks if our claims to natural-historical knowledge are justified (cf. A84–85/B116–17). In 1775, Kant can only answer in the negative.

From its preliminary definitions onward, Kant's "Introduction" signals the problematic status of geographic inquiry. Geography, Kant proposes, gives us knowledge of "the world, as the **object of outer sense**"—that is, of "**nature**" (445). The statement resonates with the "Transcendental Aesthetic," which, as I have explained, divides the forms of intuition according to outer and inner sense. Here Kant appears to have something similar in mind: he initially characterizes geography as a science of space, while natural history is described as the science of changes in time. Yet the opposition is less straightforward than it seems. Because both sciences concern the external (spatial and temporal) world, both must give an account of nature's "ancient history" (562–66). So, while it begins with "the places on earth where a thing is actually to be found" (448), geography does turn toward the past. The simultaneity that defines relations among geographic phenomena presupposes a notion of historical succession.[26] Thus, as Kant argues, "The history of occurrences at different times, which is true history, is nothing other than a consecutive [*continuirliche*] geography" (449). Similarly, "The history of nature comprehends the diversity of geography, as it has been at different times" (450). With these notions of a "consecutive," or continuous, geography and a natural history that "compre-hends" geographic "diversity," the "Introduction" complicates the divisions it had seemed to establish. Like "true history," as Phillip Sloan understands it, ge-ography inevitably "deals with the historical changes that have taken place over time and with the original state of things."[27] The objects of this spatial science belong to nature's history.

Notice Kant's appeal to "a continuous geography." The phrase implies that nature's changes might evince some underlying continuity.[28] In fact, this is the *Physical Geography*'s position, yet the "Introduction" shows that it may not be a defensible claim. Outlining the various modes of natural history, Kant ex-plains how each is attended by its own conceptual difficulties. Addressing the empiricism of his lectures, Kant remarks that he might instead have sought out a "system of nature" organized around a rational principle like "similar-ity of form" (448). Unfortunately, he goes on, there can be no such system today: "The systems of nature that have been drawn up so far are probably more properly called aggregations of nature, for a system presupposes an idea of the **whole**, from which the diversity of things is derived. Actually, we do not yet have a *systema naturae*. In the so-called systems of this type available at present, the things are simply put together and arranged in series" (448). Without a principle of "cognitive unity"—the unity, in Rachel Zuckert's terms, "of diverse, empirical properties as salient, meaningful components of justified disjunctions"—the system of nature can only be a series of facts.[29] Exempli-fied by Linnaean botany, the present-day manner of ordering natural-historical knowledge is arbitrary, a system only insofar as it contributes to the task of clas-sification. Kant asks, then, how our categories or kinds, the "units of division" that make up a science, might be related to the continuous totality of nature.[30] In the *Physical Geography*, the question finds no answer.

This is not the only methodological problem encountered by the natural historian. Of greater concern is the timescale of natural history itself—a par-ticular challenge for a science seeking evidence of nature's continuity. "Only if one were to describe the events of the whole of nature as it has been through all time, then and only then would one write a real so-called natural history," Kant remarks. "For natural history is not one whit shorter than the world itself" (450). Of course, Kant's point is that no finite being could write such a his-tory. This is a matter of time: there is no reconciling the duration of the earth with the finitude of its human investigator. Natural history and "the human standpoint" remain incommensurable. So, on the one hand, Kant contends that natural history must be continuous geography, a "narrative" of changes (449) that somehow shows lawful continuity. On the other, he insists on the impossibility of "a genuine natural history" and on the need to limit our purview to "the description of nature" (450). Confronted with an immeasurable temporal expanse, the natural historian is utterly disoriented. Without "true history," however, there is no way to know how nature's past relates to its present. In 1775, Kant demonstrates how urgently natural history needs new "epistemic warrant[s]."[31]

This is not to say that the *Physical Geography* lacks methodological coherence. Like all of Kant's earlier natural histories, the book claims fidelity to Newtonian principles. Nonetheless, Kant's geographic method is less mathematical than it is analogical.[32] Outlining the structure of the course, he explains that geography, in its "**general part**," investigates "the **earth** according to its parts and all that belongs to it, **the water, the air**, and **the land**" (468). These parts, Kant suggests, can be understood by analogical relation to each other. Thus, the atmosphere is like a sea above the earth (547), and "[a] valley winding between two rows of mountains is analogous to the channel of a river or the channel of a current in the sea" (561). These are not idle comparisons but significant observations for empirical study—aids for investigating phenomena such as atmospheric pressure and the formation of mountains.

Analogy is essential, therefore, to Kant's understanding of natural history. In the following section, I discuss its role in the *Critique of Judgment*. In the *Physical Geography*, unlike the third *Critique*, its limited use as a heuristic or "research tool" often gives way to something else—to what might be described as the search for "correspondences," or the constitutive resemblances between things. Now, Kant's nature is far from a "forest of symbols."[33] But the relations he identifies between water, air, and land are not just products of the mind. In the *Physical Geography*, analogy is a method of study and a fact of nature. Thus, Kant dwells on resemblances between ocean currents and river valleys (561), between currents at sea and in the air (551). He entertains the thought that stone might grow like an organic being and that, beneath the ground, there might be seasons "opposite to those on the surface of the earth" (527). In each of the earth's divisions, the same forces and forms can be found.

Such analogies cannot be dismissed as remnants of a magical worldview. Indeed, Kant's interest in the parallelism of natural forms was shared by many of his contemporaries, including J. G. Herder, J. W. Goethe, and F. W. J. Schelling.[34] Scholars have long considered Kant's aesthetics as an enabling condition for later romanticism. I see his natural history in much the same way. In addition to articulating an analogical method that returns in romantic nature philosophy, Kant relies on what Michael Friedman has called an "aethereal 'atmosphere'" surrounding all bodies in the universe.[35] As I show in chapter 6, such a universal ether offers Percy Shelley a model for poetic thinking. In Kant's natural histories, ether is similarly significant. Like "a sea of fluid, elastic material," the ethereal atmosphere is the continuity in nature's changes.[36] Furthermore, as the cause or mediator of forces from attraction and repulsion to light and heat, it makes sense of those correspondences—analogous products of universal forces—that Kant discovers throughout the earth and beyond.

The *Physical Geography* shows, therefore, how water, air, and land are joined together by the atmosphere. It additionally suggests that atmosphere emplaces the earth in the cosmos. During a discussion of the tides, "the prime cause of the greatest changes on the earth" (497), Kant invokes Newton's "force of attraction" (498) to explain how the moon exerts its powerful influence. In Newtonian physics, as I discuss later in this book, ethereal mediation resolves the problem of action at a distance—a problem posed by phenomena such as the influence of the moon on the earth. For Newton himself, the ether's existence is only a hypothesis. Kant is less cautious as he wonders if attraction and light might be caused by the ether. They are the only "foreign force[s] . . . felt on our earth," and light "appears to be only a vibrating motion of the aether" (498). If light is not particulate matter, as Newton had maintained, then it must be a vibration of the ether permeating the cosmos.[37]

In fact, in Kant's ethereal atmosphere, vibration is the condition of all things. Despite its (intermittent) defense of mere spatial description, the *Physical Geography* depicts a planet incessantly moving.[38] "In the entire universe there is never complete rest," Kant writes, and "bodies are always attempting to come closer together or mutually attract one another" (495). Significantly, this is not motion in a void. "Light," Kant observes, again invoking Newton, "penetrates through a medium in which the particles are placed one behind another continuously" (477–78). This account of light hews closely to Newton's own. Yet it also recalls Leibniz, who had argued for the continuity of the natural world: "All matter is connected," he wrote in 1714, and "Every natural change takes place by degree."[39] In the *Physical Geography*, which assumes such a law of nature, the continuity of matter in motion exceeds divisions between water, air, and land, between the earth and its products. Thus, Kant observes, "The circulation of water . . . takes place above the earth" (486), "Vapours rise from its interior that give the earth its fertility" (530), and "Air is consumed by the transpiration of humans, animals, and plants" (536). On this fluid planet, he contends, "Everything which appears above our heads was previously present under our feet" (536). All of natural history is a history of the atmosphere.

For Kant, as I have said, ether guarantees the continuity of nature. Yet if the earth has been "liquid" since its distant origin (530–31, 565), geography must give an account of changes.[40] It cannot confine itself to description, because the earth it describes is never the same. Kant thus observes how earthquakes, rivers, floods, and "the action of the sea" effect "gradual changes" that reshape the "figure of the earth" (559–60). Such processes confirm Leibniz's sense that change takes place by degree. Catastrophic change is harder to accommodate. From fossil remains to mountains and islands, signs of ancient revolutions can be found throughout the earth; "We only inhabit dreadful ruins," Kant writes (537). These traces of past catastrophe pose a special challenge to natural history in the mode of continuous geography. As Grant explains it, Kant's "natural history confronts the problem of how to introduce order into chaos, or how to impose the uniformity or continuity of 'causes which can now be observed in action' onto the evident catastrophism of nature's timescape."[41] When it turns toward an ancient history marked by "chaos" (565) and "revolution" (566), the *Physical Geography* undermines its own capacity to find continuity in the natural order.

Similar problems arise when Kant considers anthropogenic changes. In a striking account of weather, climate, and the seasons, he describes the deforestation of Europe and the warming climate it brings (558). Though humans are vulnerable to nature, they wield significant power over it: "They build dams against the sea and rivers and thus create dry land. . . . They drain swamps, fell forests and thus change the climate of countries considerably" (560–61). These irreversible changes occur quickly, and they are not easily characterized as evidence of continuity. Instead, they recall Friedrich Hölderlin's remark, discussed in the Introduction to this book, that "we, with nature, are fallen, and what once, one can believe, was one, now struggles against itself, and mastery and servitude alternate on both sides."[42] This vision of struggle in and against nature—of changes effected through self-division—cannot be reconciled to the law of continuity. It is not exactly Kant's vision, but it does derive from his natural history, defined as it is by the tension between continuity and change.

Once more, then, Kant confronts the limits of his earlier thought. The principle of continuity must be found within. After 1770, Kant begins to reconceive time in precisely this way. In the *Inaugural Dissertation*, he first contends that time cannot be a property of nature if it is to guarantee the "continuity in the changes of the universe." Nature makes no leap, and its changes take place by degree, because it appears to us in time—the "continuous quantity" underlying all our presentations. As I have explained, this argument is essential to the doctrine of nature in the first *Critique*. It resolves the problem of change by asserting that intuition itself is continuous and that the intuition of nature is the foundation for what we know. As an a priori form of intuition, time is unchanging. It is a transcendental condition of what Kant calls "*nature in general,*" "the law-governedness of appearances in space and time" (B165).[43] In the following section, I ask what happens to natural history after this articulation of a "nature in general." I shall argue that the separation of time from history and change generates as many problems as it solves.

Natural History within the Limits of Reason Alone

Kant's reconstruction of natural history begins in the first *Critique*. In the second chapter of the "Transcendental Dialectic," the "Antinomy of Pure Reason," Kant considers a series of what he terms "cosmological questions" (A485/B513), once central to the metaphysical tradition and now declared to be ultimately unanswerable. Among them is the question of the world's beginning in time. I see this, with Christophe Bouton, as a matter of natural history, or a "deep time" "going back before the appearance of the human species."[44] Commentators have shown that Kant's antinomic procedure—the demonstration, in this case, that a temporal beginning of the world can be proved and disproved using the same laws of logic—bolsters his notion of time as a form of intuition. In the "Antinomy," he thus gives a negative proof of claims made earlier in the first *Critique*, illustrating the contradictions attendant on any effort to transgress the limits of experience. As Kant himself stated in a famous letter to Markus Herz, such problems were a powerful motivator of his turn toward transcendental idealism.[45] Nevertheless, he adds, there are some unanswerable questions that human beings are fated to ask (A vii)—including that of the world's first beginning.

To explain why such a question is necessary and unanswerable, I must say more about the theory of time developed in the first *Critique*. In the "Transcendental Aesthetic," time is defined as a "pure intuition." It is not a concept derived from experience, but it is a condition of possibility for experience of the world. In its purest form, time cannot be said to have a past, present, or future. It has one dimension, it is unified, and it is infinite (A31–32/B47–48). Nonetheless, this notion of time as the form of inner sense does appear rooted in a perpetual present. Though time itself cannot be perceived, Kant says, it can be imagined as a line moving into infinity that somehow lacks simultaneous parts (A33/B50). Later in the first *Critique*, in the "Analogies of Experience," he elaborates on this thought of succession as he considers how the forms of intuition determine our particular experiences. Kant's argument is complex, and I will not attempt to reconstruct it here. Suffice it to say that he finds three modes of time in experience: permanence, succession, and simultaneity (A177/B219). I follow Zuckert in observing that succession underpins the others.[46] In Kant's terms, temporal succession is revealed to be a "necessary law of our sensibility, and hence a *formal condition* of all perceptions": experience requires "that the previous time necessarily determines the following one (inasmuch as I cannot arrive at the following time except through the preceding one)" (A199/B244). If the world of experience is not to dissipate in a "mere dream" (A202/B247), appearances must be unified according to the law of succession.[47]

So, for Kant, time is linear, successive, and composed of "precise fleeting instants."[48] This explains, in part, his approach to the cosmological questions. Because succession is a law of appearances and therefore of cognition in general, the world's beginning can never be made an object of experience. In a certain sense, cosmological time is "nothing but illusion."[49] Nevertheless, human reason, as the highest form of the faculty of knowledge, compels us to pose the question. It is our fate as finite beings, Kant writes, to seek totality even where it is not to be found. Thus, reason demands, "for a[ny] given conditioned, absolute totality on the side of the conditions" (A409/B436). Determined to emplace each thing in a world-whole, reason strives to account for every condition of the given. It seeks to construct a "series of conditions," beginning with time as "the formal condition of all series." Yet if time is composed of successive moments, each one assumes a prior. "According to the idea of reason," then, "the entire elapsed time, as condition of the given instant, is thought necessarily as given" (A411–12/B438–39). The present moment presupposes the entirety of the time sequence (an entirety Kant attributes to the "idea" of the world). Again, I understand these claims to bear directly on the study of natural history. Recall the discussion in the *Physical Geography* of a "real so-called natural history," no shorter than the history of the world itself. Returning to this unresolved methodological challenge, Kant sees it as expressing the inner demand of human reason.

Crucially, Kant now proposes an alternative to the dogmatic positing of truths about the deepest past and to skeptical doubt. Near the close of the "Antinomy," he observes that there is a way to think, if not to know, the world's beginning without violating the strictures of transcendental idealism. This can be done

> only insofar as I present that a regressive series of possible perceptions (either by the guide of history or by the footprints of causes and effects) leads according to empirical laws—in a word, that the course of the world leads—to a bygone time series as condition of the present time. Yet this series is then presented as actual only in the coherence of a possible experience, and not in itself; and hence all events that have from time immemorial gone by prior to my existence yet signify nothing but the possibility of prolonging the chain of experience, starting from the present perception, upward to the conditions that determine this perception as regards time. (A495/B523)

Here, in preliminary terms, Kant outlines a method for natural history rooted in the present. Beginning with perceptions of the world now existing, the natural historian seeks a limited knowledge of the past. Of course, neither first beginnings nor ancient changes can ever be objects of experience. But by following "the guide of history," or "the footprints of causes and effects," the investigator can construct an image of the past with "the coherence of possible experience." This is not to lay claim to what Kant called in 1788 "a science for gods."[50] It is rather to "prolon[g] the chain of experience" and to envision how things might have been. It is, in other words, to reason by analogy. By "starting from present perception," Kant assumes, as Sloan points out, that causes in the present resemble causes in the past; catastrophic change finds no place in this account.[51] Yet for the transcendental philosopher committed to the ideality of time, natural history is inexplicable otherwise.

Kant therefore depends on analogy to reconcile natural history with transcendental idealism. In Kant's earlier works, analogy is a form of thought and a fact of nature. In the *Critiques*, on the other hand, analogy is restricted to its heuristic, or regulative, function. It "assist[s] our cognitive power in dealing with natural things in the world," but it cannot provide determinate knowledge of those things (*Critique of Judgment*, 357). All the same, analogy is essential to the study of natural history. In the first *Critique*, Kant proposes that analogy can "prolong the chain of experience," thereby providing some basis for conjecture about the ancient past. In the third *Critique*, he envisions a new role for analogy as a way to make sense of organic nature. Identifying formal resemblances and mutual relations between organic beings, analogical thinking allows us to develop a system of nature, a rational scheme for ordering empirical findings. Even more important, analogy helps account for the inner organization of plant and animal life, an "intrinsic purposiveness" (256) inexplicable by the exact sciences. Still, Kant refuses to treat natural history as "a science for gods" or even as "a daring adventure of reason" (305n5); analogy alone can never give "complete insight" into the constitution of things (264). Kant's insistence on epistemological limits is motivated, once more, by problems of time. Neither the emergence nor the evolution of organic beings can be reconciled with the notion of time developed in the first *Critique*. In living nature, Kant encounters another timescale, incommensurate with the form of intuition.

Now known for its discussions of beauty and the sublime, the *Critique of Judgment* is not only a work of aesthetic theory. The book poses fundamental questions about the lawful unity of nature and human knowledge. In its "Introduction" in particular, Kant considers the relation between "nature in general"—the minimally coherent nature constructed by the forms of intuition and the categories of the understanding—and what Rodolphe Gasché describes as a "wild nature" that has "not yet been cognitively mastered, or that would seem to be absolutely unmasterable."[52] Now, as I have shown, the first *Critique*'s doctrine of nature is limited by design. It is what many have characterized as "underdetermined," a theory not of natural particulars but of the general conditions by which nature becomes an object of experience.[53] In the third *Critique*, Kant therefore asks how transcendental idealism should respond to natural phenomena that have not yet been conceptualized—or even encountered. Given Hegel's comments on the mastery of nature in transcendental idealism, Kant's treatment of wild nature may be surprising. Admittedly, he aims to secure the potential comprehensibility of unknown things. He seeks to fend off, as Karen Ng puts it (after Henry Allison), "the threat of empirical chaos, or disorder and contingency in nature at the empirical level."[54] Nonetheless, in searching for a principle of unity among "wild and apparently ruleless" things (*Critique of Judgment*, 94), Kant concludes that nature itself must be his guide.[55]

To follow nature, Kant says, our judgments about it must begin from the particular. Accordingly, the power of judgment itself has to take on a new role.

Confronted with the form of a wildflower or the inner unity of a bird—with any empirical thing or law unaccounted for by "nature in general"—judgment reflects on the specificity of the phenomena.[56] Unable now to subsume the particular under pregiven concepts, judgment abandons the "determinative" function that it (arguably) performs throughout the first *Critique*.[57] Nevertheless, all judgments need a rule. "Reflective judgment," as Kant terms it, is therefore "obliged to ascend from the particular in nature to the universal" (*Critique of Judgment*, 19). The principle of unity in diversity that it seeks is not yet given, so reflective judgment must develop this principle for itself: "It cannot take it from somewhere else [such as the understanding] (since judgment would then be determinative); nor can it prescribe it to nature, because our reflection on the laws of nature is governed by nature" (19). Reflective judgment begins from the specificity of empirical nature. All the same, it assumes that there is an underlying order to be found. This, in fact, is the rule that judgment gives to itself. It makes no constitutive claims about phenomena, but it presupposes a certain "harmony" (e.g., the relations between species and genera in living nature) as well as its accessibility to our cognitive powers (24). Reflective judgment thus develops a principle of "purposiveness," a rule for judging as if "a cognizable order of nature . . . is possible" (24). Though far from certain, purposiveness is the promise of unity in endless variation. It lets us feel at home among wild things.

The principle of purposiveness is an essential supplement, therefore, to transcendental idealism. It suggests that the "universal laws" articulated in the first *Critique* might be reconciled with "an endless diversity of empirical laws that [despite being laws] are nonetheless contingent as far as we can see" (22–23). Without it, there could be no transition between wild nature and nature in general, and "our empirical cognition could not thoroughly cohere to [form] a whole of experience" (23). Kant's claims have direct consequences for the scientific investigation of nature. Indeed, he identifies the principle of purposiveness as the transcendental basis for the study of natural history. Nature takes the shortest way; nature makes no leap; nature's principles are not multiplied beyond necessity—these indispensable maxims for the natural historian are rules for "how we ought to judge," grounded in "the purposiveness of nature for our cognitive powers" (21–22). Without the horizon of intelligibility that purposiveness affords, empirical research is left ultimately aimless.[58]

Purposiveness promises to transform the study of organic beings in particular. Throughout his earlier natural histories, Kant had declared that Newtonian principles alone could never explain the generation or form of a living organism.[59] The *Physical Geography*, for instance, makes no attempt to account for the origin of those "creatures of the earth" that it describes (468). Nevertheless, the book implies that a genuine system of nature must include living beings. In the third *Critique*, Kant returns to the question of the organism, suggesting that, while Newtonian physics cannot make sense of life, the principle of purposiveness may lead us to new insights. Now, Kant is famously unclear about the relationship between purposiveness in nature as a whole and the unity or lawfulness he finds in living nature; it is not obvious that the sum of empirical phenomena and a single organism display the same kind of unity in diversity. This, however, appears to be Kant's claim.[60] Thus, he contends that in "teleological judgment" the principle of purposiveness guides reflection on organic beings (33). Unlike aesthetic judgments, judgments about organisms make (limited) use of concepts. Departing thereby from pure reflection, such judgments are determined by an interest of reason; as Kant insists, our judgments about organisms, no matter how provisional, can contribute to the scientific investigation of nature. Still, teleological judgments cannot be identified with the determinative judgments of the first *Critique*. While pivotal for the study of natural history, teleological judgments are rooted in the subjective principle of purposiveness. As Joan Steigerwald explains, "However necessary a maxim for the investigation of living organisms, this remains a merely subjective principle, allowing for no objective determination of these beings."[61] Surprisingly, then, Kant continues to identify teleological judgments with "real (objective) purposiveness": in judging organic beings, he argues, "we attribute to nature our concept of a purpose in order to judge its product" (33). Teleological judgment requires that living beings be presented as natural purposes. This seeming contradiction—the simultaneous subjectivity and objectivity of teleological judgment—can be resolved only by addressing the role of analogy in the third *Critique*.

I have said that analogy is central to Kant's reconstruction of natural history. In the third *Critique*'s latter half, the "Critique of Teleological Judgment," Kant identifies the judgment of organic beings as a kind of analogical reflection. Conditioned by the "as if" of analogy, the insight it offers is effectively suspended between subjectivity and objectivity. Consider the following example. In studying the physical structure of a bird—its bones, wings, and tail—the natural historian understands its diverse parts as "utterly contingent." There is no objective basis for identifying a "special" causal relation between them (236). All the same, Kant continues,

> We are right to bring teleological judging into our investigation of nature, at least problematically, but only if we do this so as to bring nature under principles of observation and investigation by *analogy* with the causality in terms of purposes, without presuming to *explain* it in terms of that causality. Hence teleological judging is reflective, not determinative. Yet the concept of connections and natural forms in terms of purposes does at least serve us as *one more principle* for bringing nature's appearances under rules in those cases where the causal laws of nature's mere mechanism are not sufficient to allow us to do so. (236–37)

Drawing up against the limits of mechanical explanation—of physical law, in other words—the natural historian turns to the subjective principle of purposiveness. This principle cannot definitively explain organic life, yet it does allow the investigator to "brin[g] nature's appearances under rules." The natural historian reflects on organic forms with the aid of "our concept of a purpose" (33) and begins to see lawfulness where contingency had prevailed: the bird's bones, wings, and tail now appear as a complex unity, determined by the goal of flight and essential for the life of the species. Kant explains later in the "Critique" that to judge something as a natural purpose one must conceive it as "*both cause and effect of itself*" (249). In the unity of their diverse parts and in their striving for survival, organisms appear to exhibit just such a causality—a causality, Kant notes, that cannot be explained in terms of physical law.[62] Teleological judgment is necessary, therefore, but the insight it provides cannot be compared to a Newtonian demonstration. Rightly construed, judgments about organisms proceed "by *analogy* with the causality in terms of purposes." The natural historian cannot prove that a bird's body is determined by a purpose, but the assumption that it may be so lends coherence to empirical research.

Kant's argument has occasioned an enormous amount of debate, and there is no consensus concerning the part of analogy in it. In recent years, however, it has become clear that the standard reading of Kant's position—as a modified argument from design, based on the analogy between organisms and artifacts—cannot be right.[63] For one thing, Kant claims that purposes need not be external to, or imposed upon, an object. Indeed, teleological judgments depend on a notion of "intrinsic purposiveness" (245), or the recognition of a "product of nature" as "an *organized* and a *self-organizing* being" (252–53). While artifacts are certainly organized, their purposiveness is imposed by a maker from without. There is no "machine," Kant says, with the "*formative* force" required for self-organization (253). Clearly, the artifact analogy has its limits. At this point, I follow Angela Breitenbach, who argues that Kant "draw[s] an analogy not with the products of human activity but with the very capacity for that activity, namely the capacity of practical reason itself."[64] In looking inward, as it were, at the power of pure practical reason—determining and determined by purposes, self-organizing and organized, cause and effect of itself—the natural historian discovers an image of intrinsic purposiveness. In the mind's highest power, the "symbol" of the organism is found.[65]

This claim has profound implications for natural history and for the relation between nature and consciousness more broadly. Drawing out the analogy between the organism and the power of reason, teleological judgment offers, as Breitenbach puts it, "a reflective awareness of some parts of nature as alive."[66] It suggests too that our recognition of living nature might be a kind of self-recognition. In the words of Schelling, a devoted student of the third *Critique*, the "regularity," even artistry, exhibited by physical forms can only be "explained . . . by saying that it is an unconscious productivity in its origin akin to the conscious, whose mere reflection we see in Nature."[67] Kant ultimately declines to embark on the "daring adventure of reason" these thoughts invite (305n5). Resisting the implications of his own earlier use of analogy, Kant maintains that teleological judgment gives no true insight into the constitution of things—including the affinity between nature and consciousness that it suggests.

This is not to say that our analogical reflections are merely illusory. Rather, analogy can "offer the mind a ray of hope" (304). Tracing morphological resemblances in living nature, the natural historian may envision "a common archetype" for organic beings. The "analogy among them" inevitably leads to the thought "that they are actually akin, produced by a common original mother" (304). Thus, Kant observes, an entire system of nature begins to unfold before us:

> When the archaeologist of nature considers these points, he is free to have that large family of creatures . . . arise from the traces that remain of nature's most ancient revolutions, and to have it do so according to all the natural mechanism he knows or suspects. He can make mother earth (like a large animal, as it were) emerge from her state of chaos, and make her lap promptly give birth initially to creatures of a less purposive form, with these then giving birth to others that became better adapted to their place of origin and to their relations

with one another, until in the end this womb itself rigidified, ossified, and confined itself to bearing definite species that would no longer degenerate, so that the diversity remained as it had turned out when that fertile formative force ceased to operate. (304–5)

In this well-known passage, Kant returns to a central problem in the "Antinomy of Pure Reason," asking again if analogy can help us think the ancient past. Here, he poses the question in terms of the relation between teleology and mechanism in natural history. Teleology, as I have shown, supplements empirical research with a causality according to purposes. It offers limited insight into organic beings, for which no "natural mechanism" can be found.[68] Kant asks now if the "family" of living "creatures" can be unified without appealing to purposes—that is, by the laws of physics alone. Here, too, his answer is no. In the generation of diverse species and in the seemingly developmental relations between them, nature, or the *Urmutter*, hints at a purpose: "The archaeologist of nature will have to attribute to this universal mother an organization that purposively aimed at all these creatures," Kant says, "since otherwise it is quite inconceivable [how] the purposive form is possible that we find in the products of the animal and plant kingdoms" (305). On the verge of evolutionism, Kant insists on the merely regulative status of these claims. Nevertheless, there can be no system of nature without them.[69]

Once again, Kant cannot quite reconcile natural history with transcendental idealism. Notice how the system of nature unfolds entirely from the "free" reasoning of the natural historian. From "nature's most ancient revolutions" to the births of the *Urmutter*, this regulative theory of the earth is grounded in the human standpoint; the ancient past must be conceived by analogical reflection. In the "Antinomy of Pure Reason," Kant argued that analogy "prolongs the chain of experience" by assuming that causes in the present resemble causes in the past. The limits of this method now become clear. Kant insists throughout the third *Critique* that "only as far as matter is organized does it necessarily carry with it the concept of it as a natural purpose" (258). Yet organic beings themselves are born in natural-historical time from out of the "chaos" of "crude matter" (304). The principle of purposiveness gathers living nature as a "large family," but it cannot harmonize these claims.[70] If the concept of a natural purpose is usable only for judging organic beings, it cannot be invoked to explain their origin. Thus, while Kant argues for the inadequacy of mechanical explanation, he implies that "natural mechanism" must have given rise to organic beings. The thought is as inevitable as it is "absurd" (305n5). Analogical reflection unifies all of living nature—from "man, all the way to the polyp, and from it even to mosses and lichens and finally to the lowest stage of nature discernible to us, crude matter" (304)—yet it tells us nothing about how or why nature's causes change. The time of life's beginning remains unthinkable.

Remaining Time

I turn now to Kant's last major work in the philosophy of nature, the notebooks collected as the *Opus postumum*. Written between 1796 and 1803, these fragmentary meditations return to, and sometimes radically rethink, central themes in Kant's philosophy: the relation between transcendental idealism and the natural sciences; the possibility of a system of nature; the constitution of subjectivity.[71] In search of the "transition from metaphysics to physics" (37), Kant's unfinished work shows that nature's changes, at their most catastrophic, are never far from his mind. Yet the planetary upheavals that punctuate this text remain almost untheorized. In the *Opus*, "revolutions" in nature mark a limit or a threshold of cognition, about which little can be said.

Consider the following fragments from around 1800, where Kant addresses the place of organic beings in his "transition project." In the first, Kant describes a system of nature similar to that in the third *Critique*: "The organized creatures form on earth a whole according to purposes which [can be thought] *a priori*, as sprung from a single seed (like an incubated egg), with mutual need for one another, preserving its species and the species that are born from it" (57). Developing further his conjectural history of life, Kant seems to envision an ethics of interspecies existence, defined by "mutual need" and the preservation of self and other. Yet the note soon turns—absent any transition—from preservation to "revolution." "Also," he writes, "revolutions of nature which brought forth new species (of which man is one)" (57). This is the "natural mechanism" sought in the third *Critique*, an upheaval in nature that somehow gives rise to organic beings. It is also a figure for remaining time—the time of origins and extinction—as it persists before and beyond finite things. Humanity itself, Kant suggests, is implicated in its passing. In a much-discussed later fragment, he returns to this idea: "How many such revolutions (including, certainly, many ancient organic beings, no longer alive on the surface of the earth) preceded the existence of man, and how many . . . are still in prospect, is hidden from our inquiring gaze—for, according to [Petrus] Camper, not a single example of a human being is to be found in the depth of the earth" (67). Drawn to the thought of past and future catastrophe, Kant ultimately falls silent before the time of nature's revolutions. Though he alludes to ongoing controversy about "anthropolites," or human fossils, his silence is not only a matter of missing evidence.[72] The theory of the earth—grounded in the human standpoint, as I have shown—can never account for origins or extinction; it cannot think the absence of its own epistemological ground. When knowledge of nature is thus "hidden from our inquiring gaze," the transcendental philosopher is left to wonder. "To set a beginning or an end to this process," Kant writes, "wholly exceeds the bounds of human reason" (66).

So, from his earliest inquiries into the possibility of natural history, Kant conceives of nature as far more than material for human cognition. In his insistent return to the problem of remaining time—the time of change, catastrophe, emergence, extinction—Kant points to the limits of "nature in general" and to what lies beyond. In the next chapter, I turn to Hegel's treatment of these themes, which, as we shall see, makes explicit their political dimension. Hegel shows us that the apprehension of nature, as well as its failure, demands to be thought as a problem of social life.

3   Hegel in and Out of the Woods

In his 1955 *Studies on Marx and Hegel*, Jean Hyppolite observed that one could not see the brilliance of Hegel's early critical writings without first coming to terms with their economic and political underpinnings.[1] In general, Hyppolite's reminder has done little for the reception of these difficult, often tortuous essays.[2] Published in (or around the time of) Hegel and Schelling's *Critical Journal of Philosophy*, and including *The Difference between Fichte's and Schelling's System of Philosophy* (1801) and *Faith and Knowledge* (1802), they are unusually polemical, even for the contentious world of German romanticism. Yet Hegel's critiques—of an exhausted ethical and intellectual climate, of a philosophical scene caught up in solipsistic, "reflective" maneuvering—can sometimes feel as undermotivated as they are unrelenting.

In this chapter, my goal is to restore some of the urgency to these early writings of Hegel's. Beginning from remarks in Hyppolite and in Georg Lukács, for whom the young Hegel's study of economics is decisive, I stress the critical essays' confrontation not just with economic theory but with actually existing forces and relations of production.[3] Throughout the Jena period (1801–7), in published essays and more explicitly in notes and lectures, Hegel takes the measure of a nascent industrial capitalism, along with its consequences for life, consciousness, and labor.[4] He responds with equal parts awe and repulsion. Like Marx, his great disciple, Hegel is awed by capital's universalizing power, by its drive to tear down all barriers to its expansion. At the same time, he anticipates precisely what this universality will mean for most: utter dependence on an arbitrary yet worldwide "system of need"; unequal accumulation of wealth; and life under a law of the bare minimum, where wages are hardly enough for survival—no matter how productive the work.[5]

The point is not that Hegel preempts Marx and Engels. Recent commentators have shown that Hegel's Germany was in many respects still feudal, a messy conglomerate of the medieval and the modern.[6] This in itself would be enough to explain why Hegel could not have written *Capital*. Yet the misfit between the British economic theories he had so carefully studied and his day-to-day surroundings did show him something else. Among the remnants of feudalism, just after the great bourgeois revolution in France and just before the arrival of a mature industrial capitalism in Britain, Hegel writes in a Germany that, in Rebecca Comay's terms, "presents the perfect model of historical nonsynchronicity."[7] It is this historical unevenness that gives Hegel such a clear view of capitalism's logic, of its difference from past forms of life and its latent contradictions. Making a meticulous study of the new world as it comes into view, Hegel also intuits "the crises that it carries within it, as the clouds carry a storm."[8]

The atmospheric figure is apt. Among Hegel's foremost concerns is the domination of nature in capitalist modernity—ostensibly justified by an ethics of infinite freedom. For Hegel in Jena, writing against the philosophers of the self-reflecting subject, nature is always woven in with the spirit.[9] When he investigates, in a lecture course of 1803–4, the difference between the hand tool and the machine, he is concerned not only with the machine's reshaping of consciousness. Just as disconcerting is the way machinery "deceives" nature, as it hastens on the "evaporation" of a bond between worker and world.[10] If under capitalism all that is solid melts into air, for Hegel this change in the weather can be attributed to industry and its intensifying capacity for exploitation.

It is not my intention to identify romanticism in general or Hegel in particular with present-day environmentalism. Rather, my interest is in seeing what romanticism might say to us, as we look back at it from our own moment of environmental crisis. For one, romanticism reminds us that "business as usual"—now synonymous with what Andreas Malm has called the "fossil economy"—was in 1800 far from usual.[11] Romanticism takes on the status of a missed opportunity, becoming "an index of what was also possible."[12] From this standpoint, Hegel's analysis of industrial capitalism and its relation to nature has particular interest. For Hegel, nothing is yet determined. The necessity of a situation is founded only in the contingency that precedes it.[13] At the same time, he clearly anticipates, or at least faces the possibility of, the worst: all cunning of reason aside, certain problems will never be resolved. This should not be taken for an assertion of fate. In Slavoj Žižek's formulation, when faced with imminent calamity, "one should accept the catastrophe as inevitable, and then act to retroactively undo what is already 'written in the stars'"—or, in other words, to reactivate or "insert a new possibility" in the past.[14] For us now, such a sense of contingency, of the dormant possibilities occluded by the present, is increasingly indispensable.

Reflection, or the Night of Infinity

I am not the first of Hegel's readers to signal the importance of such themes to his work.[15] My contribution is to show how the writings of the *Critical Journal of Philosophy* period add to Hegel's analysis of the capitalist mastery of nature. I suggest that his uneasiness about idealism's self-reflective subject is founded in the economic and political concerns outlined above. I begin from the philosophical arguments leveled in *Faith and Knowledge*, Hegel's lengthiest contribution to the *Critical Journal* and his most substantial treatment of the "reflective philosophy of subjectivity."[16] In the following sections, my focus is more concretely historical, and I ask why Hegel deems reflection to be a "culture" as much as a concept.

Hegel was drawn to Jena by his younger friend Schelling, who had not only been recognized as a major new philosophical voice but had also attained the institutional support to prove it. Stuck in a dead-end tutoring job in Frankfurt, Hegel moved to Jena on the promise of a (probably unpaid) lectureship and some intellectual camaraderie. His first publication there, *The Difference* (1801), was an openly partisan intervention in Jena's conflict of philosophies: a book-length defense of Schelling against the subjective idealisms of Kant and J. G. Fichte. The *Critical Journal* was supposed to continue their collaboration, but Hegel found himself doing most of the work. And the response to his harried production was almost entirely negative. Adhering to, though often repurposing, Schelling's conceptual vocabulary, Hegel's writing stood out for its belligerent difficulty—for its badness even. F. H. Jacobi would thus complain, concerning one of the anonymous pieces in the *Critical Journal*, "If only the wretched Hegel could write better. . . . I often have trouble in understanding him. It is the bad style that makes me certain it is he, and not Schelling who was guiding the pen in this essay."[17]

Despite being dismissed as an ill-spoken disciple, Schelling's bulldog, Hegel was already articulating the distinctive relations among concept, language, and history that define his later work.[18] In *Faith and Knowledge*, a critical approach to reflection depends on a history of the concept's usage—by Kant, Jacobi, Herder, Fichte, Schleiermacher, and others. Hegel's sense of philosophy as, in part, a history of philosophy is captured well by the form of the critical review. Moreover, by tracing the dialectical contradictions that shape this history, Hegel shows how habitual ways of thinking about the world carry powerful, sometimes unintended, consequences. More specifically, though *Faith and Knowledge* never really defines its central term, it demonstrates that a history of reflection says more than any single definition could.

Thus, the essay's bulk is composed of detailed textual analyses, and it moves in its central chapters from Kant's already canonical *Critiques* to minor periodical pieces from the weeks before. It is united by its concern with the dualisms in contemporary thought: subject and object, freedom and nature, infinite and finite. *The Difference* had already shown that reflection manifests itself through the "positing of opposites"; as a method or pattern of thinking, reflection produces and reproduces binaries, even when mediation seems to be the goal.[19] In sounding out "the power of dichotomy" in all its varied forms, Hegel seeks to respond to "the need of philosophy": to a lack in the modern intellect and to the need for genuine speculative knowledge.[20]

Consider how *Faith and Knowledge* deals with idealism's self-reflective subject. In Hegel's telling, since the religious and philosophical revolutions of early modernity (Luther, Descartes, Locke), thought's "one self-certifying certainty" has been "that there exists a thinking subject."[21] This is the basis of the philosophy of reflection. In all its varied forms, reflection presupposes an individual consciousness, without which nothing else is thinkable. The first principle of reflection is the reflective intellect itself. Because this intellect is finite, Hegel adds, its objects of possible knowledge are limited to the finite too—to the world of appearances. The problem receives its fullest articulation in Kant's transcendental philosophy: if finite consciousness gives form to perception and to cognition, then it remakes the world in its own image.[22] In other words, the subject of reflection becomes the center and the circumference: "The world as thing is transformed into the system of phenomena or of affections of the subject" (189). After Kant in particular, then, the absolute nature of dogmatic metaphysics disappears from view.

Conceiving knowledge as a relation of subject to object, reflective thought deems everything outside that relation unknowable. There is no knowing apart from this founding dichotomy. At the same time, Hegel observes, reflection never quite shakes its feeling for the beyond. Disavowing all absolutes, it nonetheless guarantees their return (in ever more irrational forms) by offering up such a limited notion of truth. Reflective knowledge is a mere "table of contents," as he says in the *Phenomenology of Spirit*; assembled by an understanding in permanent opposition to its objects, it provokes all kinds of yearning—for enchantment, for unity, for the infinite.[23] On the level of theory, reflection must leave us dissatisfied. Thus, in the age of Kantian critique, faith returns to assert its rights.

This story strikes many familiar notes. Modern intellect, or reflective *Verstand* in Hegel's diction, has often been charged with the loss of the world. *Faith and Knowledge* recognizes that this loss and the struggle against it are part of a longer history. Indeed, the contemporary contest of reflective knowledge and faith recapitulates a whole series of earlier struggles: between enlightenment and dogmatism, Luther and the church, Judeo-Christianity and paganism.[24] In each attempt at reconciliation, however, lies the start of a new conflict. When, for instance, Protestant inwardness yearns to be united with the world, it leads only to a vulgar *Wirklichkeit*: "The poetry of Protestant grief that scorns all reconciliation with empirical existence is transformed into the prose of satisfaction with the finite and of good conscience about it" (61). Thus, Hegel claims, the Protestant renunciation of Catholicism's devotional objects inadvertently leads on to empiricism and its ethics of satisfaction, which must in turn be overcome by the idealists' self-reflective subject.[25] Displaying a powerful dialectical logic, this is not just a history of revolution and reaction. Rather, Hegel's narrative concerns the immanent tensions and unspoken oppositional tendencies that run through every cultural formation.

Such tensions are certainly Hegel's interest as he evaluates his own intellectual surroundings. In leaving so much room for faith, he remarks, idealism already begins to display its inner contradictions. They become even clearer when idealism turns, as it often does, to the problem of subjective freedom and its relation to nature. Again, as Hegel shows, the thinness of the reflective vision allows for a host of unintended effects.

What happens to freedom and nature in reflection? In a fragment of 1800, Hegel contends that "nature" itself is the product of reflective thought, of the conceptual division and fixation of an infinite vital force.[26] By the time of *Faith and Knowledge*, the coordinates have shifted. No longer positioning life against the deadness of thought, Hegel sees a more intimate relation between these terms.[27] Reading Kant's *Critiques* in such a light, he shows how the idealist subject derives a certain life from its opposition to the "infinity of sensations and . . . of things in themselves." The subject emerges through its separation from the realm of the sensible. At the same time, the latter appears to take its life from the subject: "Abandoned by the categories," he writes, "this realm cannot be anything but a formless lump" (76). From the standpoint of reflection, nature without the forms of thought is entirely indeterminate.

Reflection seems to enable the exchange of animating energies between subject and object, mind and nature. For Hegel, though, this is a half-truth. It could just as well be said that reflection destroys the forms already in nature, imposing on it external limits. Returning to the image of nature as "a formless lump," thought's raw materials, Hegel tells a philosophical fairy tale: "Objectivity and stability derive solely from the categories; the realm of things in themselves is without categories; yet it is something for itself and for reflection. The only idea we can form of this realm is like that of the iron king in the fairy tale whom a human self-consciousness permeates with the veins of objectivity so that he can stand erect. But then formal transcendental idealism sucks these veins out of the king so that the upright shape collapses and becomes something in between form and lump, repulsive to look at" (77). Hegel's story shows how consciousness treats the natural world.[28] In binding together a manifold of sensations and things in themselves "with the veins of objectivity," the subject builds not a living being but an automaton. The life bestowed on nature by reflection is the life of a machine, where the semblance of animation bespeaks the absence of an innate formative drive. Hence, as Hegel observes elsewhere, the overvaluing by reflection of mechanism as a mode of causal explanation. Because it denies that any force could "dwell" in nature, reflection must maintain "that inert matter is moved always by an external impulse, or what amounts to the same thing, by forces alien to matter itself."[29] To build an automated appearance-nature is to empty out the living forces of the world. Reflection gives objectivity and stability, but in exchange for inert uniformity.[30]

All this is no accident, Hegel argues. The theoretical claims of reflection—the insistence on the absolute separation of subject and object, on the primacy of subjectivity, on the relative nothingness of nature—are motivated by a single practical end. Indeed, the reflective philosophy of subjectivity sees itself as a philosophy of freedom. As Rodolphe Gasché notes, it avows its "eminently emancipatory function": "By severing the self from the immediacy of the object world, reflection helps give the subject freedom as a thinking being."[31] In Kant, then, the finitude of human knowledge finds its counterpart in the infinity of freedom—in the capacity to self-legislate, or to be autonomous. If freedom is attained at the price of nature's own liveliness, so be it.

Yet the subject-object dichotomy again has unintended consequences.[32] By locating freedom in the antithesis between subjectivity and the world, Hegel notes, reflection condemns itself to a futile search. Such opposition is invariably felt as constraint, as the presence of an otherness or finitude supposed to be transcended. The subject of idealism therefore "has a being of its own only in its tie with the finite" (63). Defined by its relation to a natural world theoretically determined as finite (even if this relation is strictly negative), the subject becomes a finite thing itself: "If infinity is thus set up against finitude," Hegel says, "each is as finite as the other" (63). As it strives for self-legislation, the idealist subject discovers the dependence, or heteronomy, in its inmost heart. The idealism of infinite freedom, having voided nature of its essence, finds itself reduced to nothing too.[33]

Thus, where "so-called man and his humanity . . . form philosophy's absolute standpoint" (65), we find a surprising vision of dejected humanity. Claiming superiority to all things, the idealist subject is tormented by its own, necessarily failed efforts to master, and thereby free itself from, nature. In another vivid image from *Faith and Knowledge*, "It is as if art, considered simply as portraiture, were to express its ideal aspect through the longing it depicts on an ordinary face and the melancholy smile of the mouth, while it was strictly forbidden to represent the gods in their exaltation above longing and sorrow, on the grounds that the presentation of eternal images would only be possible at the expense of humanity" (65). This passage anticipates the *Aesthetics*'s account of romantic art, in which the infinite or absolute is made present only in the signs of its absence.[34] Hegel sees in idealist subjectivity a similar portrait of loss, or *Sehnsucht*. Reflection, particularly in its idealist form, seeks to elevate the human being. But it does so with a dichotomous method that is ultimately self-subverting. Rather than open up a divine freedom from or control over the natural world, reflection condemns us to longing and sorrow—to a melancholic existence in the "nothing and pure night of infinity" (190).[35]

The Culture of Reflection

These are philosophical matters. As *Faith and Knowledge* shows in painstaking detail, none of the reflective philosophers can give an adequate account of nature or freedom. But reflection is more than bad theory. It is also a "culture," or *Kultur*. Thus, as Hegel says, "These philosophies have to be recognized as nothing but the culture of reflection raised to a system" (64). Like the other romantics discussed in this book, Hegel raises here the question of the relation between consciousness and social life. He asks, in other words, how spiritual forms arise from and intervene in the economic and political realms.[36] Famously, Hegel is supposed to get this all wrong. In the words of Marx and Engels, the Hegelian philosophy "descends from heaven to earth": it begins with spirit, while materialist thinking should "set out from real, active men." It is only by first grasping the human "life-process," they argue, that we can explain its ideological projections, in which "men and their circumstances appear upside down . . . as in a camera obscura."[37]

At times, Hegel himself seems to support such an account. The "Introduction on the Essence of Philosophical Criticism," from the first issue of the *Critical Journal*, even anticipates its language by claiming that "in its relationship to common sense the world of philosophy is in and for itself an inverted world."[38] I think that Hegel is closer to Marx and Engels than they admit. For one thing, common sense is not knowledge; it merely gives a "concept-name to what has long been familiar in everyday [*bürgerlich*, or bourgeois] life." Claiming the status of wisdom, common sense is the coercive justification of bourgeois norms and practices. What the popular philosophers and the empiricists call "healthy common sense" is just another way for "*Reflexionskultur*" to shore up its existence.[39]

So, what would the inversion of common sense reveal? How is it to be done? Hegel recommends a certain cultural study, an analysis of common sense and idealist philosophy in terms of their historical—even material—significance. The concept of the culture of reflection already brings spirit and the "life-process" together. Though this culture is a complex entity, changing over time, it depends on a single economic system, capitalism. As Fredric Jameson observes in a similar context, culture implies more than art, religion, and philosophy. It should be taken in a broad sense "as the organization of daily life and of the production of subjectivities designed to function within a specific mode of production."[40] This last part is crucial. For Hegel, the philosophy of reflection and the subjectivities it produces are inseparable from the capitalist mode of production. To put it simply: no reflection without capitalism.

These terms collude in another way, as they intensify the domination of nature. Reflection condemns nature to formlessness in the absence of the subject. This is one of several "connection[s] of domination" that Hegel identifies with the culture of reflection. As I showed in the previous section, "the domination of the concept over what appears as the real and the finite" (*Faith and Knowledge*, 60–61) is self-subverting, and it dialectically reverses into an assertion of finitude. In striving to master or to free itself from nature, the subject becomes less free. Its infinite freedom is anything but, because it depends on a dominative relation to the finite. This reversal expresses "the *Zeitgeist* of an absolutization of finitude," according to which all things, from human life and labor to the natural world, become quantifiable and exchangeable. For Hegel, this is a matter of life-processes as much as any philosophical position.[41]

As a concept, culture has a storied past. In the eighteenth and nineteenth centuries, it often signified a formative or an educational process. Friedrich Schiller's notion of aesthetic education, or *Bildung*, exerted a powerful hold on the young Hegel, who wrote about art's potential to shape enlightened minds.[42] In *Faith and Knowledge*, however, he describes something different. Here Hegel anticipates Adorno, who presents culture in a 1958 lecture as "the molding of reality"—as "the human being's coping with nature in the sense of its mastery; that is, domination of both the external nature that opposes us as well as domination of the natural forces in the human being itself."[43] On this view, culture is not aesthetic education—or the reconciliation with nature Schiller hoped it might entail. Rather, the "molding" that Adorno describes is the progressive domination of the world.

This captures well Hegel's own sense of the term—especially as it features in *Faith and Knowledge*, which remarks on the calculating spirit of modernity. "What is here called Reason," Hegel writes, "consists solely in calculating the worth of each and every thing" (61).[44] He contends that the philosophies of reflection are defined by such an impulse. Empiricism and idealism alike are "manifestations [*Erscheinungen*] of this realism of finitude (to which the non-philosophical manifestations, all the hustle and bustle of contemporary civilization, still belong)" (63). Both the enjoyment of and the flight from the finite express a preoccupation with the calculable. More than a worldview, this realism of finitude is coterminous with "the hustle and bustle of contemporary civilization." For Hegel in 1802, in the years of his closest engagement with the works of James Steuart and Adam Smith, this is the "hustle and bustle" of "commerce."[45]

A second look at the *Critical Journal*'s rejection of common sense makes clear that capitalism is at issue. According to empiricist common sense, happiness is the goal of human life. The claim's self-evidence is testament to its coercive force. Defining happiness as "sensual enjoyment" and the indulgence of our capacity to consume (*Faith and Knowledge*, 60–61), common sense eternalizes commercial society. It implies that there is no other way to live.[46] With the ethics of happiness and desire, common sense aims to justify the system of need: the dependence of all on all, working not for subsistence but to produce a surplus exchangeable on an inherently unpredictable and increasingly unfathomable market.

The connections between idealism and the capitalist system of need are harder to see. Yet Hegel maintains that the philosophies of Kant and Fichte are the highest expressions of reflective culture. This is puzzling because the idealists strive to transcend the realism of finitude. In their striving, however, Hegel identifies the dialectic of concrete and abstract, finite and infinite that defines the culture of reflection. As we have seen, the promise of immediate sensuous fulfillment shores up an intangible, and near-unimaginable, system of need, exchange, and accumulation. (The system's abstractness might explain the lack of *capitalists* in Hegel's account.) Conversely, idealism's spontaneous self-generating freedom demands, and even intensifies, the mastery of the natural world.

Such is Hegel's argument when he turns to Fichte in the final part of *Faith and Knowledge*. In *The Difference*, Fichte had been praised for his attempt to overcome the limits of individual consciousness through the concept of "the absolute I." One year later, Hegel's criticisms are relentless. He focuses on Fichte's "utterly vulgar view of nature" (176).[47] Mocking the idealist attempt to deduce nature from within subjectivity, Hegel writes, "The ordinary sort of formal knowledge has the manifold of experience as its ground but it draws up many a peak of concepts from the ground into the ideal atmosphere. Fichte's formal knowledge reverses [the pattern of] this ordinary knowledge. It begins in the atmosphere where the very same thing is encountered but only negatively and ideally; and being aware of this ideality, it lets down its negatively present content with a plus sign as reality" (160). Hegel charges subjective idealism with descending from the heavens to the earth—from the "atmosphere" of subjectivity, or "the I," to a natural world that is present only in the negative, as "the not-I." Today, after nearly two centuries with *The German Ideology* (1845–46), such language has particular resonance. And Hegel's atmospheric image can be read like Marx and Engel's: as a figure of mystification.[48] In looking down from the heavens, Fichte's I proclaims its own ungrounded freedom.

This is not Hegel's only point, however. Consider the language he uses to characterize the emptiness of the Fichtean deduction, which resembles nothing more, he says, than the deduction of a sum of money from the mere existence of a money bag.[49] "Speculative" in the economic more than the philosophical sense, Fichte's thought purports to make something out of nothing.[50] Its value (freedom) is spontaneously self-generating, and it disavows all ties to the natural world.

Indeed, Fichte's nature is only negatively present, a necessary but indefinite counterpart to the free activity of the subject. The two terms never get nearer than this antithetical relation. As Hegel sees it, Fichte seeks to isolate the subject in an ideal heaven. "The monstrous arrogance," Hegel writes, "the conceited frenzy of this self who is horrified, filled with loathing and sadness, at the thought that he is one with the universe" (176). Because the subject's striving for freedom undermines itself, such isolation is never complete. But not for lack of trying—and this striving has certain consequences.

These become clear in Fichte's discussions of teleology. We may be surprised, Hegel says, that a thinker so contemptuous of nature also asserts its purposefulness. But nature has a purpose for him only insofar as it is manipulable. In being mastered, nature contributes to our rational ends, and it thereby becomes rational itself. For Fichte, he adds, nature is only "present for the sake of something else, namely to constitute a sphere and provide elbowroom for free beings and to be capable of falling into ruins above which the free beings can raise themselves and so fulfil their vocation" (177). Subtending the miracle of the Fichtean I is a natural world used up and led to ruin.[51]

Recall that, for Hegel, the culture of reflection describes a form of social life as well as a set of philosophical positions. The idealism of freedom cannot be understood apart from the world in which it emerges and in which it also intervenes. In making this claim, Hegel goes well beyond the critique of ideology. He shows how abstraction itself has concreteness, a capacity to determine the world.[52] What, then, is the intervention of the idealism of freedom? For one, it denies nature any inherent value, apart from a calculable quotient of utility for human purposes. As the tale of the iron king showed, reflection defines matter as raw material, nature as a natural resource. Because for Hegel abstractions are real, such definitions exceed ideology.[53] What Fichte demonstrates is that instrumentality in theory is always also borne out in fact.

In itself, an instrumental attitude toward nature is not remarkable. From the earliest prehistory, human beings have used tools to work on and draw sustenance from the world.[54] In the culture of reflection, however, the metabolic process undergoes fundamental change. Earlier, I drew an analogy between the self-reflective subject of idealism and the self-valorizing value of capital—itself "an automatic subject," in Marx's famous phrase.[55] For both, reflexivity is a vehicle of "systemic amplification": through its self-activity, the I strives to free itself from, and extend its mastery over, nature, while, according to its own laws of motion, capital accumulates and extends its reach.[56] Now, Hegel suggests, this logic of amplification transforms the human use of nature. The energy systems and the environmental degradation of the nineteenth century find their roots in reflection.

Early on in *Faith and Knowledge*, Hegel signals what is at stake. In his first account of the reflective philosophy, he observes, "Precisely through its flight from the finite . . . subjectivity turns the beautiful [in nature] into things—the grove into timber, the images into things that have eyes and do not see, ears and do not hear" (58). Kant's reflective knowledge and Fichte's striving for freedom are identified as modes of iconoclasm. Reflective consciousness, by its opposition to the world, evacuates nature of motion and force. It smashes all "images" of nature's liveliness. This leveling of "grove into timber" should be taken quite literally: "the hustle and bustle of contemporary civilization" demands the intensifying exploitation of nature.

Hegel's editors note that this image of the leveled grove recurs throughout his early career, from the first fragments to the final chapters of the *Phenomenology*; they read in it allusions to Horace and the Psalms.[57] We might look closer to home for the source of this oddly persistent figure. In 1803, with Schelling's scandalous departure from Jena, the *Critical Journal* folded. Holding out once more, as so often in his youth, for something else to come along, Hegel stayed. And luckily he did find work—with the Jena Mineralogical Society.[58] Part of Hegel's job was to venture into the nearby forests of the Harz Mountains to collect samples. He took these journeys seriously: on the title page of the *Phenomenology*'s first edition, he even identifies himself as "assessor in the Ducal Mineralogical Society." There is no knowing if these are the precise forests Hegel imagined clear cut several years before. But he would surely have known in 1802 about Goethe's sojourn in the Harz, memorialized in the 1789 poem "Harzreise im Winter." Devoted follower of current affairs that he was, Hegel might also have had in his sights heated and urgent debates about fuel-wood shortages in the German principalities; the long history of rational forestry in the Harz, known since the seventeenth century as an "indispensable" source of wood and coal energy and for "the conservation and improvement of [forest as] a capital good"; or even Frederick the Great's more recent initiative to install coal-burning steam pumps in his Harz Mountain mines.[59] No image of longing for a pristine and untouched nature, Hegel's leveled grove is an emblem of capitalism itself—of its management and mastery of the world, of its appetite for energy, and of its relentless drive to expand. And indeed, in the last year of his reign, Frederick succeeded in bringing steam power to the Harz.[60]

Living Labor, Living Dead

I turn now to Hegel's lectures on spirit of 1803–4. Given at Jena, after the collapse of the *Critical Journal,* in the precise years of his forest wandering, these lectures contain Hegel's most explicit and extended treatment of capitalism in its new industrial form. Famously, Germany lags behind here; despite Frederick's modernizing push, coal- and steam-powered industry would not be a widespread feature of German economic life until late in the nineteenth century. Nonetheless, I think Hegel grasps something of the radical break that industrialization will constitute in the history of production.[61]

Now, the final aim of Hegel's course is difficult to discern, not least because his elliptical notes never reach a conclusion. It is certain, however, that the lectures develop a history of human consciousness, represented by its external forms—from speech to hand tools to modern machinery. In the last of these movements, from agricultural and handicraft to machine labor, Hegel stumbles on a set of contradictions:

> [All labor] is essentially the putting [of the object] to death, ripping it out of its living context, and setting it up as something to be nullified as whatever it was before; in the MACHINE man supersedes just this formal activity of his own, and lets it do all the work for him. But this deceit that he practices against nature . . . takes its revenge upon him; what he gains from nature, the more he subdues it, the lower he sinks himself. When he lets nature be worked over by a variety of machines, he does not cancel the necessity for his own laboring but

only postpones it, and makes it more distant from nature; and his living labor is not directed on nature as alive, but this negative vitality evaporates from it, and the laboring that remains to man becomes itself *more machinelike*; man *diminishes* labor only for the whole, not for the single [laborer]; for him it is increased rather; for the more machinelike labor becomes, the less it is worth, and the more one must work.[62]

Here Hegel offers an early articulation of the "iron law of wages," their tendency under capitalism to hew to the bare minimum.[63] He explains the law as a function of technology: the more efficient labor becomes, the less it is worth, and the less it is worth, the more we must work. Mechanization has other effects, too, and it changes the essence of labor. Machinery makes labor and the laborer machinelike: "The labor becomes that much deader, it becomes machine work, the skill of the single laborer is infinitely limited, and the consciousness of the factory laborer is impoverished to the last extreme of dullness."[64] These anxieties are a familiar feature of the liberal tradition since Adam Smith. For Hegel, though, the worker's exploited and stupefied condition cannot be ameliorated. The domination of the worker by the machine (and presumably by its owner) is the necessary outcome of capitalism's promise of freedom.[65] The dialectic resembles that in *Faith and Knowledge*, where the idealism of freedom in reflective culture ends only in longing.

As unsettling as these human costs is the new energy economy that machinery puts to work. To produce a surplus, as Hegel observes, the machine needs more and more energy. It requires "living labor": the life of the worker that it consumes and turns into product. But machinery also takes more from nature, the vital force of which is absorbed into the industrial process. For Hegel, this is tantamount to "deceit," a violation of the bond between consciousness and the world. If in all labor humanity commits violence against nature ("His activity is essentially the putting of the object to death"), machinery gives this violence a new quality. Thus, in the *Philosophy of Right* (1821), Hegel will uneasily comment, "In our day agriculture is conducted on methods devised by reflective thinking, i.e. like a factory. This has given it a character like that of industry and contrary to its natural one."[66]

The energy enabling these transformations is not simply wasted. Taking vital force from the worker and the world, machinery produces a new and nightmarish form of the system of need. This is industrial capitalism as "a monstrous system of community . . . a life of the dead body, that moves itself within itself, one which ebbs and flows in its motion blindly, like the elements, and which requires continual strict dominance and taming like a wild beast."[67] Once more, Hegel evokes the living death of the automaton. Unlike in *Faith and Knowledge*, however, here the "life of the dead body" is somehow self-moving. With its insatiable appetite for vital force, the machine gives back a life in, or after, death.[68]

Yet the operation leaves a remainder. In machine labor, as Hegel notes, the vitality of the bond between worker and world flees, or "evaporates." Where does this vapor end up? What happens to this atmospheric trace of industry? Hegel has no answer. But a hint might be found in the work of his contemporary Charles Babbage. In 1832, Babbage asked these same questions, as an aside to his account of the steam engine and with no real awareness of their significance. He writes, "Water is converted into elastic vapour by the combustion of fuel. The chemical changes which thus take place are constantly increasing the atmosphere by large quantities of carbonic acid and other gases noxious to animal life. The means by which nature decomposes . . . these elements . . . are not sufficiently known."[69] For Babbage, the steam engine is cause for great wonder, an emblem of all modernity's triumphs. Still, he registers for an instant the possibility that these triumphs will leave a noxious trace.[70]

Today, such an image of danger hits hard, as a portent of our history in the making. But as Hegel knew, historical necessity is only retrospective. Rather than endlessly interpreting the omens of disaster, the point now is recovering the contingency occluded by our present.

4 Wollstonecraft in Ruins

This chapter turns from the problem of abstraction—as a mechanism of appropriative apprehension—to the poetics of wilderness. For the most part, the romantics position poetry against abstraction; poetic form and figure promise an alternative to the deadening abstractions of modernity. But the opposition is not always complete. For Mary Wollstonecraft, poetic language can enact a violence of its own, humanizing and thereby laying claim to the natural world.

Wollstonecraft's 1796 narrative of a journey north, *Letters Written during a Short Residence in Sweden, Norway, and Denmark*, has been recognized as a masterpiece of romantic memoir. Here I read it as a significant contribution to poetics. Mediating between the philosophical critique of abstraction and the aesthetic effort to mitigate its harms, Wollstonecraft's writing opens up the problem of wilderness for poetry. Throughout the *Letters*, she joins intricate figurative descriptions of the Scandinavian landscape with philosophical reveries on the origin and end of human life and language. Speculating about "the first dwelling of man" and "the origin of many poetical fictions," she is led, again and again, to visions of "devastation"—of the earth, of humanity, and of her own life.[1] Wollstonecraft's thinking about poetry and violence pivots on the figure of anthropomorphism. Long seen as integral to the romantic lyric, anthropomorphism signifies the appropriative humanization of nature; it prompts, in the realm of poetry, some of the same questions addressed by Kant and Hegel. In the *Letters* as well as the closely related essay "On Poetry" (1797), Wollstonecraft registers the damage wrought by anthropomorphism while reconceiving it as a memorial to violence. According to Wollstonecraft, this figure attests to the ruinous history of nature in "commerce"—her term for the circulation of raw materials, commodities, and human bodies.[2] Her experiments in anthropomorphism thus present, with surprising specificity, "an image of human industry in the shape of destruction" (*Letters*, 79). This vision is pessimistic; the *Letters* does not propose a better way of being in the world. Nevertheless, by insisting on the critical possibilities of poetic language, Wollstonecraft anticipates the poetry of wilderness to follow.

Anthropomorphism and "the Materiality of Actual History"

Anthropomorphism was central to late eighteenth-century theories of poetic language for the same reason that it matters to ecocriticism today: it speaks to the relationship between humanity and nature. In recent ecocriticism, anthropomorphism is often regarded as a betrayal of the nonhuman world.[3] To anthropomorphize is to obscure nature's true shape, or even, as Jonathan Bate suggests, "to begin to destroy it." Ecocritics have sought to dispel the fantasies attendant on the anthropomorphizing of nature; they aim to protect it from misrepresentation.[4]

In general, I affirm these ecocritical claims. But if anthropomorphism is an error, it is a powerfully persistent one—particularly in the romantic discourse of mind and nature. This is the wager of Paul de Man's 1983 essay "Anthropomorphism and Trope in the Lyric." Returning to the theme of the "marriage of mind and nature," de Man inquires into the figurative language that makes such a marriage seem possible. He thereby unsettles the basic categories upon which anthropomorphism depends.[5] De Man's essay responds to the humanism of M. H. Abrams, discussed earlier in this book: to say, as Abrams does, that the romantic lyric "humanizes" nature is to understand it as inherently anthropomorphizing. This also implies that "human" and "nature" can be taken as givens—in their separation and in their identification. De Man thus famously argues that "'anthropomorphism' is not just a trope."[6] An "identification on the level of substance," it is a figure that disavows its own figural status.[7] By positing an immediate identity between humanity and nature, anthropomorphism denies its proximity to tropes like prosopopoeia, or "face-making." It leads to (erroneous) metaphysical conclusions: "It takes one entity for another and thus implies the constitution of specific entities prior to their confusion, the *taking* of something for something else that can then be assumed to be *given*."[8] In pursuing this ideal unity, anthropomorphism petrifies, or "freezes," the categories of human and nature; it obscures, while never completely effacing, their "actual history," just as it promises to unite them.[9]

At issue in de Man's essay is not only the (catachrestic) imposition of human features on the natural world. He is also concerned with the way that "human" and "nature" take on a monumentality that elides their historical existence. As de Man's readers have shown, this is a political matter. Sara Guyer, for instance, invokes anthropomorphism in a discussion of the phantasmatic relations between a people and its language in romantic nationalism. For Guyer, who builds on de Man's account, anthropomorphism is "a mode of explication" that relies on "a self-affirming tautology."[10] The anthropomorphisms of romantic nationalism suggest that a language can be defined by its people and a people can be defined by its language. Both categories are treated as monolithic and ahistorical, and they acquire an exclusionary force with devastating consequences.

Like ecocriticism, rhetorical reading insists on anthropomorphism's political stakes. Yet it does not claim that the figure can or should be avoided. The error of anthropomorphism is a kind of knowledge. Elsewhere, Guyer proposes that rhetorical reading can help us "to approach romanticism (and readings of romanticism) as neither evasion nor cover-up."[11] This is something like my point here. As a poetic figure for the relation between humanity and nature, anthropomorphism idealizes and testifies to their continuing historical interchange. It presents as an ideal unity what de Man describes as the "materiality of actual history."[12] Anthropomorphism speaks, if not quite openly, about the history of which it is the figure.[13]

In the Scandinavian *Letters*, as I have said, Wollstonecraft is concerned with the ruinous history of nature in commerce. She uses anthropomorphism to reflect on this history. This chapter is not a critique of the anthropomorphisms in her poetic prose. Rather, I read these experiments in anthropomorphism as a way of commemorating nature's devastation.[14] In so doing, I show that attention to ruin is a primary mode of historical thinking for Wollstonecraft. If anthropomorphism signifies the violent grasping of the natural world, then ruin describes the consequences of that violence. For Wollstonecraft, ruin is history's material trace. In what follows, I show how the "actual history" at first obscured by the figure of anthropomorphism returns through the ruination of figure.

Origin, Figure, Destruction

Though rarely regarded as a poetic theorist, Wollstonecraft often thought and wrote about poetry. On her return from Scandinavia, she composed a brief

essay that William Godwin called, in the 1798 *Posthumous Works*, "On Poetry."
At the same time, she drafted a set of fragments on aesthetics entitled, perhaps wrongly, "Hints, chiefly designed to have been incorporated in the second
part of the Vindication of the Rights of Woman."[15] These elements of a poetic
theory are closely related to the Scandinavian *Letters*. Moreover, they position
Wollstonecraft as a participant in the ongoing debate about the origin of poetic
language. For her, as for many of her contemporaries, the conjectural history
of poetry is necessarily a theory of anthropomorphism. In this section, I read
Wollstonecraft alongside two of her main interlocutors, Jean-Jacques Rousseau
and Hugh Blair. Each sees poetic language as involved in the progress of civilization. For Wollstonecraft, who is closest to Rousseau on this point, historical
progress is always potentially harmful. As the *Letters* makes clear, when Wollstonecraft imagines history, she is often imagining a history of destruction.

A decade before writing her own essay on poetry, Wollstonecraft studied
with enthusiasm Hugh Blair's *Lectures on Rhetoric and Belles Lettres* (1783). The
culmination of the eighteenth-century rhetorical tradition, Blair's *Lectures* suggests that the desire to personify has "its foundation laid deep in human nature."[16] For Blair, language must have been most figurative at its origins: "The
early Language of men being entirely made up of words descriptive of sensible
objects, it became, of necessity, extremely metaphorical."[17] Equipped with a limited set of names and with a powerful imagination, human beings used the
same words to speak about different things. Language was thus metaphoric,
even poetic, at its beginning. The impulse to trope, Blair continues, resulted
in the personification of everything in nature. There is a "proneness in human
nature," he writes, "to animate all objects."[18] These anthropomorphisms are not
simple errors. In the form of myth and religion, they are the foundation for all
human culture.[19]

Blair's story of poetic language and civilization is profoundly important to
Wollstonecraft. Nevertheless, she is skeptical about progress—in the arts and
otherwise.[20] In her skepticism, she resembles Rousseau, another thinker of poetic origins. Rousseau's significance for Wollstonecraft is well established.[21] A
critical engagement with his thought was a constant of her writing life: she re-
viewed his memoirs in the *Analytical Review*, contested his theory of education
in *A Vindication of the Rights of Woman* (1792), and alluded throughout her
writings to his *Discourse on the Origin of Inequality* (1755) and *Reveries of the
Solitary Walker* (1782). The essay "On Poetry" shows his influence too, though
it often challenges his ideas. Notably, Wollstonecraft refuses nostalgia for a
state of nature that she terms "Rousseau's golden age of stupidity" (*Letters*, 60).

Without any faith in progress, she argues that nothing is gained by idealizing poetry's origins.

In two major essays of the 1750s, the *Discourse on Inequality* and the *Essay on the Origin of Languages*, Rousseau elaborates the themes addressed by Wollstonecraft in her critical prose. Like Blair, Rousseau argues that language enabled the development of human knowledge and culture. Imagining a prelinguistic, and thus a presocial, state, Rousseau asks, "To what extent could men improve themselves and acquire knowledge by mutual endeavour when, having neither fixed abodes nor the least need for one another, they would perhaps hardly meet twice in their lives, without recognizing or speaking to one another?"[22] Without spoken language, he insists, human beings could not build or dwell, could not live together, and could not even think.[23] Language is the condition of possibility for everything from abstract thought to the development of social forms like the family and the nation.

This history appears progressive, yet it ultimately ends in ruin. In his *Essay on the Origin of Languages*, written at the same time as the *Discourse on Inequality*, Rousseau points to poetry's role in this history of destruction. The *Essay* tells and retells the story of language at its beginnings. It insists that language has no single origin. Rousseau imagines the earliest human beings dispersed across the earth, and he argues that the passions proper to its different climates gave rise to different languages.[24] In the deserts of the south, for instance, where young men and women came together at a well, love surely prompted speech. Surprised by the sight of desirable strangers, their "ardent youth gradually forgot its ferocity, gradually they tamed one another; through endeavoring to make themselves understood, they learned to explain themselves."[25] For Rousseau as for Blair, poetry is the first language: "Poetry was discovered before prose," he writes, and "this had to be so, since the passions spoke before reason."[26]

Despite such a promising beginning, Rousseau's history takes a ruinous course. Once poetry has made human life social, the cultivation of the earth proceeds with haste. "I see Palaces and Towns raised; I see the arts, laws, commerce born; I see peoples forming, extending, dissolving, succeeding one another like the waves of the sea," Rousseau proclaims.[27] This apparently triumphal vision soon reveals itself as something else: "I see men gathered together at a few dwelling places in order to devour each other there, to make a frightful desert of the rest of the world; a worthy monument to social union and the usefulness of the arts."[28] In a single paratactic sentence, Rousseau follows civilization from its origins to its seeming end. He leaves us with a metropolis and a desert, the two faces of uneven development. To put it differently, he develops in the *Essay* a certain dialectic of enlightenment. In the words of the critical theorists, which read almost as a gloss on Rousseau, "The wholly enlightened earth is radiant with triumphant calamity."[29]

Wollstonecraft's own history of "arts, laws, [and] commerce" has a markedly similar form. In her essay "On Poetry"—composed in 1797 for the *Monthly Magazine* and included by Godwin in the *Posthumous Works*—she echoes Rousseau and Blair in telling the story of poetic language and civilization.[30] She brings together a skepticism about progress with a close attention to figuration. Yet Wollstonecraft's essay is more than a synthesis. As its (few) present-day readers have remarked, "On Poetry" anticipates some of the best-known statements of romantic poetics. In diagnosing as a social ill the conventionality of much modern poetry, it lays the basis for similar claims in Wordsworth's "Preface to *Lyrical Ballads*" (1800/1802) and Shelley's *A Defence of Poetry* (1821)—which were both likely influenced by Wollstonecraft.[31] As do these later texts, "On Poetry" traces affinities between imagination and understanding, and it suggests that poetry is a distinctive form of thought. In Harriet Jump's words, it "point[s] forward irresistibly to the more famous examples of Romantic literary theory."[32]

These commonalities help draw out what is distinct about Wollstonecraft's essay. Her poetic theory is far more pessimistic than Wordsworth's or Shelley's. Near the close of "On Poetry," she writes despairingly that "the beauties of nature are not forcibly felt, when civilization, or rather luxury, has made considerable advances."[33] This picture of modernity returns in the "Preface to *Lyrical Ballads*," as Wollstonecraft's indictment of luxurious consumption finds a counterpart in Wordsworth's view of production, or "occupation"—of the modern worker's "savage torpor" and his "degrading thirst after outrageous stimulation."[34] Rather than seek to restore the poetic sense, Wollstonecraft wonders if poetry is a thing of the past.

In many ways, this theory is expressive, in Abrams's sense of the term.[35] Wollstonecraft appeals to the spontaneity of expression as a measure of aesthetic value, and she asks "why the poetry written in the infancy of society, is most natural . . . the transcript of immediate sensations, in all their wildness and simplicity" (7). Here she relies on familiar contrasts between ancient and modern poetry: the former is natural, or wild, while the latter is artificial. In such moments, she seems almost to hope for a new poetry of "immediate sensations." "In the present state of society" (7, 11), can we learn to feel naturally again?

Surprisingly, Wollstonecraft's answer seems to be no. For a true poetry of nature, she writes, "the understanding must bring back the feelings to nature, or the sensibility must have such native strength, as rather to be whetted than destroyed by the strong exercises of passion" (11). Neither of these paths is open to us. The understanding has been dulled by luxury and by the conventionality of modern poetry. Meanwhile, the culture of sensibility has dissolved in libertinism. In the final lines of her essay, which chime with her unfinished novel *The Wrongs of Woman* (also 1797), she argues that "the same sensibility, or quickness of senses, which makes a man relish the tranquil scenes of nature, when sensation, rather than reason, imparts delight, frequently makes a libertine of him" (11). The powerful feelings that once inspired poetry express themselves now as a "fondness for the sex," which "often gives an appearance of humanity to the behaviour of men, who have small pretensions to the reality."[36] In the absence of a poetry of nature, we can only look to the past—not for inspiration, but for evidence of what went wrong.

Wollstonecraft's history of poetry is thus a narrative of decline. It is also a story about figuration, which becomes in modernity a mere ornament or effect. For the ancients, figuration was essential for knowledge. Like Blair, Wollstonecraft assumes that poetic language began with naming: "The first observers of nature, the true poets, exercised their understanding much more than their imitators. But they exercised it to discriminate things" (9). Such poetic knowledge, Wollstonecraft stresses, enabled the cultivation of the earth. It was anthropomorphism in particular that made the earth a home:

> The imagery of the ancients seems naturally to have been borrowed from surrounding objects and their mythology. When a hero is to be transported from one place to another, across pathless wastes, is any vehicle so natural, as one of the fleecy clouds on which the poet has often gazed, scarcely conscious that he wished to make it his chariot? Again, when nature seems to present obstacles to his progress at almost every step, when the tangled forest and steep mountain stand as barriers, to pass over which the mind longs for supernatural aid; an interposing deity, who walks on the waves, and rules the storm, severely felt in the first attempts to cultivate a country, will receive from the impassioned fancy "a local habitation and a name." (8)

These spontaneous metaphors—clouds imagined as chariots; a deity felt in every forest, sea, or storm—were the elements for future poetry. But they also consoled the first cultivators of the earth, as they attributed to wild nature a distinctly human form. The anthropomorphisms of ancient poetry preceded the humanizing labor of the agriculturalist. In a fragment from the "Hints," Wollstonecraft puts it thus: "I am more and more convinced, that poetry is the first effervescence of the imagination, and the forerunner of civilization."[37]

Cultivation is a key term in Wollstonecraft's essay. Rather than invoke it to naturalize culture, she uses this language to ask how a civilization might appropriate the natural world. In "On Poetry," as we have seen, she argues that the cultivation of art and knowledge preceded the cultivation of the earth. That said, her overall vision of history is far from triumphant. As Deidre Lynch observes, Wollstonecraft's appeals to cultivation evoke a political-economic "luxury debate that had long worried over the refinements implemented by the commercial classes and by women."[38] So when Wollstonecraft defines modern history as a process of cultivation, she is not offering praise. Rather, she implies that cultivation must become "overcultivation"—as exemplified by the development of commerce, by the miseducation of women, and by the artificiality of modern poetry.[39]

Her figure for overcultivation is the greenhouse. In the *Vindication of the Rights of Woman*, as Lynch notes, "Wollstonecraft depicts her miseducated ladies as beautiful 'exotics.' They are tender plants, whose 'sensations,' she says, have been 'heightened in the hot-bed of luxurious indolence.'"[40] Similarly, in "On Poetry," greenhouse gardening is a figure for writing poetry in the present. Unlike the ancients, who cultivated the earth with vital metaphors, the moderns have no expressive power. Today, nature is reduced to its representations and poetry is the recirculation of images. "In a more advanced state of civilization," Wollstonecraft writes, "a poet is rather the creature of art, than of nature. The books that he reads in his youth, become a hot-bed in which artificial fruits are produced, beautiful to the common eye, though they want the true hue and flavor" (9). Like fruit grown in a greenhouse, modern poetry is deprived of "real, native roots." It is the outgrowth of an uprooting commercial society.[41]

This is not Wollstonecraft's only way of presenting modern poetry. In the essay's following sentences, she depicts the modern poet as a figure painter. Insisting now on the cold artifice of his work, she writes that "his images do not arise from sensations; they are copies; and, like the works of the painters who copy ancient statues when they draw men and women of their own times, we acknowledge that the features are fine, and the proportions just; yet they are men of stone; insipid figures, that never convey to the mind the idea of a portrait taken from life, where the soul gives spirit and homogeneity to the whole" (9). Once more, she finds a superficial refinement in modern poetry. She also signals an ongoing controversy about figurative representation in the visual arts. The passage suggests that poets who rely on conventional imagery are like painters who copy classical artworks. Such painters would have been women. In eighteenth-century England, women artists were discouraged from using nude models, and they had no choice but to paint after sculptures. Unlike their male contemporaries, they would never move on to life studies.[42] Wollstonecraft's modern poet—whose "insipid figures" recall the "men of stone" in neoclassical paintings by women—would have been read as a feminized type. He is underdeveloped and overcultivated, much like a "miseducated lad[y]."[43] Too civilized for authentic expression and "deformed" by the culture of luxury, this poet can only present nature as a lifeless copy.[44]

If Wollstonecraft's greenhouse connotes a nature transformed by commerce, her ancient statue seems less dynamic. Yet it too presents poetic language as a measure of history. Jonah Siegel has noted that, for artists in training in the period, "the major pedagogic materials . . . were the remains of antique statues."[45] Eighteenth-century artists and writers received the past via fragments and ruins. Such a "disquieting intimacy with the broken manifestations of antiquity" is illustrated, according to Siegel, in a drawing by Wollstonecraft's onetime friend and lover Henry Fuseli, *The Artist in Despair before the Magnitude of Ancient Ruins* (1778–79; fig. 1).[46] Dominated by a giant hand and foot, the remains of a missing sculptural whole, this drawing shows an artist overcome by the grandeur of classical fragments and by his distance from the past. These fragments stand for an absent aesthetic ideal. To "copy ancient statues," in Wollstonecraft's phrase, would mean making a record of loss. The expressive limitations of modern art and poetry, for Fuseli as well as for Wollstonecraft, are a testament to history, understood as the progress of ruin.

When Wollstonecraft imagined ancient sculpture, was a ruin what she saw? Might we read her claim about poetry's diminishing powers as a claim about how figurative language responds to or records history? Certainly, this is something like the point of Fuseli's drawing. Remnants of a bygone world, reminders of loss, and a measure of time's inexorable passing: Fuseli's ruins articulate an immanent historicism. On one hand, these fragments of an anthropomorphic form fail to convey their aesthetic ideal (except perhaps in the negative). On the other, they speak eloquently about the history that guarantees this failure.

Like Fuseli, then, Wollstonecraft attends to ruin as a mode of historical thinking.[47] In the *Letters*, she reflects on "the contemplation of noble ruins":

FIGURE 1. Henry Fuseli, *The Artist in Despair before the Magnitude of Ancient Ruins* (1778–79). Source: Wikimedia Commons.

"We take a retrospect of the exertions of man, the fate of empires and their rulers; and marking the grand destruction of ages, it seems the necessary change of time leading to improvement" (48). Sometimes destruction means the coming of a better world. This is not how Wollstonecraft usually understands it. In *The Wrongs of Woman*, she appeals to "the most terrific of ruins—that of a human soul." "What is the view of the fallen column, the mouldering arch, of the most exquisite workmanship," she writes, "when compared with this living memento of the fragility, the instability, of reason, and the wild luxuriancy of noxious passions?"[48] Here Wollstonecraft meditates on a ruined life—a ruin that interrupts aesthetic pleasure with real "anguish."[49] Such a human ruin is no less historical, "exhibiting the misery and oppression, peculiar to women, that arise out of the partial laws and customs of society."[50] Wollstonecraft's poetics are defined by this view of history as ruin. Moreover, it is through figuration that poetry expresses its historical being. In what follows, I argue that Wollstonecraft's history of ruin entails the ruination of figure. This is not the end of representation or reference but a way of remembering history's ruinous course.

Nature in Ruins

Since its first publication, Wollstonecraft's *Letters* was seen as fundamentally poetic in style. In a 1797 letter, Robert Southey distills the book to pure imagery when he writes that it "made [him] in love with a cold climate, and frost and snow, with a northern moonlight."[51] In the years following, both Samuel Taylor Coleridge and Percy Shelley read Wollstonecraft's prose as aspiring to the condition of verse—an aspiration to be fulfilled by poems such as "Kubla Khan" (1798/1816) and "Mont Blanc" (1816), which draw on the language of the *Letters*.[52] Of course, Wollstonecraft's memoir of her Scandinavian journey, in search of a missing cargo ship licensed by her lover Gilbert Imlay, is not a poem. The *Letters* join confession with political economy, travel narrative with conjectural history, poetic theory with poetic practice. A romantic book in Novalis's encyclopedic yet fragmentary sense, the *Letters* reflects on, as much as it performs, the poetic.[53]

Like works of picturesque art, the book's descriptive passages emphasize the incompleteness of efforts to humanize the land.[54] On her first arrival in Scandinavia, Wollstonecraft gazes at the rocky coast near Gothenburg and thinks of "the rude materials of creation forming the barrier of unwrought space" (7). This image of creation's limits positions Wollstonecraft at the periphery of the developed world. Here, she writes, "only so much is cultivated . . . as is absolutely necessary to supply the necessaries of life; and near the seashore . . . there scarcely appears a vestige of cultivation" (17). Scandinavia is not outside of history, she observes, so much as at its threshold. In a zone of encroaching and uneven development, the violence of "improvement" (21, 38, 61) is glaring. While praising some signs of civilization, Wollstonecraft remarks that the first peasants she meets are "scarcely human in their appearance" (6). Like the land itself, these peasants are both unfinished and already damaged, vestiges of "barbarism" (17) and victims of the commercial society materializing around them.[55]

As in "On Poetry," then, in the *Letters* history is progressive and destructive. The discourse of cultivation again helps Wollstonecraft convey this. Near the Norwegian border, in "the most uncultivated part of the [Swedish] country" (25), she imagines "that the first dwelling of man happened to be a spot like this which led him to adore a sun so seldom seen" (29–30). Born in an inhospitable climate, these human beings must have "worship[ped]" and "run after the sun, in order that the different parts of the earth might be peopled" (30). The anthropomorphic sun of ancient religion allowed for the population of the earth. Further, as Wollstonecraft notes, population is a force of culture: "The increasing population of the earth must necessarily tend to its improvement, as the means of existence are multiplied by invention" (61). The earth is thereby remade in humanity's image. Once again, Wollstonecraft argues that cultivation is an anthropomorphizing process. She maintains that it will end in ruin. Envisioning a future earth, "perfectly cultivated" and "completely peopled," she cannot help "pictur[ing] the state of man when the earth could no longer support him. Where was he to fly from universal famine?" (68). If cultivation must become overcultivation, and subsistence must become luxury, then a future "universal famine" is the inevitable end of history.

Torn between her views of improvement and her visions of future ruin—to say nothing of her memories of loss—Wollstonecraft observes that poetic description might not do justice to this land.[56] "There is an individuality in every prospect," she writes, "yet we cannot find words to discriminate that individuality so as to enable a stranger to say, this is the face, that the view" (25). How to describe a place so rapidly changing? Can poetic language portray its singular face? These are questions about the limits of the picturesque, which privileges wild nature but in a thoroughly generalized form. Ostensibly opposed, as Thomas Pfau has explained, to "a Whiggish ideology of improvement and commercial speculation," the picturesque view of landscape—as an accumulation of general aesthetic effects—mirrors closely "the *appearance of value*" in a capitalist society.[57] Reflecting on her own use of poetic language, Wollstonecraft shows her awareness of these relations.

In this context, too, Wollstonecraft turns to anthropomorphism. At its least developed, she writes, Scandinavia "seemed to remind me of the creation of things, of the first efforts of sportive nature" (27). In such a setting, the origin of poetic language is an unavoidable question. Wandering on the grounds of an abandoned estate near Tonsberg in Norway, Wollstonecraft thus remarks, "How often do my feelings produce ideas that remind me of the origin of many poetical fictions" (57). Like one of the first poets, she anthropomorphizes the things around her: "The continual recurrence of pine and fir groves, in the day, sometimes wearies the sight; but, in the evening, nothing can be more picturesque, or, more properly speaking, better calculated to produce poetical images. Passing through them, I have been struck with a mystic kind of reverence, and I did, as it were, homage to their venerable shadows. Not nymphs, but philosophers seemed to inhabit them—ever musing; I could scarcely conceive that they were without some consciousness of existence—without a calm enjoyment of the pleasure they diffused" (57). In a moment of transport, Wollstonecraft sees these ancient groves as figures for her own "philosophical day-dreaming."[58] Her reverie is an indulgence in "unrestrained" imaginative play (57–58), whereby the projection of consciousness onto nature is experienced as immediate unity. There is no distinction here between the theory and practice of anthropomorphism.

Such moments of identification rarely last in the *Letters*. In the same episode, Wollstonecraft comments on the deforestation of Norway. "The destruction, or gradual reduction, of their forests, will probably meliorate the climate," she remarks, "and their manners will naturally improve in the same ratio as industry requires ingenuity" (60). Thus, she pivots from a fantasy of unity to an anticipation of destructive improvement (in the climatic, economic, and cultural senses).[59] This improvement depends on what Marx will call the "formal subsumption" of forestry under capital: "Half a century ago the Dutch . . . only paid for the cutting down of the wood, and the farmers were glad to get rid of it without giving themselves any trouble. At present they form a just estimate of its value" (60). In other words, the forest will still be cleared away, but it is now a raw material or a capital good.[60]

So is Wollstonecraft's forest dreaming an occasion for imaginative play or a prelude to political economy? The letter's structure suggests that it is both—and that anthropomorphism is the link between imagination and "actual history." Something similar is the case in a later passage, where the ruination of anthropomorphism commemorates a history of ruin. The view that Wollstonecraft describes was a celebrated one in Norway (see fig. 2). I quote from her letter at length:

Approaching, or rather descending, to Christiania, though the weather continued a little cloudy, my eyes were charmed with the view of an extensive undulated valley, stretching out under the shelter of a noble amphitheatre of pine-covered mountains. Farm houses scattered about animated, nay, graced a scene which still retained so much of its native wildness, that the art which appeared, seemed so necessary it was scarcely perceived. Cattle were grazing in the shaven meadows; and the lively green, on their swelling sides, contrasted with the ripening corn and rye. The corn that grew on the slopes, had not, indeed, the laughing luxuriance of plenty, which I have seen in more genial climes. A fresh breeze swept across the grain, parting its slender stalks; but the wheat did not wave its head with its wonted, careless dignity, as if nature had crowned it the king of plants.

The view, immediately on the left, as we drove down the mountain, was almost spoilt by the depredations committed on the rocks to make alum. I do not know the process.—I only saw that the rocks looked red after they had been burnt; and regretted that the operation should leave a quantity of rubbish, to introduce an image of human industry in the shape of destruction. (79)

Once more, Wollstonecraft locates an anthropomorphized landscape alongside a vision of destruction. Less ambivalent now, she mourns the ruin of the earth. As I have said, Wollstonecraft is alert to correspondences between the impositions of poetic language and the appropriative violence of commerce. One might therefore argue that this description of an alum mine rewrites or revises the picturesque imagery that precedes it.[61]

But no such separation between these moments can be maintained. If the mine is "an image of human industry in the shape of destruction," the landscape presents a different sort of ruin. This anthropomorphized landscape is not only a wishful fantasy of art and wilderness harmonized—of their "identification on the level of substance" (de Man). It is also a ruin on the level of figure, as the anthropomorphisms that populate the landscape have all been rendered inoperative. Thus, farm houses "animated, nay, graced" the scene, a rhetorical gesture that anthropomorphizes, then turns substance (life) toward accident (ornaments or graces), while leaving behind the mark of negation. Similarly, the crops growing on the mountain slopes "had not . . . [a] laughing luxuriance" and "did not wave [their] heads." Throughout the passage, the ruination of figure insists on the failure of anthropomorphic identification; it demonstrates the

FIGURE 2. John William Edy, *Alum Mine at Egeberg* (1820). Source: Wikimedia Commons.

violence of the attempt. These ruined anthropomorphisms testify to a ruined nature that is just out of sight.

Such "impossible" figures, to borrow Nancy Yousef's apt description, are a defining feature of Wollstonecraft's indictment of commercial society.[62] In the *Letters*, ruinous violence is not only inflicted on the earth. Just as nature is humanized, or improved, in destructive ways, human life is made less livable by the progress of commerce. In a direct address to Imlay, Wollstonecraft attributes his failures of feeling to an uncontrolled desire for gain: "You—yourself, are strangely altered," she writes, "since you have entered deeply into commerce—more than you are aware of—never allowing yourself to reflect, and keeping your mind, or rather passions, in a continual state of agitation" (126). The psychology of the commercial speculator is not so different from that of the libertine or any other devotee of luxury; each is driven by "the strong exercises of passion" ("On Poetry," 11), and each leaves a ruined life in his wake.

Wollstonecraft's sense of ruin therefore intensifies as she returns from the peripheries. In her penultimate letter, on the metropolitan "whirlpool of gain" that is Hamburg (129), Wollstonecraft observes, "The sword has been merciful, compared with the depredations made on human life by contractors, and by the swarm of locusts who have battened on the pestilence they spread abroad.

These men, like the owners of negro ships, never smell on their money the blood by which it has been gained, but sleep quietly in their beds, terming such occupations *lawful callings*; yet the lightning marks not their roofs, to thunder conviction on them, 'and to justify the ways of God to man'" (130). The circulation of commodities and wealth cannot be understood apart from these human costs; as Wollstonecraft puts it, there is no money that is not soaked in blood.[63] If commerce is a force of civilization, it is one of devastation too—dependent on the far-reaching and intensifying degradation of human life. To make the world over in a human form is to condemn much of humanity to ruin.

Regarding the *Letters* from its bleak end, it becomes clear that such knowledge is never far from Wollstonecraft's mind. In an earlier discussion of hereditary land rights in Norway, she remarks that "England and America owe their liberty to commerce, which created a new species of power to undermine the feudal system" (86). She predicts that as archaic property laws are abolished, Norway will follow a similar trajectory. Of course, this is not a narrative of achievement: "Let them [all] beware of the consequence; the tyranny of wealth is still more galling and debasing than that of rank" (87). Wollstonecraft's claim here is yet another effort to present history's progressive and destructive form. In the *Letters*, anthropomorphism bears the trace of this history. For Wollstonecraft, the ruination of figure commemorates the devastation of nature and humanity alike. But even if she understands poetic language as a record of violence, she proposes no alternative. For Wordsworth and Shelley, however—to whom I look in the following chapters—the alternative is poetry itself.

5   Accidental Revelation in Wordsworth

In the remainder of this book, I show how Wollstonecraft's sense of poetic language is developed by poets like Wordsworth and Shelley. Adopting, in various ways, the social critique integral to Wollstonecraft's *Letters*, these romantics seek a language that circumvents the domination of nature. For Wordsworth, as I suggested in the first chapter, poetry can disclose nature in flight from intentional consciousness; it opens onto a world at the threshold of apprehension. Now I develop that earlier discussion of Wordsworth's poetics of wilderness by turning to a celebrated lyric of nature and consciousness in "concourse wild," "There was a Boy."[1] Drafted in 1798 as an autobiographical fragment and published as a self-standing poem in *Lyrical Ballads* (1800/1802) and *Poems* (1815), these lines find a resting place in Book V of *The Prelude*, an episode in that "book of 'Books.'"[2] The poem is well known. Its description of a boy in conversation with the owls on Lake Windermere's shore has long been seen as illustrating Wordsworth's own thought about nature, consciousness, temporality, poetry, and much besides.[3]

I shall argue that in "There was a Boy" and related verses from *The Prelude* and elsewhere Wordsworth reconceives the apprehension of nature as an "accidental revelation." The phrase is De Quincey's, and it speaks well to the inconsequentiality of experience central to Wordsworth's poetry.[4] Neither sublime nor traumatic, accidental revelation concerns nature as it simply appears, or reveals itself, in all its ordinariness—which is not to say in its "fittedness" to the human mind.[5] Rather, by redirecting or suspending its own apprehensive power, Wordsworth's poetry feels its way toward a familiar though genuinely nonhuman nature. What Wordsworth calls the "gentle shock of mild surprise" (V.407)—a feeling as inconsequential as potentially destabilizing—is the feeling of nature in its difference from, or nonidentity to, consciousness. In this gentlest of shock experiences, nature appears, and consciousness finds itself free, if only for a moment, from the compulsion to grasp.

My discussion of "There was a Boy" begins from De Quincey's. I am especially interested in what De Quincey terms, in his 1839 memoir, the "psychological principle" (160) pivotal to the poem: a "principle" of frustrated expectations, withdrawn attention, and sudden manifestation. I am not alone here. Many readers of "There was a Boy" have looked to De Quincey, who tells a striking anecdote related to the poem. Recalling an evening spent with Wordsworth in expectation of the mail carrier, De Quincey reports the poet speaking at length on the vagaries of attention and perception. "I have remarked," says De Quincey's Wordsworth,

> that, if under any circumstances, the attention is energetically braced up to an act of steady observation, or of steady expectation, then, if this intense condition of vigilance should suddenly relax, at that moment any beautiful, any impressive visual object, or collection of objects, falling upon the eye, is carried to the heart with a power not known under other circumstances. Just now, my ear was placed upon the stretch, in order to catch any sound of wheels. . . . At the very instant when I raised my head from the ground, in final abandonment of hope for this night, at the very instant when the organs of attention were all at once relaxing from their tension, the bright star hanging in the air above those outlines of massy blackness fell suddenly upon my eye, and penetrated my capacity of apprehension with a pathos and a sense of the infinite, that would not have arrested me under other circumstances. (160)

De Quincey sees these comments as a general statement of the "psychological principle" shaping "There was a Boy." His profound appreciation of the poem, which follows on this anecdote, suggests he is right. Other critics have agreed, identifying in the same conjuncture of memoir and poem a "phenomenology of perception and consciousness" (Anne-Lise François) and a poetics of "the intervals *between* acts of attention" (Lily Gurton-Wachter).[6] I find little to disagree with in these statements; Wordsworth's poetic practice is clearly informed by such a phenomenology.

In what follows, though, I will be particularly concerned with what De Quincey's Wordsworth calls the "capacity of apprehension." The Kantian resonance is notable, given Wordsworth's supposed ignorance of "German metaphysics."[7] Still, as De Quincey tells it, Wordsworth describes how the power of apprehension is rendered receptive, no longer grasping a world before it, but "penetrated" and "arrested" by an unanticipated "pathos and a sense of the infinite." The capacity to apprehend becomes a capacity to receive.[8] This transformation is sudden and impermanent, a hiatus in appropriative perception allowing the most inconsequential things to "fal[l] upon" us. Wordsworth first associates these mild surprises with beauty, before settling on the understated "impressive." Recall, here, the philosophical sense of *impression*; far from sublime, "sheer sense impressions," as Kant says, fade almost to nothing in the span of a day.[9] All the same, these transient experiences are repeatable. It is, in fact, through repetition that Wordsworth and the Winander boy learn to perceive—or better, to feel—nature differently. Thus, what I am calling a hiatus in apprehension is something like the "double take" William Galperin finds in Wordsworth's poetry: a structure of looking and looking again that discloses a material world "unrealized and overlooked."[10] Moreover, because these mild surprises nearly fail to register in terms of cause or consequence, they do not participate in the narrative of "abundant recompense" often associated with Wordsworth.[11] If an accidental revelation is a gift of nature, it is a gift given without reason—without, that is, the economic justification of "an ennobling interchange / Of action from within and without" (XII.376–77). Nature appears when we ask nothing of it.[12]

Chance Appearances

Throughout his 1839 memoir, De Quincey poses the question of "Wordsworth's attachment to nature" (164). He seeks, in the manner of a nascent depth psychology, the hidden sources of the poet's character. Attending to all those "indirect effect[s] growing gradually upon" the young Wordsworth, De Quincey remarks that a love of nature can never arise from "a direct conscious anticipation of imaginative pleasure" (159). Rather, attachments like Wordsworth's have "unconscious" origins: "that which happened to the boy in mimicking the owls," De Quincey argues, must have "happened also to him" (164). One need not accept the biographical claim to appreciate the insight. In Wordsworth's poetry, especially in "There was a Boy," nature reveals itself when "direct conscious anticipation" halts. As De Quincey puts it, the night's "solemn spectacle" impresses itself on the Winander boy only after his attention "giv[es] way" (161).

Like De Quincey, I understand the revelation of nature in Wordsworth's poetry as a matter of "passive" or "semi-conscious" states (161). But before turning directly to "There was a Boy," I consider the broader philosophical and poetic implications of this claim. De Quincey is eager to generalize from his literary and biographical observations. Writing in a lengthy footnote, he offers "an illustration . . . of those accidental revelations that unfold new aspects of nature: it was one that occurred to myself" (164). De Quincey proceeds to describe his habitual walks in the mountains above Great Langdale. "On a favourable day," he writes,

> this accident occurred; and the scene which I then beheld, was one which I shall not wholly forget to my dying day. The effects arose from the position of the sun and the spectator, taken in connexion with a pendulous mass of vapour, in which, however, were many rents and openings, and through them, far below, at an abyss-like depth, was seen the gloomy valley, its rare cottages, and "unrejoicing" fir-trees. I had beheld the scene many times before; I was familiar with its least-important features, but now, it was absolutely transfigured, it was seen under lights and mighty shadows that made it no less marvellous to the eye than that memorable creation amongst the clouds and azure sky, which is described by the Solitary in "The Excursion." And, upon speaking of it to Wordsworth, I found that he had repeatedly witnessed the same impressive transfiguration; so that it is not evanescent, but dependent upon fixed and recoverable combinations of time and weather. (165)

For De Quincey, a chance appearance in nature—the interplay of light, shadow, and fog above a valley—bears comparison with visionary poetry; the footnote draws no distinction between natural phenomena and their representation. Thus, the accidental occurrence or "revelation" above Great Langdale is "no less marvellous to the eye" than the Solitary's vision in book II of *The Excursion*. As De Quincey tells it, Wordsworth is familiar with the phenomenon, having "repeatedly witnessed" it himself. Neither wholly "evanescent" nor a singular "vision of glory," in Geoffrey Hartman's phrase, the experience can be recovered, "time and weather" permitting.[13] Though "impressive," the "transfiguration" of the landscape is repeatable.

De Quincey's note evokes, more than any particular event, a mode or quality of experience that might be called "Wordsworthian." The prose contributes powerfully to this effect. "I had beheld the scene many times," he writes, "but now, it was absolutely transfigured, it was seen under lights and mighty shadows." Shifting into the passive voice, De Quincey joins the grammatical with the perceiving subject (no longer a specific individual, but an anonymous "spectator"). The "occlu[sion]" of agency at the level of the sentence bespeaks a related transformation of perception.[14] As De Quincey rightly suggests, such formal and conceptual maneuvers are essential to Wordsworth's thinking.

Yet De Quincey's poetic example is rather odd. Consider the lines from *The Excursion* to which he alludes.[15] After the discovery in a ruined chapel of the "homeless Pensioner" (II.770) whose funeral begins book II, the Solitary is struck by a vision: "The Appearance, instantaneously disclosed, / Was of a mighty City," he recalls, "A wilderness of building, sinking far / And self-withdrawn into a wondrous depth, / Far sinking into splendor—without end!" (869–73). The description that follows of a city of gold and gemstones draws on the book of Revelation and its apocalyptic vision of the New Jerusalem. As discussed in the first chapter of this book, M. H. Abrams argues that the romantics reconceived biblical apocalypse as a revelation of the imagination, "a marriage between subject and object, mind and nature, which creates a new world out of the old world of sense."[16] Something similar seems to be at work here, as the Solitary remarks that "By earthly nature had the effect been wrought / Upon the dark materials of the storm / Now pacified" (881–83). Revelation is thus naturalized, become an "effect" of time and weather. Like De Quincey's own vision of "mountain-steeps and summits" (884), "vapours" (885), and "cerulean sky" (886), the Solitary's is

> an unimaginable sight!
> Clouds, mists, streams, watery rocks and emerald turf,
> Clouds of all tincture, rocks and sapphire sky,
> Confused, commingled, mutually inflamed,
> Molten together.
> (887–91)

This is not, however, an accidental revelation. Far from it: the Solitary's vision is a painful reminder of imaginative power and a chastisement for political and personal despair. It leaves him utterly destroyed: "'I have been dead . . . And now I live! Oh! wherefore do I live?'" (910–11), he cries. In other words, the Solitary's vision is narratively significant, a pivotal event in his story of "Despondency" and "Despondency Corrected" (as the titles of books III and IV have it). To read the episode as De Quincey does, narrative must be pared away.

I take this misreading as a reminder that accidents need not be catastrophes. Some accidents—whether painful or pleasing—barely rise to the level of narratability.[17] Scaling down both "accident" and "revelation," De Quincey stays true to the unemphatic appearances and repeatable transformations of Wordsworth's poetry—against the grain of *The Excursion* itself. He asks if the Solitary's vision, freed from its narrative surrounds, might be just an accidental sight: a moment of unprivileged seeing, "entirely accidental," that can only be "fortuitously sustained."[18] Read in such a way, the Solitary's vision in the clouds shows us, with many of Wordsworth's finest poems, that "pleasure is spread through the earth / In stray gifts to be claimed by whoever shall find."[19] Neither sublimely elevating nor calamitous, accidental revelation indicates a milder quality of experience. When De Quincey chances to see Great Langdale transformed, he resolves not to change his life but to gaze into the "mass of vapour" once more.

To put it differently, accidental revelation belongs to that realm of experience Rei Terada has defined in terms of "mere phenomenality."[20] Attending to the post-Kantian fascination with "perceptions that seem below or marginal to normal appearance," Terada argues that such experiences offer "fleeting relief" from the coerciveness of the given world and the demand to affirm things as they are.[21] For the "phenomenophile," she writes, "the most transient perceptual objects come to be loved because only they seem capable of noncoercive relation."[22] I would add that, for Wordsworth, the coercion implicit in "normal appearance" has consequences for the object too. According to the critical theorists discussed earlier in this book, perception is conditioned by the value abstraction, the ground of those categories of the understanding that make experience possible. Meanwhile, the categories—abstract movement, substance, space, and time, to follow Alfred Sohn-Rethel—enable the intellectual and practical apprehension of nature required for the valorization process. In Wordsworth's own terms, the sheer uniformity of modern experience, the loss of "the discriminating powers of the mind," cannot be separated from the "intellectual mastery" of nature.[23] So when the lover of mere appearances recoils from what is, in all of its normative force, this act of "looking away" (Terada) suggests a lighter, less demanding relation to the world.

If book II of *The Excursion* thus offers a counterintuitive instance of accidental revelation, an earlier related poem treats the phenomenon with particular directness. Written sometime after 1795 and commonly regarded as the germ of "The Ruined Cottage," the fragment called "Incipient Madness" was never incorporated into *The Excursion*'s main text (unlike "The Ruined Cottage" itself). I read it as a preliminary account of that form of appearance De Quincey identifies in the later poem.[24] The fragment begins with a ruin, the remnants of a "wretched hut" (47) on a "dreary moor" (1). Inside, the speaker—who prefigures *The Excursion*'s Wanderer—happens upon "a broken pane which glittered in the moon / And seemed akin to life" (6–7). Afflicted by persistent "grief" (8), he finds solace in this chance appearance. The reflection of moonlight in broken glass becomes an external image of his grief. But it also recalls him to the shared life in things, "the persistence of vital powers," felt even in a glimpse of light.[25]

To be clear, I am not posing once more the question of Wordsworth's vitalism.[26] Rather, my interest is the appearance, or the "seem[ing]," of this something "akin to life," which I see as the poem's main concern. Consider these lines from an alternate draft:

> I found my sickly heart had tied itself
> Even to this tiny speck of glass—it could produce
> A feeling as of absence []
>   [] on the moment when my sight
> Should feed on it again. Many long months
> Confirmed this strange incontinence; my eye
> Did every evening measure the moon's height
> And forth I went before her yellow beams
> Could overtop the elm trees oer the heath,
> I went, I reach'd the cottage, and I found
> Still undisturb'd and glittering in its place
> That speck of glass.
> (MS, quoted in note to 12)

Expanding on the speaker's "strange" attachment to the "glittering" glass, Wordsworth describes a practice of perception and a form of appearance. The speaker wanders back repeatedly, over "many long months," to the site of his encounter and faithfully recreates the conditions of its initial occurrence (moon, elm trees, ruin, glass). All the same, he is surprised by every return: inside the ruined cottage, he invariably finds, but as if for the first time, the broken pane and the reflected moonlight. He cultivates an openness to accidental appearances—even when, as in this case, the accident is repeatable. "Still undisturbed," untouched and somehow unanticipated, the glittering glass appears without ever amounting to much. Yet the speaker's powers of perception are strangely remade. Struck by an inner "absence," he feels the world of nonhuman things impinge upon him: the sound of a horse's hooves "still following in the wind" (13–24), the short-lived light of the glow worm (25–28), a blackbird's nest (28–31), the linnet's "pleasant melancholy song" (33). Each emerges and then vanishes in turn, a transient manifestation of "being."[27] In looking away and looking again, the speaker makes no demands, even as he "feed[s]" on what the world gives him. For Wordsworth's editor, who titled the fragment, this is a kind of madness. For Wordsworth himself, it might be characterized as an ethics, a first effort to remake the relation between consciousness and the world.

Surprised by Silence

Classed among the "Poems of the Imagination" in 1815's *Poems*, "There was a Boy" indeed concerns consciousness's highest power. It also concerns, as De Quincey notes, the suspension of that power. Unlike "Incipient Madness," then—which performs a related, though fragmentary, phenomenological investigation—"There was a Boy" envisions a hiatus in appropriative perception from within.[28] The "Preface" to *Poems* suggests something like this. Dedicated in large part to the classification system organizing his collected poems, the "Preface" also offers detailed commentary on the faculties of imagination and fancy and on their poetic expression.[29] Thus, Wordsworth remarks that "There was a Boy" "represent[s] a commutation and transfer of internal feelings, co-operating with external accidents to plant, for immortality, images of sound and sight, in the celestial soil of the Imagination."[30] Anticipating De Quincey's 1839 account, Wordsworth glosses his poem in psychological or phenomenological terms: it shows how "images" derived from "internal feelings" and "external accidents" are impressed upon or "plant[ed]" in the "soil of the Imagination." His sentence's labored grammar insists, surprisingly, on the passivity of the imagination, described earlier in the essay as an inherently active power. If "There was a Boy" is a "poem of the imagination," it is one in which that power looks very different from the world-negating consciousness I discussed in chapter 1. As Wordsworth puts it, while "the Poems next in succession [in the volume] exhibit the faculty *exerting itself upon various objects of the external universe*," this poem depicts a boy who is "surprised into a perception."[31] Nature appears to the Winander boy when he gives up "exerting [him]self upon" it.

For Wordsworth as for De Quincey, then, "There was a Boy" presents a hiatus in appropriative perception that is the condition for any accidental revelation. In Wordsworth's poem, this is a matter of form as well as theme. Recall the well-known description of the boy as "he stand[s] alone / Beneath the trees, or by the glimmering Lake" (V.393–94):

> And there, with fingers interwoven, both hands
> Pressed closely, palm to palm, and to his mouth
> Uplifted, he, as through an instrument,
> Blew mimic hootings to the silent owls
> That they might answer him.—And they would shout
> Across the wat'ry Vale, and shout again,
> Responsive to his call, with quivering peals,
> And long halloos, and screams, and echoes loud
> Redoubled and redoubled; concourse wild
> Of mirth and jocund din!
> (395–404)

The poem lingers for three full lines on the image of fingers and hands brought together, then raised to the mouth like "an instrument." The boy resembles a kind of musician, playing on the world as well as his hands. Often supposed to figure an immediate identity with nature, the boy is actually a skilled manipulator. He acts and expects a reaction from a world he has learned to imitate. Regardless of the passage's shifting tenses and moods, the grammatical voice is appropriately active: "he . . . / Blew mimic hootings to the silent owls / That they might answer him." Then, the birds "shout / Across" the vale and "shout again, / Responsive to his call." Nevertheless, it is the boy who initiates this interchange by "exerting [him]self upon . . . the external universe." There is no echo, no "concourse wild" without him. Even at the level of the line, where enjambment ("shout / Across") suggests separation as much as unification with nature, the poem refuses the claim to immediacy.[32]

So the Winander boy's imitative action is not necessarily a sign of his identity with nature. In fact, his bearing toward the world is basically instrumental—a point made clearer by Wordsworth's revisions, which introduce the image of the instrument sometime after 1798.[33] This is not to say that the poem presents us with a scene of violence (though another "poem of the imagination," "Nutting," also from 1798, does just that). Nonetheless, it does insist on the distance between the boy and his surroundings, without which neither imitation nor manipulation would be possible. While Hartman sees the Winander boy as expressing a "joyfully unselfconscious mode of being" and a potential "absorption by nature," and Paul de Man finds in the image of echo "an intimate and sympathetic contact between human and natural elements," I understand the boy's call as at least a latent acknowledgment of nature's difference.[34] At the same time, the boy seeks to overcome that difference—to master it, even—through creative imitation.

From the poem's start, therefore, the Winander boy is a figure of reflective consciousness, defined by distance from the world. While "the mind of man," as Wordsworth writes elsewhere, may "naturally [be] the mirror of the fairest and most interesting qualities of nature," the capacity to "mirror"—and thereby to apprehend—presupposes reflective distance.[35] In their discussion of mimesis in *Dialectic of Enlightenment*, Horkheimer and Adorno make a related point. "Civilization," they write, "replaced the organic adaptation to otherness, mimetic behavior proper, firstly, in the magical phase, with the organized manipulation of mimesis, and finally, in the historical phase, with rational praxis, work."[36] This little history—from "organic adaptation" to ritual, from art to a "rational praxis" that replicates and represses "mimetic behavior proper"—bears interestingly on Wordsworth's poem, which evokes several forms of mimetic behavior. Indeed, the boy's imitation of the owls' cries is simultaneously an organic adaptation, an imaginative representation, and a technique for the manipulation of nature. The latter point is emphasized in *The Prelude*, where "There was a Boy" is located alongside an account of a child prodigy, who with "telescopes, and crucibles, and maps / . . . can read / The inside of the earth, and spell the stars" (V.330, 332–33). Now, the prodigy obviously differs from the Winander boy; he is a product of that modern system of "education which 'cures' children of childishness," as Horkheimer and Adorno put it.[37] All the same, his bearing toward the world is not entirely distinct from the boy's. With his array of scientific instruments, the prodigy puts "all things . . . to question" (V.341). Meanwhile, with instruments of his own, the Winander boy demands an answer from the birds.[38] Calling from "across the wat'ry Vale," he lays claim to their animal language and turns to advantage "the distance of subject from object" that, according to Horkheimer and Adorno, enables all "controlled reflection."[39]

Read in this way, "There was a Boy" appears less a narrative of youth and (interrupted) maturation than a lyric study of consciousness in fraught relation to nature. This is so even as the poem's final lines reframe it as "a beautifully

extended epitaph."[40] In part, then, my reading aligns with the classic phenomenological and deconstructive accounts. Hartman, for example, also presents "There was a Boy" as a meditation on poetic consciousness: "The poet is
mourning the loss of a prior mode of being but meditates on the necessity of a
loss which leads into matured awareness," he writes.[41] Yet this familiar narrative
of loss and recompence risks eliding, by its very form, the accidental revelations
that do register in Wordsworth's poetry.[42] My aim is to show how Wordsworth
holds open possibilities for consciousness—rather than consigning them to an
irrecoverable narrative past. For Wordsworth, it is always possible, if only for a
moment, to think and feel otherwise.

So when the poem turns to the failure of the boy's exertions, the "gentle
shock" that befalls him need not be understood in terms of loss. Rather, in the
suspension of the boy's call and the accidental revelation that follows, the poem
opens onto a nonhuman nature that has always been close by:

> And when it chanced
> That pauses of deep silence mocked his skill,
> Then sometimes, in that silence, while he hung
> Listening, a gentle shock of mild surprize
> Has carried far into his heart the voice
> Of mountain torrents; or the visible scene
> Would enter unawares into his mind
> With all its solemn imagery, its rocks,
> Its woods, and that uncertain Heaven, received
> Into the bosom of the steady Lake.
> (V.404–13)

These lines show how nature, without compulsion, might appear. The interruption of "direct conscious anticipation," in De Quincey's terms, is not singular
but a recurrent accident. Thus, the boy confronts a surprising, if not unprecedented, failure of his mimetic technique, and he is struck by "pauses of deep silence." The image of listening as hanging, extended over the line break ("hung /
Listening"), captures precisely his condition of perceptual suspension.[43] Following another pause, an initial caesura, something suddenly appears. Yet the
structure of Wordsworth's sentence is such that one cannot be sure what it is.
For a moment, feeling is all: "a gentle shock of mild surprize" falls upon the boy
and moves "far into his heart." Loosening his hold on inner experience, the boy

surrenders his mastery of the scene. The appearance of loss is fleeting, however, as nature's voice floods in to fill the silence. Following a stronger medial caesura, "the visible scene" takes over. Its "solemn imagery" dilates across the next three lines: rocks, woods, and an "uncertain Heaven" reflected not in a human consciousness, or awareness, but in "the bosom of the steady Lake"—near presences on the threshold of apprehension.

In these images, in particular, of a voice heard in silence and a "visible scene" perceived "unawares," Wordsworth presents consciousness differently. Frustrated in the effort to master his surroundings, the boy feels nature impinge upon him. This is not an imitable nature but one that "mock[s] his skill" as it nearly mocks the poet's, who resorts to paradox as the form of the inexpressible. Without directly grasping the scene before it, consciousness reveals itself as a capacity to receive. Once again, this hiatus in appropriative perception registers grammatically as the boy's heart and mind become the passive objects of the sentence unfolding across these ten lines. Thus, nature's voice is "carried far into his heart," while its vision "enter[s] unawares into his mind." Despite the intimation of inner depths, the feelings that fall upon the boy are less than profound. A gentle shock, a mild surprise: this is not the "deepest feeling" that confirms "the mind / Is lord and master" (XI.272).

Ultimately, Wordsworth says little about the consequences of such experience. Neither sublime nor obviously traumatic, nature's appearance is a gift amounting almost to nothing. The blank space that follows, a pause between verse paragraphs, suggests as much. But if accidental revelation proves inconsequential, it is nevertheless repeatable. From its opening, the poem establishes an indeterminate temporality that forecloses all sense of crisis. The boy's birdcalls are themselves a habit, practiced "many a time / At evening" (V.390–91). Moreover, repetition allows for their failure. Like the "double take" Galperin finds in Wordsworth's poetry—an act of looking again that discloses a world once overlooked—the boy's repeated calling and listening is the occasion for the overhearing of nature. In the silence of a call without a response, "the voice / Of mountain torrents" is heard. There is something mildly destabilizing, even bewildering, about this failure of technique.[44] It is also, as I have shown, the condition for nature's appearance. Still, the poem does not present accidental revelation as admonishment. In fact, it never offers a clear moral lesson. Unlike "Nutting," which responds to the "merciless ravage" of a forest "nook" with an imperative—"with gentle hand / Touch,—for there is a Spirit in the woods"—"There was a Boy" declines to adopt the voice of morality.[45] To lighten our demands upon the world, to dwell in thought's wilderness—this will require more than a moment of conscience.

At the Grave

Of course, in its published form, "There was a Boy" does not end with nature's accidental revelation.[46] It ends with a grave. Here are the poem's concluding lines:

> This Boy was taken from his Mates, and died
> In childhood, ere he was full ten years old.
> —Fair are the woods, and beauteous is the spot,
> The Vale where he was born; the Churchyard hangs
> Upon a Slope above the Village School,
> And there, along that bank, when I have passed
> At evening, I believe that oftentimes
> A full half-hour together I have stood
> Mute—looking at the Grave in which he lies.
> (V.414–22)

How should this final moment be understood? For many readers, the boy's untimely death and the speaker's reverie at his grave make sense of all that comes before. To cite Hartman once again, these lines show us how "the survivor contemplates his own buried childhood."[47] At the boy's grave, the "halted traveler" confronts, and fails to recognize, the death of his former self. In short, death, not nature, seems to be the meaning of the poem.[48] Following the logic of Hartman's account, one might also say that the poem's epitaphic close presents death as a mark of history. For Hartman, this is personal history, or a history of individual consciousness. For others, the boy's death recalls another history: the history of capital. As David Simpson has argued, the "abbreviated chronology" so characteristic of children's lives in Wordsworth's writing "is exactly what Marx finds in the operations of capital and Engels in the condition of the working class in England: children old before their time, men and women dying earlier than they should."[49] Read in this fashion, the grave and the body within it signify in several ways: as literal reminders of "the shrunken lives of the coming proletariat" and as figures for history itself, the buried referent of the lyric as a whole.[50]

That history might be somehow buried or encrypted in Wordsworth's po-etry, waiting to be unearthed by the critic—this has been a powerful and per-vasive idea. In Alan Liu's influential work, "burial" captures precisely Words-worth's use of history. Discussing the poet's early love of Virgil, Liu remarks that "georgic is the supreme mediational form by which to bury history in nature."[51] The critic, he continues, must therefore learn to dig: "There are, after all, those protruding 'bones' in the soil, which . . . cannot be easily covered. Too much energy of repression must be expended to keep the georgic mirror from turn-ing transparent to history."[52] Nature, Liu insists, is nothing but the soil in which history is buried, a convenient cover for poetry's enabling conditions. More recently but not so differently, Anahid Nersessian has approached Words-worth as a poet of "obscurity," or the stylistic difficulty by which he "record[s], repress[es], and transmute[s] traumatic experience into a morality that is in-sistently apolitical."[53] To read for obscurity is, for Nersessian too, a kind of ex-humation. Thus, in its "stutter[s]" and breaks, Wordsworth's poetry "remind[s] us that 'the world' is not just that which is present and accounted for but also that which is intrusively absent or else held off, blocked out. The world is the fact of dead bodies disappeared and the blankness that still entombs them; it is the labor of remembering them and . . . making that memory tolerable."[54] Less committed than Liu to a notion of poetry as ideology, and far less committed to the false opposition between nature and history, Nersessian still reads Words-worth for the buried referents of his verse.

Would it be possible to think differently about the history in Wordsworth's poetry? In the case of "There was a Boy," this would mean reading its final lines not as an allegory of buried hurt—psychic or social—but simply as an ending. "Fair are the woods, and beauteous is the spot, / The Vale where he was born": this line and a half softens considerably the distinction between life and death. The boy is buried in the very "spot" of his birth, and his incon-sequential life ends where it began. Like Lucy among the "rocks, and stones, and trees," he is a mute presence, inseparable from the vale that gave him life.[55] If the boy is ever truly unified with nature, it is now, in the absence of con-sciousness. There is, however, a mind here—that of the speaker, or the halted traveler. Significantly, Wordsworth posits no direct relation between the boy and the traveler. The latter is known only by his passage through the church-yard and his silent reverie before the grave. He is almost disembodied, a figure of minimal consciousness—reduced, as in Kant's "Transcendental Aesthetic," to the forms of space and time.[56] In the nonrelation between the boy and the traveler—between, that is, an immediate unity with nature achievable only in death and a pure consciousness that barely resembles life—the poem recalls, without attempting to resolve, the problems of nature and consciousness it had earlier addressed.

In other words, these lines offer narrative closure without philosophical resolution, a sight of "fair . . . woods" from within thought's wilderness. This is not to say that Wordsworth obscures or represses the shock of accidental revelation. The poem's ending is neither an answer to nor a mystification of what precedes it, and the consolations it does offer are largely generic. Unlike Thomas Gray's "Elegy Written in a Country Church Yard" (1751), however, "There was a Boy" suggests that not all paths "lead but to the grave"—or better, that the end of something need not be its only meaning.[57] Despite the undeniable closure of the grave, the moment of possibility—of nature's accidental revelation—remains. History is far from buried in Wordsworth's verse. Rather, his poetry becomes historical precisely at the level of consciousness. In the interrogation of instrumentality, in the reimagining of apprehension, in the effort to think nature's silence: for Wordsworth, history is there.

6 Shelley's Ethereal Poetics

In his 1878 biography *Shelley*, John Addington Symonds observes that "all was of one piece in Shelley's nature." This includes the poet's voice, noted for its highness of pitch and its "thrilling," even "piercing," tone. For Symonds, there is nothing surprising in such a detail. "Like all finely tempered natures," he writes, Shelley "vibrated in harmony with the subjects of his thought": "This peculiar voice, varying from moment to moment and affecting different sensibilities in divers ways, corresponds to the high-strung passion of his life, his fine-drawn and ethereal fancies, and the clear vibrations of his palpitating verse. Such a voice, far-reaching, penetrating, and unearthly, befitted one who lived in rarest ether on the topmost heights of human thought." Voice and verse alike vibrate in harmony with an ethereal thought; all partake of a single atmosphere.[1]

What would it mean to take Symonds's intuition seriously? To really listen for the "clear vibrations" of Shelley's verse? In this final chapter, I aim at something of the sort, as I follow Shelley into the ether. Once more, I invoke the ethereal atmosphere of natural philosophy, which profoundly shaped Shelley's thought. In this context, as I have discussed, ether is the subtle mediator of forces such as gravity, light, and magnetism. By way of ethereal vibration, forces move between distant bodies without transgressing the laws of nature. Ether forms a common atmosphere, encompassing and making place for all that exists.[2]

For Shelley, ether is an indispensable image. (Think only of the "solid atmosphere" or the "aery surge" that F. R. Leavis found so objectionable.)[3] But in the ether, Shelley also finds an ideal for poetic thinking. Irreducible to either spirit or matter, ether suspends the distinction between them. Since at least the late seventeenth century, ether had been considered not just as a vehicle for physical forces but also as involved in the movements of thought and feeling.[4] According to the ether hypothesis, spirit cannot be separated out from matter. It gave Shelley new ways of thinking about the relation between spirit, or consciousness, and material nature. In reading Shelley as the poet of "rarest ether," I propose that the very terms of debate about his philosophical poetics must be reconceived.[5]

To be sure, Shelley is not a philosopher. He is fascinated by philosophical and scientific problems, but his thinking takes place in poetry. It is therefore to the vibratory movements of Shelley's verse that we must look. In a 1971 letter, J. H. Prynne observes in Shelley a tendency toward "overlapping figurational transformation." As Prynne explains it, "In the sequence of overt or implied metaphor or simile the initial ground for comparison from which the figure rises often has less primacy in the direction of later development than the new areas of reference introduced by the figure."[6] This letter describes a general movement of Shelley's figures, whereby the vehicle or vehicles of a comparison take on an autonomous life and develop free from subordination to the initial tenor. Rather than call this a stylistic flaw, Prynne insists that such figural and rhythmic unfolding is integral to Shelley's thought: "At its best, this produces a power and vigour of creative intelligence in the working out of ideas astonishingly disregarded at the present time."[7] Shelley's thought is inseparable from the form in which it takes place.[8]

In what follows, I specify such figurative transformations as ethereal. I pay particular attention to an early work, *Queen Mab* (1813), in which the movement of figure insistently draws spirit and matter together. This is a recurring effect in Shelley's poetry. From *Queen Mab* and *Prometheus Unbound* (1819) to the late love lyrics for Jane Williams (1822), Shelley seeks a form of thought liberated from the "dead" abstractions of modernity.[9] The complex metaphors so characteristic of his style do serious conceptual work.[10]

Shelley's challenge to metaphorical and metaphysical hierarchies has political consequences. *Queen Mab* dedicates itself to undoing anthropocentric power, founded on the domination of nature. In this sense, Leavis's notorious description of Shelley is correct: "There is nothing grasped in his poetry."[11] Projecting a utopian future, in which humanity might be reconciled to nature, Shelley (like Wollstonecraft) identifies an obstacle to its realization: "commerce" and the world-destroying labor that makes it possible. To be freed from the laws of commerce is to inhabit a new relation to need and to activity altogether. For Shelley, utopia realized will be "a paradise of peace," achievable only by relinquishing the pursuit of mastery.[12] He imagines an end to the seemingly infinite task of making the world anew. Once more, Shelley summons the ether as the spirit of nature and the sign of paradise's imminent arrival. The life and "eternal breath" (I.274) of a utopian natural history, ether reconciles inactivity and freedom, and nature and humanity, as much as matter and spirit. In *Prometheus Unbound*—to which I return in closing—Shelley therefore offers "common . . . love" as another name for such an atmosphere to come.[13]

The Subtle Spirit

Though not the first, the most significant modern ether theory is Isaac Newton's. It develops out of a difficulty in his account of gravity: How does the force of attraction act between bodies distant from one another in space? This is the problem of action at a distance. As formulated by Newton in a letter of 1692/93, "It is inconceivable that inanimate brute matter should, without the mediation of something else, which is not material, operate upon and affect other matter without mutual contact."[14] Universal gravity assumes an agent of mediation. Newton continues by remarking that attraction itself "must be caused by an agent acting constantly according to certain laws; but whether this agent be material or immaterial, I have left to the consideration of my readers."[15] Because it is not inherent in matter, and because it cannot be communicated through a vacuum, gravity must be attributed to some other obscure agent, whether "material or immaterial."

In the "General Scholium" added to the *Principia* in 1713, Newton speaks again about gravity's unknown cause. Here it is described as "a certain very subtle spirit pervading gross bodies and lying hidden in them."[16] The subtle spirit resolves the problem of action at a distance by filling space between physical bodies. This is not all it does. In a nearly rhapsodic passage, Newton proposes that, "by its force and actions, the particles of bodies attract one another at very small distances and cohere when they become contiguous; and electrical bodies act at greater distances, repelling as well as attracting neighboring corpuscles; and light is emitted, reflected, refracted, inflected, and heats bodies; and all sensation is excited, and the limbs of animals move at command of the will, namely, by the vibrations of this spirit being propagated through the solid fibers of the nerves from the external organs of the senses to the brain and from the brain into the muscles."[17] The spirit joins distant planetary bodies. But it also explains the cohesion of matter and the action of electricity and light. By its vibrations, the spirit transmits sensations too, from the perceptual organs of living beings to their brains and muscles. While he knows that the spirit's existence will never be experimentally verified, Newton maintains that it flows through everything in nature, from the minutest "particles of bodies" to the inmost pathways of the human brain.

In the *Principia* as well as the later "Queries" to the *Opticks*, Newton invokes the subtle spirit to unify the natural world. Yet a 1675 letter to Henry Olden-burg, secretary of the Royal Society, insists upon its ultimate heterogeneity.[18] Proposing that light might travel through some ethereal medium in motion— "that light and aether mutually act upon one another"—Newton wonders about the composition of the ether.[19] The subtle spirit cannot be "one uniform matter," he says, but it is perhaps "compounded, partly of the main phlegmatic body of æther, partly of other various æthereal spirits, much after the manner, that air is compounded of the phlegmatic body of air intermixed with various vapours and exhalations: for the electric and magnetic effluvia, and gravitating prin-ciple, seem to argue such variety."[20] With its manifold of powers, ether may be composed of as many rarefied and imperceptible substances. Newton's appar-ent holism gives way to a thought of irreducible difference.[21]

At the same time, Newton argues for the "community" of these spiritual substances.[22] In the same letter, he suggests that "the whole frame of nature may be nothing but various contextures of some certain aethereal spirits, or vapours, condensed as it were by precipitation . . . and after condensation wrought into various forms; at first by the immediate hand of the Creator; and ever since by the power of nature."[23] Conceived as a "contexture" of spirits, ether joins— or weaves together, to follow Newton's metaphor—all creation in an unending process of formation. It does this without rendering nature an undifferentiated mass. While it cannot be reduced to a "uniform" element or power, ether per-mits "the whole frame of nature" to be thought of as one. For Shelley, as we shall see, this ethereal vision has poetic and political significance.

Through reading Newton, the romantic fascination with ether becomes easier to understand. For poets and philosophers alike, it offered more than a resolution to certain problems in physics. Vibrating in sympathy with the most fleeting of physical impulses—with feelings as well as with thoughts— ether brings together the routinely divided: force and substance, spirit and matter, mind and body. For romantics including Shelley, it demonstrates the inadequacy of our abstract categories, of our very language for speaking about nature. As Friedrich Hölderlin would put it, at the turn of the century, "I understood the silence of Aether / But human words I've never understood."[24]

Shelley's study of ether began early. His youthful enthusiasm for the physical and chemical sciences is well known, and his reading in Newton, David Hartley, Leonhard Euler, Pierre-Simon Laplace, and others has been carefully documented.[25] It is no coincidence, then, that *A Refutation of Deism* (1814), the culmination of his early scientific research, proclaims that "inert matter" does not exist.[26] As Shelley maintains, "matter deprived of qualities," such as the "mechanist" purports to discover, is a mere "abstraction, concerning which it is impossible to form an idea."[27] Forces, he continues, including light, electricity, and magnetism, prove nature to be "infinitely active and subtile." These spirits each "possess equal claims with thought to the unmeaning distinction of immateriality."[28] Shelley's ether, like Newton's, suspends the distinction between materiality and immateriality entirely. It shows too that the abstract nature of modernity is a "learned error" with devastating effects.[29] Evacuated of "'sensible qualities,'" nature is deprived, in Ross Wilson's terms, of "the meaning of a lived life rather than an objectified one."[30] In the subtle spirit, the atmosphere of feelings as well as forces, Shelley finds a way to think nature differently.

During this same period, he first conceived of ether as a poetic principle. At Oxford, as Thomas Jefferson Hogg reports in his memoir, Shelley announced his devotion to chemistry, "the only science that deserve[s] to be studied."[31] Hogg recalls the poet's claims for the boundless potential of chemical knowledge. One day soon, says Hogg's Shelley, human beings will generate their own water, heat, and electricity and thus find new ways to dwell upon the earth. Through the "chemical agency" of such "useful fluid[s]," humanity will "transmute an unfruitful region into a land of exuberant plenty"; make clay and stone into sources of warmth; and channel the "omnipotent energies" of electricity.[32] Here, Shelley's thought tends toward the instrumental; he understands "chemical agency" as an extension of human power. Still, he intuits the liberatory possibilities latent in scientific knowledge. For these to be realized, as he argues in the *Defence*, the science of fluids and forces must become poetic.[33]

To put it otherwise, Shelley adheres to "the romantic imperative," in Frederick Beiser's sense of pursuing "a *synthesis* of science and art" that would transform both.[34] In an 1811 letter to Elizabeth Hitchener, he remarks on the affinities between ether and the feeling of beauty. Deeply skeptical about religion and philosophy, Shelley points out the limits of our moral and aesthetic categories. To look for the causes of nature's grandeur and "enchantment"—to "analyze a feeling," as Shelley puts it—is to seek "knowledge" where it cannot be found.[35] This is not to say that beauty transcends understanding. Rather, Shelley's claim is that sensations, or "qualities," in the terms of the *Refutation*, cannot be grasped in the abstract: "Thus does knowledge lose all the pleasure which involuntarily arises by attempting to arrest the fleeting phantom as it passes. . . . Vain, almost like the chemist's ether it evaporates under our observation."[36] If nature's beauty is a "fleeting phantom" or an "ether," then our fixed "signs for portions or classes of thoughts" do violence in their efforts to "arrest" it. These instruments are the death of all "nobler purposes," as Shelley will later comment.[37] The ether demands an answerable style.

In the *Defence*, Shelley claims for the poetic imagination precisely this power to develop an ethereal language. Only "the most delicate sensibility and the most enlarged imagination" will allow the "self [to] appea[r] as what it is, an atom to a Universe."[38] Rather than affirm the poet's identity, the force of inspiration joins the mind with nature as a whole. The poet's self is nearly dissolved into "the eternal, the infinite, the one," where "conceptions" such as "time and place and number are not."[39] Still, the poet has a gift for communicating from within this standpoint. In Shelley's words, poets "can colour all that they combine with the evanescent hues of this etherial world."[40] Inspired and impersonal, poetry communicates the common atmosphere in which we live and breathe.

For Shelley, then, poetry can renew our sense of inhabiting a shared world. "It reproduces the common universe of which we are portions and percipients," he writes, "and it purges from our inward sight the film of familiarity which obscures from us the wonder of our being."[41] What would it mean to do this ethereally? Elsewhere, Shelley describes poetry as a "subtler language within language wrought."[42] Unlike the dead and deadening abstractions of the letter to Hitchener, it gives life and form to the "fleeting phantoms" of feeling. Poetry is a language of sensible qualities, responsive to the subtlest of spirits. Once again, Shelley anticipates Horkheimer and Adorno, who argue that exchange society makes "dissimilar things comparable by reducing them to abstract quantities" and that quality is therefore "consign[ed] . . . to poetry."[43] Shelley's thought is similar, yet he attributes to poetry a renovating force that the critical theorists do not allow. In fact, Shelley claims for his ethereal poetics the capacity to transform apprehension itself. Like Wordsworth, he imagines a poetic "apprehension of life" freed from the compulsion to grasp.[44] Turning to *Queen*

Mab, where ether is both image and formal principle, I show how Shelley puts this thought into practice.

The Ethereal World

Often called Shelley's "first major poem," *Queen Mab* has received comparatively little scholarly attention.[45] At the same time, it is perhaps Shelley's most influential work. Throughout the nineteenth century, this philosophical poem was widely circulated in a series of illegal editions. The volume itself—half poetry, half prose treatise—contains provocative discussions of religion, sexuality, astronomy, and animal rights. It constructs a history of radical political thought extending back to ancient Greece. Needless to say, it is a difficult work to treat as a whole. But in this unwieldy form, as E. P. Thompson demonstrated, it became an important vehicle for the transmission of radical thought in nineteenth-century England.[46] Its influence was also felt in Europe: Friedrich Engels began translating it into German in the 1830s, and he later proclaimed, "Oh, we all knew Shelley by heart then." Later in the Marx-Engels circle, it would form, with *Laon and Cythna*, the poetic heart of Eleanor Marx and Edward Aveling's "Shelley and Socialism" (1888).[47]

So natural philosophy is not the only way to approach Shelley's poem. *Queen Mab* is a committed political work. One of its most compelling characteristics is the intimacy it builds between natural philosophy and politics.[48] For Shelley, the two are inseparable: even at its most philosophical, *Queen Mab* uses verse technique to destabilize hierarchies of spirit and matter. Before looking to its utopian horizon, I consider the poem's form, focusing on those figurative transformations that draw spirit and matter together.

Let me begin with an overview: *Queen Mab* narrates the encounter between a young woman, Ianthe, and the queen of the fairies, Mab. At the poem's start, Mab descends from the evening sky. Ianthe's spirit leaves her sleeping body and the two of them journey to the outermost reaches of the universe. The imagery of ether is pervasive. Ianthe travels in an "etherial car" (I.65) to Mab's "etherial palace" (II.29). Beyond the reach of "matter, space, and time" (91), this palace of "flashing light" (32) and changing colors can only be entered on "etherial footsteps" (46). Once she is within, Ianthe looks through "etherial eyes" (III.3) upon the world's past, present, and future. The fairy queen reveals to her a prophetic vision, showing the formation of the cosmos; the origins of political and economic exploitation; and a utopian scene of freedom from compulsion and of harmony between humanity and nature.

To put it simply, ether permeates the poem. In Shelley's words, *Queen Mab* is painted in "the evanescent hues of [an] etherial world." It strives to transcend the standpoint of the self, to speak about a common atmosphere. Its world is lively, even sensate, but no human being occupies its center. Ianthe's vision precludes anthropocentrism. Freed from the "chains of earth's immurement" (I.188) and granted an "apprehension uncontrolled" (193), she sees that all of nature thinks, feels, and lives. As Mab explains,

I tell thee that those viewless beings,
Whose mansion is the smallest particle
Of the impassive atmosphere,
Think, feel and live like man;
That their affections and antipathies,
Like his, produce the laws
Ruling their moral state;
And the minutest throb
That through their frame diffuses
The slightest, faintest motion,
Is fixed and indispensable
As the majestic laws
That rule yon rolling orbs.
(II.231–43)

Mab reveals to Ianthe the formation and the laws of nature. The throbbing atoms, from which all bodies are composed, possess their own powers of sensation. This is not to anthropomorphize each "particle." Rather, Shelley invokes a thinking, feeling world to contest the dominance of the human being. "How strange is human pride!" Mab exclaims, when "there's not one atom of yon earth / But once was living man" (II.225, 211–12). No less significant is Shelley's translation of physical forces into affects. Rendering attraction and repulsion as "affection" and "antipathy," he draws out the affective dimension of Newtonian law. These feelings are not reserved for human or even animal beings. In Shelley's telling, all of nature feels itself.[49]

Thus, in *Queen Mab* as in his philosophical prose, Shelley refuses the conceptual distinction between spirit and matter. His claim that nature thinks and feels—that it is "infinitely active and subtle," in the terms of the *Refutation*—is clearly inspired by the ethereal atmosphere of the natural philosophers. Shelley, however, is not content with abstractions. Philosophical arguments, even when they aim to overcome false oppositions, can reinforce the divisions they would suspend. Though "merely nominal," as he argues elsewhere, the distinction between "ideas" and "external objects" is fixed by its "reiteration."[50] Acutely aware of our concepts' deadening effects, Shelley turns to poetic language—to an ethereal poetics, through which he seeks to convey the subtle interweaving of spirit and matter.[51]

Midway through the poem, Mab speaks again about the formation of the universe. Her claims echo those made in earlier cantos, but Shelley's figurative language becomes increasingly complex:

> Throughout this varied and eternal world
> Soul is the only element; the block
> That for uncounted ages has remained
> The moveless pillar of a mountain's weight
> Is active, living spirit.
> (IV.139–43)

These images of soul and spirit are striking. Writing against the notion of matter without qualities, Shelley insists on nature's activity and variety. In so doing, he seems to replace inert matter with "active, living spirit." A closer reading complicates our sense of the exchange. For Mab, soul is the world's "only element," yet it is somehow "varied" too. It is both one and many things. Furthermore, while nature's soul or spirit is "active" and "living," it "remain[s]" a stony, "moveless" "block." This is not to say, with William Empson, that Shelley's "muddle of ideas clog[s] an apparently simple lyrical flow."[52] Rather, Shelley's metaphors develop in that manner outlined by Prynne, who comments not only on the complexity of such evolving figures but on the relative autonomy and intellectual significance of "the new areas of reference" they introduce. In this case, Shelley presents the soul of nature as, in sequence, an element, a block, a pillar, and a mountain. The objects of comparison increase in mass and size, from the imperceptibly small to the sublimely large. Then, at last, the sequence dissolves in spirit, lending to immateriality the weight of a mountain.

The same movements characterize Shelley's treatment of the individual soul. In the first lines of the poem, Mab commands Ianthe's spirit to leave her body behind: "Soul of Ianthe! / Awake! arise!" (I.128–29). Ianthe's soul seems to shake free of her physical form, doomed to break down "like an useless and worn-out machine" (155). Yet, as the poem shows, there is no real division between spirit and matter. Mab proclaims that spirit

> aspires to Heaven,
> Pants for its sempiternal heritage,
> And ever changing, ever rising still,
> Wantons in endless being.
> (148–51)

Seemingly a description of spiritual transcendence, these lines exert a countervailing force. When Ianthe's spirit rises, it "aspires" and "pants," in an etymological play on *spiritus*, or breath, that restores to the word *spirit* a certain materiality. Shelley implicates the breathing body in spirit's "endless being." At the same time, he insists that it inevitably "rots, perishes, and passes" (156). Here, however, Shelley's breathy plosives (pants, perishes, passes) find the trace of spirit even in a rotting corpse. Through these "figurational transformations," Shelley not only suspends the distinction between spirit and matter but also conveys the feeling of their intertwinement. His verse communicates the atmosphere that philosophy struggles to describe. Spirit and matter, soul and body are woven together by the movement of the poem.

For Shelley, as I have said, ethereal poetics has a politics. Remarking on the transience of kingly power, Mab calls on "nature's silent eloquence" (III.197) in answer to empire's falsehoods. She announces "that all fulfill the works of love and joy,— / All but the outcast man" (198–99). Her claim is more interesting than it appears; Mab is not proposing that modern civilization has somehow left nature behind. Once more, Shelley's figurative language is essential to his thinking. As Mab summons the "Spirit of Nature!" she declares,

> The pure diffusion of thy essence throbs
> Alike in every human heart.
> Thou, aye, erectest there
> Thy throne of power unappealable:
> Thou art the judge beneath whose nod
> Man's brief and frail authority
> Is powerless as the wind
> That passeth idly by.
> (215–22)

Shelley's image of an "essence" throbbing in all hearts recalls that subtle spirit "propagated through the solid fibers of the nerves." Mab's spirit of nature is much like Newton's. Yet this spirit builds a weighty "throne of power" that renders kings and tyrants naught. It transforms the might of empires into a "wind / That passeth idly by." Again, Shelley's evolving metaphors contest the separation of spirit from matter—the latter now presented, with great irony, as the realm of "human justice" (224). Defined by infinite activity and life, spirit is the throne and judge that will dissolve all palaces and prisons. It is, too, a common atmosphere, diffused through every human heart and every "particle" of the world. This is what "the outcast man" must deny. As Horkheimer and Adorno explain, mastery depends on alienated distance: "The distance of subject from object, the presupposition of abstraction, is founded on the distance from things which the ruler attains by means of the ruled."[53] Thus, for Shelley, the end of sovereign power and the liberation of humanity are inseparable from reconciliation with nature—a nature to which humanity also belongs.

Regeneration's Work

In its middle cantos, *Queen Mab* turns to the historical present and offers a devastating vision of social life around 1813. Shown a world made sick by greed, Ianthe mourns "the venal interchange / Of all that human art or nature yield" (V.38–39). Mab explains that "commerce" has made all things interchangeable. "All things are sold," she remarks (177), her grim aphorism condensing the whole of commercial society. Of course, "the wealth of nations" is not spontaneously generated (80): commerce requires work, and "slaves by force or famine driven" (72) become the "scarce living pullies of a dead machine, / Mere wheels of work and articles of trade" (76–77). Like many of the poets and philosophers addressed in this book, Shelley sees how the mechanization of labor and the circulation of wealth transform living beings into automatons, "mere wheels" that revolve until they break down.[54]

Ianthe's vision does not end in despair: Mab promises the coming of another, better era. The "paradise of peace" will necessarily arrive, she says, but no heroic action can bring it into being. Utopia will be realized only through "the happy ferment" of nature in itself (IX.49). This language of fermentation is drawn from Newton, for whom it describes the slow unfolding of the cosmos from the ether.[55] Mab's utopia thus relies on an ethereal movement, whereby humanity and nature are led toward harmony and repose. History's final end, according to Mab, is the achievement of such unconstraint. This is possible only with the acceptance of natural-historical necessity. Liberation demands an end to the pursuit of mastery. Like Adorno, Shelley imagines that, in "the true society," "*rien faire comme une bête*, lying on the water and look[ing] peacefully into the heavens ... might step in place of process, doing, fulfilling." As the final cantos of *Queen Mab* suggest, "None of the abstract concepts comes closer to the fulfilled utopia than that of eternal peace."[56] Crucially, this is not the peace of death but that of a life without "unprofitable toil" (V.129)—a utopia of free time.

Throughout *Queen Mab*, Shelley struggles against the separation of humanity from nature.[57] Ianthe's final vision, in particular, shows that the highest human goods will be achieved only in the course of natural history. Glutted with their "all-polluting luxury and wealth" (VIII.180), the rulers of humanity run athwart of nature's own activity. The consequences are planetary. From the poles to the tropics, human beings must suffer, victims of "famine, cold and toil" (160) or "earthquake, tempest, and disease" (171)—of all "that earth's revenge / Could wreak on the infringers of her law" (163–64). The good of humankind, properly understood, is identical to the good of nature. Such knowledge can reconcile human beings with their world. Happiness is to be found not by mastering nature, Mab says, but by finding oneself a part of it:

> How sweet a scene will earth become!
> Of purest spirits, a pure dwelling-place,
> Symphonious with the planetary spheres;
> When man, with changeless Nature coalescing,
> Will undertake regeneration's work,
> When its ungenial poles no longer point
> To the red and baleful sun
> That faintly twinkles there.
> (VI.39–46)

This is not only a call to cease laboring against nature, using it as a mere means. Mab also insists that humanity's "coalescing" with the world is inseparable from certain natural-historical processes. It will not be human action that brings us together with nature but rather the cessation of activity or work—of that which pits us against the world by setting it up over against us.[58]

The poem's notes say more. Commenting on these lines, Shelley explains that the earth's present state, including its variable and often unhealthy climate, is conditioned by the angle of its axis. Now oblique, he observes, this angle is changing, and it "will gradually diminish until the equator coincides with the ecliptic; the night and days will then become equal on the earth throughout

the year, and probably the seasons also."[59] Shelley's natural history has consequences for humanity. "There is no great extravagance," he writes, "in presum-
ing that the progress of the perpendicularity of the poles may be as rapid as the
progress of the intellect; or that there should be a perfect identity between the
moral and physical improvement of the human species."[60] As the poles shift,
the climate will ameliorate itself and the conditions of human life will be transformed. Human freedom, the liberation from "disease" promised by so many
utopias, depends for Shelley on the movement of the earth.[61] In turn, the earth's
movement depends on the ferment of the ether.

Near the poem's end, Ianthe sees the effects of such geological and atmospheric changes. Heralding an end to tyranny, her vision reveals the distant
future as if it had already come to pass. Mab triumphantly predicts the destruction of palaces, cathedrals, and prisons. As she speaks, her voice moves into the
past tense:

> These ruins soon left not a wreck behind:
> Their elements, wide scattered o'er the globe,
> To happier shapes were moulded, and became
> Ministrant to all blissful impulses:
> Thus human things were perfected, and earth,
> Even as a child beneath its mother's love,
> Was strengthened in all excellence, and grew
> Fairer and nobler with each passing year.
> (IX.130–37)

Ianthe's vision culminates with this proleptic glimpse of a utopia fulfilled,
where the "elements" of oppression have been alchemically turned toward bliss.
Throughout, her prophetic vision has wavered temporally between past, present, and future. But the language used now is unique, in that it presents history's utopian end as a thing of the past, as a matter of fact; in the words of the
theologian and philologist J. D. Michaelis, it brings futurity into "the *prophetic
present*."[62] This peculiar temporality is evoked by a rhetoric of necessity, which
corresponds on the level of language to the inexorable movement of the earth.
Shelley's prolepsis, in other words, is the poetic form of a utopia inevitably to be
realized. It makes felt the pressure of natural history.

The intuition of history's end is therefore the condition of its arrival. This is
not only because necessity promises a perpetual peace to come. In taking necessity as a law, human beings can make liberation a present possibility. Nature's

progress toward the good is independent of human activity. This alone, Shelley suggests, should trouble our instrumental orientation to the earth, which need not be remade for human purposes to be realized. In fact, natural history frees humanity from the obligation to perform all manner of world-transforming labor. "Regeneration's work," as Shelley calls it, begins only when the work of commerce ends. Shelley's utopia is indeed a "paradise of peace."

To inhabit such a paradise means reimagining the good. Some things once held necessary for human happiness cannot be reconciled with necessity's law. This becomes clear when necessity is conceived in terms of need. In a world defined by commerce, Shelley notes, the most excessive of wants can be taken for a need. Yet, as he argues elsewhere, "No man has a right to monopolize more than he can enjoy; what the rich give to the poor, whilst millions are starving, is not a perfect favor, but an imperfect right."[63] This is not an argument for renunciation, or a generalized poverty "distribut[ed] . . . over the whole surface of society."[64] Rather, Shelley imagines that our human needs, along with the needs of the earth, might be met in common. He proposes, therefore, that at the end of history humanity will adopt a vegetable diet:

> No longer now
> He slays the lamb that looks him in the face,
> And horribly devours his mangled flesh,
>
> . . . .
>
> No longer now the winged habitants,
> That in the woods their sweet lives sing away,
> Flee from the form of man;
>
> . . . .
>
> All things are void of terror: man has lost
> His terrible prerogative, and stands
> An equal amidst equals.
> (VIII.211–13, 219–21, 225–27)

The liberatory promise of Shelley's natural history is fulfilled in the homeliest of practices, eating. And the vegetable diet is truly a metonym for a host of changes: a bond of respect among living beings; an end to private luxury and its destructive mass production; a rethinking of necessity, or need, in terms of shared freedom; and the recognition that nature provides for and sustains us, if only we let it. Each of these entails an interweaving, or a suspension of divisions, that might again be called ethereal, as Symonds in fact suggested when he remarked on Shelley's "ethereal diet."[65]

Common Love

Throughout his short life, Shelley returned repeatedly to this paradise of peace, seeking always a subtler language for the freedom to be found there. And despite the beauty of its final cantos, *Queen Mab* has its limits—limits of which Shelley became increasingly aware. At the close of Ianthe's dream, for instance, Mab states, "My spells are past: the present now recurs. / Ah me! a pathless wilderness remains / Yet unsubdued by man's reclaiming hand" (IX.143–45). Mab's lament comes as a shock, as it urges Ianthe to subdue the "pathless wilderness" of the present. Searching for an ethereal language that would circumvent the mastery of nature, Shelley struggles here to conceive freedom without domination. The same tensions can be felt in *Queen Mab*'s depiction of equality as universal sovereignty: "each unfettered o'er the earth extend / Their all-subduing energies, and wield / The sceptre of a vast dominion there" (VIII.232–34). In such moments, Shelley's utopian vision is betrayed by what Walter Benjamin terms the "false dialectics" of "lawmaking and law-preserving forms of violence," or the cycle by which revolution leads to the founding of just another legal order.[66] While *Queen Mab* shows that freedom cannot be the reclamation of sovereignty—over nature or humankind—the language proper to this insight must still be woven finer.

I return, then, to Shelley's great work *Prometheus Unbound*, which begins from precisely these problems. Often discussed in terms of the "failure" of the French Revolution, *Prometheus Unbound* indeed describes the trajectory from democratic insurrection ("a disenchanted Nation / Springs like day from desolation" [I.567–68]) to new imperial order ("Despair smothers / The struggling World—which slaves and tyrants win" [576–77]).[67] At the same time, the poem is concerned with domination, or "force" (127), in general. Like Benjamin, Shelley identifies that false dialectic which turns freedom toward mastery—a dialectic that, in certain moments, conditions his earlier writing. For Shelley, this interplay between freedom and domination is not only a matter of political revolutions. As he writes in the *Defence*, in a passage repeatedly invoked in this book, "Man, having enslaved the elements, remains himself a slave."[68] The freedom promised by capitalist modernity can never be realized, because it depends on the mastery of nature and of humankind. Of course, this is not just Shelley's insight. It is central to the romantic argument I have been tracing throughout. Recall Hegel's claim, discussed in chapter 3, that in machine labor nature takes its "revenge" upon the worker: "What he gains from nature, the more he subdues it, the lower he sinks himself . . . for the more machinelike labor becomes, the less it is worth, and the more one must work."[69] Remember, too, Wollstonecraft's depiction of the ruinous humanization of nature, inseparable from the dehumanization of peasants and the enslaved. Each of the poets and philosophers I have addressed feels the urgency of disentangling liberation from domination.

It is far from obvious, in this respect, that Shelley would turn to the myth of the Titans. His friend John Keats understood it as a lesson in political despair.[70] Yet Shelley is not alone in looking to Prometheus for an exit from the dialectic of force. In her own rereading of the classical tradition, Simone Weil articulates a related desire for an end to mastery. Her celebrated 1939 essay on the *Iliad* remarks on "the nature of force": "Its power to transform man into a thing is double and it cuts both ways; it petrifies differently but equally the souls of those who suffer it, and of those who wield it."[71] Weil's thought resonates deeply with Shelley's poem, which, in its first act, lingers on the unbroken embrace of Prometheus, the "sufferer," and Jupiter, his "torturer" (I.286–91). Despite the symmetry between these two, the point is not that those who suffer are somehow at fault. The trouble with force, as Weil explains elsewhere, is its tendency to perpetuate "the oppression-domination cycle."[72] The failure of Prometheus's revolt—first against his fellow Titans and then against Jupiter—lies in its reconstitution of the very power that it resists. "One doesn't bring power back down to earth in order to raise oneself above the heavens."[73] Furthermore, as Shelley reminds us, no freedom founded on the domination of nature is true freedom. In the words of Asia, Prometheus's companion, the gift of fire liberates "the race of man" (II.iv.49) only to the extent that it "torture[s] to his will / Iron and gold, the slaves and signs of power, / And gems and poisons, and all subtlest forms / Hidden beneath the mountains and the waves" (68–71). The history of freedom, Shelley's poem insists, has so far been a history of failure, a straight path leading from "the clear knowledge" bestowed upon humanity to the "million-peopled city" that "vomits smoke in the bright air" (I.542, 551–52).

According to Weil, there is little in European literature or thought that escapes this dialectic. But in a striking discussion of Aeschylus's late drama, she appeals to Prometheus as a figure for the suspension of mastery. This is surprising, given the familiar interpretation of the myth.[74] For Weil, however, "Prometheus suffers because he has loved men too well." Fated to be reconciled with his oppressor, he still chooses to "suffe[r] in man's stead."[75] His sacrifice is an act of love that heralds an end to domination. As Weil sees it, Prometheus, like Christ, "is the Lamb slain from the foundation of the world."[76] He is the force of love itself, the only force that might undo the false dialectic depicted in the *Iliad*. "Love does not exercise nor submit to constraint," Weil writes.[77]

Likewise, for Shelley, love is the meaning of the Prometheus myth. It is "common . . . love," he says, that can suspend the pursuit of mastery. In the poem's rhapsodic final act—following the fall of Jupiter and the reunion of Asia and Prometheus—he portrays a world in the light of love. This is a world without constraint, where freedom does not require domination. Common love weaves all things together. As the Chorus of Spirits sings at the celebration of love's arrival, "oh weave the mystic measure / Of music and dance and shapes of light, / Let the Hours, and the Spirits of might and pleasure / Like the clouds and sunbeams unite" (IV.77–80). The song interweaves nature's forces with poetry's "mystic measure"; waves of sound and light vibrate in time with the verse. Love is a physical force, the Spirits say, like gravity or magnetism or even poetry. In her duet with the earth, the moon therefore sings of being "Borne beside thee by a power / Like the polar Paradise, / Magnet-like of lovers' eyes" (464–66). Remember that for the younger Shelley all of nature thinks and feels, and Newtonian law is the law of nature's affects. Now, Shelley presents love as a force and an atmosphere, as action at a distance and "all-sustaining air" (II.v.42). In the words of the earth, who sings ecstatically to the moon, "Ha! ha! the animation of delight / Which wraps me, like an atmosphere of light, / And bears me as a cloud is borne by its own wind!" (IV.322–24). Earth and moon alike are animated, enveloped, and sustained by common love.[78]

So Prometheus is not the only figure of love in Shelley's poem. In fact, as Colin Jager has observed, love is most completely "embodied" by Asia, who, in entering the cave of Demogorgon—that "Power" beneath the earth (II.iii.11)—becomes the catalyst for Jupiter's fall.[79] There is, however, no direct relation between these events and love's arrival. According to Jager, the love of the poem's final act is "already present in the figure of Asia," and its liberatory promise travels with her as she journeys toward Prometheus.[80] In other words, love is external to the dialectic of force. It appears, as Asia's sister Panthea proclaims, "like the atmosphere / Of the sun's fire filling the living world" (II.v.26–27). Irreducible to erotic desire or to familial attachment, love shines through all things. In Asia's words,

> all love is sweet,
> Given or returned; common as light is love
> And its familiar voice wearies not ever.

Like the wide Heaven, the all-sustaining air,
It makes the reptile equal to the God . . .
(39–43)

In these pivotal lines, love first appears as a gift freely given, apart from or in excess of the exchange relation. The laws of commerce cannot account for its value or its movement. If *Queen Mab* depicts a world in which "even love is sold" (V.189), Shelley now insists that love and commerce are essentially incommensurate. Midway through the second line, the gift of love becomes a "common" thing. Like light or the sky or "the all-sustaining air," love belongs to no one. It holds together and is held by all.

This principle of mutuality—of "correspondence" or "community," as Shelley says—must not be confused with the abstract equivalence of exchange society.[81] The atmosphere of common love is a "contexture" of spirits, interwoven in their irreducible qualitative difference. Such a "love *in* and *of* the world" is a love of things in their nonidentity, in their flight from apprehension.[82] In her notebooks, Weil feels her way toward a similar thought: "The beautiful is that which we cannot wish to change," she writes. "To assume power over is to soil. To possess is to soil. To love purely is to consent to distance, it is to adore the distance between ourselves and that which we love."[83] The adoration of distance that Weil describes is at once epistemological, aesthetic, and political. It is the very heart of the romanticism with which I have been concerned. Like Kant in the *Critique of Judgment* or Wordsworth in "There was a Boy," Weil sees the violence in the negation of distance—in the interminable pursuit of possession. Like Shelley, she knows that love is a word for letting be.

It is not easy to consent to distance. The appropriative apprehension of nature, as the romantics recognized, is more than a habit of mind. For the poets and philosophers featured in this book, consciousness is inseparable from commerce, and nature pays the price. Despite the continuities that I have observed across two and a half centuries of fossil capital, I have not looked to romanticism for a plan or a course of action. At its best, poetry is a reminder that things could be different, that other forms of life are possible. Transported by the "sweet singing" (II.v.74) of a spirit, a spirit of love and imminent freedom, Asia says something much like this: "My soul is an enchanted Boat . . . It seems to float ever—forever— / Upon that many winding River / Between mountains, woods, abysses, / A Paradise of wildernesses" (72, 78–81). Romanticism may not teach us how to get there, but it recalls us to the necessity of trying.

Notes

Introduction

1. Shelley, *Prometheus Unbound*, I.764.

2. Shelley, "Ode to the West Wind," 1–2.

3. Shelley, *Prometheus Unbound*, I.742. In Shelley's poem, "thought's wildernesses" is a figure for poetic consciousness; it is often understood—as in Bloom, *Shelley's Mythmaking*, 115, and in Armstrong, *Language as Living Form*, 128—to suggest that the poet transcends nature. For an alternative reading, closer to my own, see Wilson, *Shelley*, 96–100.

4. Shelley, *Prometheus Unbound*, I.661.

5. See Rigby, *Reclaiming Romanticism*, on the "wild" as "agentic or 'self-willed' . . . rather than pinned down as the passive object of human knowledge and power" (15). Rigby's claim, which I affirm, is that the encounter with wild nature need not be sublime and is not a precursor to colonization or control. For the critique of wilderness as a myth of the frontier, see Cronon, "Trouble with Wilderness." For an overview of the debate, see Speitz, "Conceptualization of Wilderness."

6. For the history, see Malm, *Fossil Capital*.

7. For the critique of romantic nature, see Levinson, *Wordsworth's Great Period Poems*; Liu, *Wordsworth*; and Morton, *Ecology without Nature*. For an influential call to abandon the distinction between human and natural history, see Chakrabarty, "Climate of History." In newer work, Levinson has returned to the topic of nature, situating Wordsworth's poetry in the tradition of a "dynamic materialism" that includes Spinoza; the science of complex systems; affect theory; and Morton's ecology. See "Motion and a Spirit." There are notable similarities between this dynamic materialism and the contemporary "spirit of capitalism," defined by a logic of self-organization,

delocalization, adaptability, and so on. For more on this, see Malabou, *What Should We Do*.

8. See Nassar, "Romantic Empiricism"; Latour, *We Have Never Been Modern*, 142–45; Morton, *Ecology without Nature*, 17; and Morton, "Coexistence and Coexistents."

9. Nassar, "Romantic Empiricism," 309.

10. Nassar, "Romantic Empiricism," 309.

11. Terada, "Racial Grammar," 277–78. Terada (277) comments on the following ecological thought: "Everything in the universe gets to access everything else, and the way that everything accesses everything is such that nothing is ever exhausted, everything is always completely sparkling with some kind of unfathomable, vivid, bristly reality, you know? And ultimately that's funny" (Morton, "Conversation").

12. Adorno, *Aesthetic Theory*, 73. Morton claims the notion of the nonidentical for an "ecology without nature"—even though nature is a central category in Adorno's thought. See *Ecology without Nature*, 13–14.

13. Malm, "In Defence."

14. Adorno, *Kant's "Critique of Pure Reason,"* 176.

15. Kant, *Critique of Pure Reason*, A99; here and throughout, I cite the first *Critique* using A and B page numbers, which refer respectively to the 1781 and 1787 editions.

16. From the Latin *apprehensio*; the word is the same in German and in English. For a brief historical overview of the term, see Wilson, *Shelley*, 13–14, 176–77. See also *Oxford English Dictionary*, s.v. "Apprehension."

17. J. G. Schlosser, *Plato's Briefe nebst einer historischen Einleitung und Anmerkungen* (Königsberg, 1795), 182, as quoted in Malabou, *Before Tomorrow*, 6. On machinery as the model for psychic and social life in the transition to capitalism, see Federici, *Caliban and the Witch*, 145–46.

18. In fact, the association of knowledge with physical grasping, or manipulation, has a longer history beginning in classical antiquity. See, for instance, Cicero's account of the Stoic theory of *katalêpsis* in *On Academic Scepticism*, 84.

19. Hölderlin, "Being Judgement Possibility," 191–92.

20. Friedrich Hölderlin, "Preface to the Penultimate Draft of *Hyperion*," in *Sämtliche Werke, Kritische Textausgabe*, ed. D. E. Sattler (Darmstadt: Luchterhand, 1982), 10:162ff., as quoted in Frank, *Philosophical Foundations*, 116.

21. See Merchant, *Death of Nature*, which outlines this precise relation between separation and control: "As European cities grew and forested areas became more remote, as fens were drained and geometric patterns of channels imposed on the landscape, as large powerful waterwheels, furnaces, forges, cranes, and treadmills began increasingly to dominate the work environment, more and more people [from the sixteenth and seventeenth centuries onward] began to experience nature as altered and manipulated by machine technology" (68).

22. Shelley, *Defence of Poetry*, 530.

23. Buck-Morss, *Hegel, Haiti*, 57–58. Buck-Morss presents Hegel's dialectic of lordship and bondage (*Herrschaft und Knechtschaft*) as a response to the Haitian Revolution.

24. See Federici, *Caliban and the Witch*, 97: "In the new organization of work *every woman (other than those privatized by bourgeois men) became a communal good*, for once women's activities were defined as non-work, women's labor began to appear as a natural resource." See also 18n2. On the structural similarities between unwaged reproductive labor and slave labor, see 100–115. On plantation slavery as "a process that transforms people of African origin into living *ore* from which *metal* is extracted," see Mbembe, *Critique of Black Reason*, 40. For a similar claim in Shelley about slavery as the conversion of "human will" into "gold," see *Queen Mab*, VIII.172–80.

25. See Marriott, "Rites of Difficulty," on the challenge of disentangling poetry (even at its most "resistan[t] to the yield of 'apprehensible truths'" [125]) from the forms of "false communication" characteristic of capitalist society.

26. McGann, *Romantic Ideology*, 2. McGann's influential claim is that a "*critical* view of Romanticism" must come from without (1)—specifically, from the present-day historicist critic.

Chapter 1

1. See, for instance, the work of Kaufman ("Legislators," "Red Kant," and "Intervention & Commitment Forever!"), Jarvis (*Wordsworth's Philosophic Song*), François (*Open Secrets*), Terada (*Looking Away*), and Wilson (*Shelley*). Robinson, in *Adorno's Poetics of Form*, reconstructs Adorno's thinking about aesthetic form, with reference to the return to formalism in literary studies.

2. By *critical theory*, I refer to a body of philosophical work also sometimes described as belonging to the Frankfurt School or to the tradition of Western Marxism. I use *critical theory* because it is the term employed by the thinkers themselves.

3. On the fortunes of Adorno's "'domination of nature' thesis," see Ronda, "Mourning and Melancholia."

4. One could also point to the earlier work of Bloom, and I do refer intermittently to *Visionary Company* (1961; revised and republished in 1971). Even at this early stage of his career, Bloom imagines a literary history defined largely by relationships among individual poets. For Bloom, the self-sufficiency of the literary—correlative to the "internal movement" of poets withdrawing from the world (xvi)—is a defining feature of poetic modernity. Thus, he has little to say about romanticism's philosophical and political dimensions.

5. Shelley, *Defence of Poetry*, 520. On real abstraction, see below. For a survey of the debate in Marxist theory, see Toscano, "Open Secret."

6. Rather than treat romanticism as a symptom, reducible to an underlying historical dimension left implicit in the poetic text, I am concerned with romanticism's avowed poetic and political thinking. For the former approach, see especially McGann, *Romantic Ideology*. But the tendency to overlook romanticism's own critique of political economy is widespread. For some recent exceptions, see Löwy and Sayre, *Romanticism against the Tide*; Simpson, *Wordsworth, Commodification*; Wang, *Romantic Sobriety*; Goodman, "Conjectures on Beachy Head"; and Nersessian, "Romantic Difficulty."

7. Allusions to Benjamin and Adorno begin to appear in de Man's work around 1967. Szondi, a friend of Adorno's and later of de Man's, would begin to engage seriously with critical theory in the mid-1950s. On de Man's reading of Benjamin, see Waters, "Paul de Man," liv–lvii.

8. Hartman, in *Scholar's Tale*, recalls being introduced to Benjamin's writings, in Adorno's edition, by Szondi himself during a 1966 visit to Berlin (184). For the broader institutional history, see Redfield, *Theory at Yale*, 19–61.

9. See Waters, "Paul de Man," xi–xiii, xxxii–lx, on the French context. It may be worth noting that, before World War II, Paul de Man's uncle—the socialist politician, social psychologist, and Nazi collaborator Hendrik de Man—taught at the University of Frankfurt alongside Horkheimer and Adorno. On Hendrik de Man, see Adorno's (only recently published) 1964 lecture course, *Philosophical Elements*, 49–50, 151n9.

10. See, for instance, his skeptical (and somewhat repetitious) questioning of de Man during the 1983 Messenger Lectures at Cornell. Their back-and-forth is captured in the lecture transcripts in de Man, *Aesthetic Ideology*.

11. On the "peculiar power [*The Mirror and the Lamp*] had for many readers in its first decade"—as a philosophical reconstruction of romanticism and in its surprising attention to the workings of figurative language—see Culler, "Mirror Stage," 149.

12. Abrams, "Correspondent Breeze," 25–26.

13. Abrams, *Mirror and the Lamp*, 66.

14. Bloom, *Visionary Company*, vii.

15. Abrams, *Mirror and the Lamp*, 66.

16. Hartman, *Wordsworth's Poetry*, 33. See Redfield, *Theory at Yale*, 84–86, for more on the consolidation of academic romanticism in the 1950s and '60s.

17. For that story, see Redfield, *Theory at Yale*.

18. Balfour locates in the later de Man, in essays such as "Anthropomorphism and Trope in the Lyric," a sense of history resonant with Benjamin's and Adorno's accounts of a critical philology. See "History against Historicism."

19. In 1966, the now-legendary conference "The Languages of Criticism and the Sciences of Man" took place at Johns Hopkins; as is well known, de Man was in attendance. For the conference proceedings, see Macksey and Donato, *Structuralist Controversy*. In the years following, de Man's work took on characteristics of the rhetorical analysis for which he is best remembered. See de Man's own account of this shift in the 1983 foreword to the revised edition of *Blindness and Insight* and in the 1983 preface to *Rhetoric of Romanticism*.

20. De Man, "Foreword," xii.

21. See, especially, Rajan, "Displacing Post-structuralism." On Hartman's engagement with Heidegger, see Vermeulen, *Geoffrey Hartman*.

22. See Sohn-Rethel's biographical preface in the belatedly published *Intellectual and Manual Labour* (first drafted in 1951, the book was published in a German version in 1970 and then in an English version in 1978).

23. Adorno's 1964 lectures, the *Philosophical Elements*, provide an overview of some of this activity. See Terada, *Looking Away*, 153–98, on the status of appearance, or *Schein*—a basic category in Adorno's aesthetics—in the sociological research.

24. Of course, many still see the *Dialectic of Enlightenment* (coauthored with Horkheimer and with "the most valuable assistance" of Gretel Adorno, Theodor's wife [xii]) as Adorno's most significant work. I read the *Dialectic* as a crucial backdrop to the aesthetic writings, especially in its account of abstraction.

25. Kaufman, "Legislators," 710.

26. Adorno, *Aesthetic Theory*, 16.

27. Adorno, *Aesthetic Theory*, 32–33.

28. Adorno, *Aesthetic Theory*, 2.

29. Here and throughout, I follow Rigby in recognizing "a wider European romanticism" that encompasses "*Sturm und Drang, Klassik, Romantik, . . . Idealismus,*" and more (*Topographies of the Sacred*, 11).

30. Hammer, *Adorno's Modernism*, 85.

31. Adorno, *Aesthetics*, 72–73. For a related claim about the romantic folksong revival, see "On Lyric Poetry," 45.

32. Adorno, *Aesthetic Theory*, 62.

33. Hartman, *Wordsworth's Poetry*, xvii.

34. Adorno, *Aesthetic Theory*, 62.

35. Adorno, *Aesthetic Theory*, 68. See also 78: "If the language of nature is mute, art seeks to make this muteness eloquent; art thus exposes itself to failure through the insurmountable contradiction between the idea of making the mute eloquent, which demands a desperate effort, and the idea of what this effort would amount to, the idea of what cannot in any way be willed."

36. Adorno, *Aesthetic Theory*, 62. On the interplay between natural and art beauty in *Aesthetic Theory*, see Hammer, *Adorno's Modernism*, 45–64, and Robinson, *Adorno's Poetics of Form*, 189–94.

37. For "material content," see Adorno, *Aesthetics*, 73, 137. For a fuller treatment of the relations among form, content, and material in Adorno's aesthetics, see Robinson, *Adorno's Poetics of Form*, especially 133–62. For a skeptical account of the objective side of Adorno's aesthetics, see Lehman, "Formalism, Mere Form," 257–58. According to Lehman, Adorno "blur[s] the distinction between phenomenal form and [a Kantian subjective] mere form" and thus falls back into a kind of pre-Kantian aesthetics. One might also read Adorno's insistence on objectivity in aesthetics as Hegelian. See Hegel, *Aesthetics*.

38. Adorno, *Aesthetic Theory*, 5. See also "Parataxis," 128: "Instead of vaguely appealing to form, one must ask what form itself, as sedimented content, does."

39. Adorno, *Aesthetics*, 151.

40. Adorno, *Aesthetics*, 151.

41. Of course, artistic materials cannot be immediately identified with nature. On the historical quality of material, see Adorno, *Aesthetic Theory*, 147–49. For the mediated presence of nature in artistic materials, see Wilson, *Shelley*, 86–90, and Robinson, *Adorno's Poetics of Form*, 190–91.

42. Adorno, *Aesthetic Theory*, 67.

43. Adorno, *Aesthetic Theory*, 73. See the fuller treatment of Goethe's poem in "On Lyric Poetry," 41–42. Adorno turns to Beethoven in a related discussion of the "spirit"

of art as "the spirit of the thing itself that appears through the appearance" (*Aesthetic Theory*, 87). Again, Adorno's example of artistic material speaking for itself is a romantic one: "the sensual constellation of two chords" (88) across Beethoven's sonata.

44. The phrase is McGann's; see the Introduction to this book for more. One could demonstrate that Adorno adopted this view from Benjamin. See *Concept of Criticism*, along with the essential analysis of Hölderlin from the same period. For related discussion of romanticism's critical reflection on its own presuppositions, see Hamilton, *Metaromanticism*, and Chai, *Romantic Theory*.

45. Adorno, *Aesthetic Theory*, 63. On "mastery over material," see Geulen, "Adorno's *Aesthetic Theory*," 401–2.

46. Adorno, *Aesthetic Theory*, 63. For a reading of contemporary elegy oriented by this same idea, see Ronda, "Mourning and Melancholia."

47. Adorno, *Aesthetic Theory*, 66.

48. Here I differ with the basic premise of the new historicist polemic. See Levinson, *Wordsworth's Great Period Poems*, which argues that "Imagination and Nature are not only not distinct (and therefore not liable to prolific marriages) but are, equally, indifferent avatars of historical consciousness and its severe conditions" (10–11). For Levinson, the field of romantic studies at the midcentury is defined by its evasion of history.

49. Abrams, *Mirror and the Lamp*, 64–65.

50. Abrams, "Correspondent Breeze," 42.

51. Abrams, "Correspondent Breeze," 43.

52. On these themes, Adorno, in *Philosophical Elements*, refers to Weber's famous 1917 lecture "Science as a Vocation," while Schmitt's fullest account of modernity as a process of disenchantment or secularization is *Political Theology* (1922). Abrams's grandest retelling of the secularization narrative is undoubtedly *Natural Supernaturalism*. For a rethinking of romanticism's relation to a secular modernity instituted and policed by the emergent nation-state, see Jager, *Unquiet Things*.

53. Horkheimer and Adorno, *Dialectic of Enlightenment*, 2.

54. Horkheimer and Adorno, *Dialectic of Enlightenment*, 4.

55. Shelley, *Defence of Poetry*, 529.

56. Abrams, "English Romanticism," 64–65.

57. Abrams, "English Romanticism," 65.

58. Abrams, "English Romanticism," 66.

59. Adorno, *Aesthetics*, 22. See also *Aesthetic Theory*, 62.

60. Bloom, *Visionary Company*, vii, 2.

61. Hartman, *Wordsworth's Poetry*, 351.

62. Hartman, *Wordsworth's Poetry*, 39.

63. Gordon, *Adorno and Existence*, 66.

64. Hartman, *Wordsworth's Poetry*, 41.

65. Wordsworth, *Prelude* (1850), VI.591–99; in what follows, I cite the poem parenthetically by line number.

66. Hartman, *Wordsworth's Poetry*, 15.

67. Hartman, *Wordsworth's Poetry*, 17. In *Wordsworth's Poetry*, as Redfield remarks, "Hartman . . . discards the effort to imagine imagination apart from consciousness" (*Theory at Yale*, 89). The terms are treated as basically synonymous. Earlier in his career, Hartman had tried to differentiate imagination from consciousness and self-consciousness.

68. Hartman, *Wordsworth's Poetry*, 49.

69. Hartman, *Wordsworth's Poetry*, xxii.

70. Hartman, *Wordsworth's Poetry*, 17.

71. See Wilner, "Pitching Apocalypse."

72. Kant, *Critique of Judgment*, especially sections 25–27 on the mathematical sublime.

73. Hartman, *Wordsworth's Poetry*, xv. On nature, nonviolence, and deferral in Hartman, see François, "'A Little While' More."

74. Hartman, *Wordsworth's Poetry*, 18.

75. Hartman cites Hegel's 1830 *Encyclopaedia Logic*: "The principle of restoration is found in thought, and thought only: the hand that inflicts the wound is also the hand that heals it" (quoted in "Romanticism and Anti-self-consciousness," 301). But Hegel has something different in mind—namely, the fulfillment of reflection in speculative philosophy.

76. See Rajan, "Displacing Post-structuralism," 453–63, and Redfield, *Theory at Yale*, 84–102. For Rajan, de Man's "earliest work is phenomenological in its emphasis on the consciousness which produces the text. This consciousness may lack the transcendental autonomy of existing outside language, and in this sense the *epoché* [the bracketing of 'all expressions that imply thetic existential positings of things,' as Edmund Husserl puts it in 1911 ("Philosophy as Rigorous Science," 89)] some may associate with phenomenology has been deconstructed" ("Displacing Post-structuralism," 460).

77. Redfield, *Theory at Yale*, 226n16.

78. Hartman, *Unmediated Vision*, 165. See also 184n60, 197n15. In Jaensch, eidetic perception is a psychological phenomenon related to visual images. In Husserl, the eidetic has a strict transcendental significance and refers to a process of abstraction from experience to a general essence of things. See Husserl, "Philosophy as Rigorous Science," 111.

79. Hartman, *Unmediated Vision*, 165.

80. Husserl, "Philosophy as Rigorous Science," 90.

81. Adorno, "Husserl," 14.

82. Hartman, *Unmediated Vision*, 5.

83. Hartman, *Unmediated Vision*, 9, 35. See Vermeulen, *Geoffrey Hartman*, 14–17, for a discussion of the Heideggerian aspects of passivity in *Unmediated Vision*, focusing on Heidegger's notion of "letting go," or *Gelassenheit*. On "whether or in what sense perceptual experience *ever* constitutes a relation to the object experienced," see Siewert, "Consciousness and Intentionality," sec. 3. To be clear, I am not offering an interpretation of Husserl, Heidegger, or Sartre; my concern is with Hartman's and de Man's views of their work.

84. See Gordon, *Adorno and Existence*, 80. As Gordon relates, phenomenology was a constant preoccupation for Adorno. From his 1924 dissertation to the major studies published in 1956 and 1964, Adorno was engaged in critical dialogue with Husserl and Heidegger. See, for example, Adorno's lucid discussion in "Husserl." Adorno's lifelong study of Hegel is better known. See Adorno, *Hegel*.

85. Hegel, *Phenomenology of Spirit*, 19.

86. It has often been noted that de Man's title alludes to a 1938 essay by Sartre: "The Intentional Structure of the Image" (see Waters, "Paul de Man," xliv–xlv; Rajan, "Displacing Post-structuralism," 458, 462–63; Redfield, *Theory at Yale*, 224n10). Less remarked upon is the other allusion in de Man's title—to Wimsatt's "Structure of Romantic Nature Imagery" (included in 1954's *The Verbal Icon*). De Man engages at length with Wimsatt in the later "Rhetoric of Temporality" (1969), where he rehearses Wimsatt's account of the "closer, more faithful observation of the outside object" that defines romantic poetry (194). Returning to a central claim of the 1960 essay, de Man observes, "This finer attention given to the natural surfaces is accompanied, paradoxically enough, by a greater inwardness, by experiences of memory and of reverie that stem from deeper regions of subjectivity.... How this closer attention to surfaces engenders greater depth remains problematic" (194). Here de Man sets up the problem in order to dissolve it; "When we interpret the romantic image in terms of a subject-object tension," he argues, we adopt an utterly mystified position regarding romantic language (198). In 1960, on the other hand, "subject-object tension" plays a crucial role in the analysis.

87. De Man, "Intentional Structure," 6.

88. Rajan, "Displacing Post-structuralism," 458.

89. See de Man, "Criticism and Crisis," 18: "One hesitates to use terms such as nostalgia or desire to designate this kind of consciousness, for all nostalgia or desire is desire of something or for someone; here, the consciousness does not result from the absence of something, but consists of the presence of a nothingness. Poetic language names this void with ever-renewed understanding and ... it never tires of naming it again." On the return of the object world in de Man's "Rhetoric of Temporality," see Galperin, *History of Missed Opportunities*, 41–44.

90. De Man, "Intentional Structure," 7.

91. See Abrams, *Mirror and the Lamp*, 201–13.

92. De Man, "Intentional Structure," 8–9.

93. I allude here to de Man's 1960 dissertation, which often resonates with the "Intentional Structure" essay. In the dissertation, "the post-romantic predicament" (exemplified by Mallarmé and Yeats) is that of a poetry constantly striving to articulate its own justifications—partly by stylistic means and partly by a rethinking of historical consciousness. See de Man, *Post-romantic Predicament*, 33–35.

94. De Man, "Intentional Structure," 4.

95. De Man, *Post-romantic Predicament*, 77.

96. I have mentioned Hyppolite's 1939 translation of the *Phenomenology*. As was common in the period, de Man's reading of Hegel was conditioned by the influential lectures of Alexandre Kojève (*Introduction* [1947]) and the commentaries of Jean Wahl

(*Malheur de la conscience* [1929]) and Hyppolite (*Genesis and Structure* [1946]). De Man knew Wahl and Hyppolite personally. In 1956, de Man delivered a talk titled "Process and Poetry" to Wahl's philosophy seminar in Paris. See also Macksey and Donato, *Structuralist Controversy*, 184–85, for the highly relevant 1966 exchange between de Man and Hyppolite, focused on the status of death in Hegel.

97. Hegel, *Phenomenology of Spirit*, 149.

98. De Man, *Post-romantic Predicament*, 77.

99. De Man, "Intentional Structure," 14.

100. De Man, "Intentional Structure," 16.

101. Rajan, "Displacing Post-structuralism," 455; Redfield, *Theory at Yale*, 86.

102. De Man, "Intentional Structure," 13–14. Since Wimsatt and Abrams, readers of romantic poetry have commented on this "use of the faint, the shifting, the least tangible and most mysterious parts of nature" (Wimsatt, "Structure," 111). See *Unmediated Vision*, 164–66, where Hartman describes the romantic imagery of "atmospheric media," "luminosity," and "ether" as figuring "immediation," or the interplay of immediacy and mediation that he sees defining modern poetics. I consider such phenomena myself in chapters 2 and 6 of this book.

103. De Man, "Intentional Structure," 15.

104. François, *Open Secrets*, 3.

105. Adorno, "Parataxis," 130.

106. Adorno, "Parataxis," 136.

107. Adorno, "Parataxis," 138.

108. Hartman, *Wordsworth's Poetry*, 33.

109. De Man, *Post-romantic Predicament*, 77.

110. Hartman, *Wordsworth's Poetry*, xvi.

111. Horkheimer and Adorno, *Dialectic of Enlightenment*, 4.

112. Horkheimer and Adorno, *Dialectic of Enlightenment*, 4.

113. See Hartman, *Scholar's Tale*, 42: "In critiques of the Enlightenment, before Adorno and Horkheimer, Blake was." Löwy and Sayre make a similar point; they attend, as do I, to Horkheimer and Adorno's "critiques of rationalist abstraction" in the name of a "substantive human rationality" (40).

114. See, for instance, Rigby, *Topographies of the Sacred*, 9.

115. This may be changing. Recent literary critical approaches to real abstraction include Cunningham, "Capitalist Epics"; Ngai, "Visceral Abstractions"; and Nathan Brown, *Limits of Fabrication*. For an effort to align Marxist theories of abstraction with the figures of haunting and spectrality in the late Derrida, see Simpson, *Wordsworth, Commodification*.

116. I distinguish here between the earlier Marxist phase of critical theory and a later (ongoing) liberal/social-democratic phase. See the discussion of Adorno's contested inheritance in Endnotes, "Communisation," which also points out that Sohn-Rethel and Alfred Schmidt were Adorno's sources for knowledge of the *Grundrisse*. Adorno had probably not studied the 1857–58 drafts of *Capital* himself (98–99).

117. See Horkheimer and Adorno, *Dialectic of Enlightenment*, 9.

118. See, most famously, the first chapter of *Capital*, vol. 1, especially 138–63. Horkheimer and Adorno are clearly informed by Marx's notion of the value-form as encompassing the entirety of "social relations": "The general form of value . . . can only arise as the joint contribution of the whole world of commodities. A commodity only acquires a general expression of its value if, at the same time, all other commodities express their values in the same equivalent; and every newly emergent commodity must follow suit. It thus becomes evident that because the objectivity of commodities as values is the purely 'social existence' of these things, it can only be expressed through the whole range of their social relations" (K. Marx, *Capital*, 1:159). In other words, the form of value is determined by *and* determines social life as a whole. The *Grundrisse*, published in the 1930s, deepens the analysis, in ways that would greatly influence the critical theorists. Here Marx describes a "social bond expressed in *exchange value*" (156): "The general exchange of activities and products, which has become a vital condition for each individual—their mutual interconnection—here appears as something alien to them, autonomous, as a thing" (157). The notion of value as an autonomous subject is central to Adorno's later work. On "forms of value subjectivity" in contemporary aesthetics and social life, see Vishmidt, *Speculation*.

119. Horkheimer and Adorno, *Dialectic of Enlightenment*, 8.

120. Horkheimer and Adorno, *Dialectic of Enlightenment,* 8; Shelley, *Defence of Poetry*, 512, 520.

121. Horkheimer and Adorno, *Dialectic of Enlightenment, 9.*

122. Horkheimer and Adorno, *Dialectic of Enlightenment,* 31.

123. Horkheimer and Adorno, *Dialectic of Enlightenment,* 23; my emphasis.

124. Shelley, *Defence of Poetry,* 530. On Shelley's "dialectic of calculation," see Kaufman, "Legislators," especially 713–16.

125. Marcuse, *One-Dimensional Man*, xvi.

126. Schmidt, *Concept of Nature*, 163.

127. Postone, *Time, Labor*, 119.

128. Postone, *Time, Labor*, 119.

129. For Postone, Sohn-Rethel recognizes the historical transformations of exchange, while relying on a relatively abstract idea of the labor process. Thus, Sohn-Rethel can "claim that a society is potentially classless when it acquires the form of its synthesis directly through the process of production and not through exchange-mediated appropriation" (Postone, *Time, Labor*, 178). This explains, in part, Sohn-Rethel's utopian perspective on communist China.

130. See Toscano, who observes that, for Sohn-Rethel, abstraction "lies in the prosaic activity, the doing of commodity-exchange, and not . . . in the individual mind of the doer" ("Open Secret," 281). Thus, he contends, drawing on Slavoj Žižek's related discussion of Sohn-Rethel, that "the secret of real abstraction is precisely *an open secret*, one that is to be discerned in the operations of capitalism rather than in an ideological preoccupation with the concrete truth or hidden essence that the abstractions of capital supposedly occlude" (282).

131. On idealization, see Levinson, *Wordsworth's Great Period Poems*, 2. None of the major statements of new historicist methodology mention Sohn-Rethel. Nor do they treat Adorno's thought in depth. Levinson has more recently argued, in "Motion and a Spirit," that the new historicism was continuous with the tradition of critical theory. She suggests that the new historicism's "view of meaning as brought about by processes of internal negation," which occur only in "genuine work[s] of art" and which refer to an absent historical object, derives from Adorno (396–97). But this is precisely the view of art that McGann rejects in *Romantic Ideology*: "Adorno's idea that art is the negative knowledge of reality," he writes, "reflects the persistent hold which certain types of Romantic idealism [for McGann, a term of disapproval] have even in the Marxian wings of the academy" (156). For McGann, art has no special status; it is simply another form of false consciousness.

132. Sohn-Rethel, "Intellectual and Manual Labour," 32.

133. Mascat, "Hegel," 30.

134. Sohn-Rethel, "Intellectual and Manual Labour," 31.

135. Sohn-Rethel, "Intellectual and Manual Labour," 31.

136. Sohn-Rethel, "Intellectual and Manual Labour," 31.

137. Sohn-Rethel, "Intellectual and Manual Labour," 33.

138. Sohn-Rethel, "Intellectual and Manual Labour," 36n6.

139. Sohn-Rethel, "Intellectual and Manual Labour," 35.

140. Moore, in *Capitalism*, has recently returned to the question of how "regimes of *abstract social nature*" make capital accumulation possible: "If the substance of abstract social nature is the production of 'real abstractions'—of time (linear), space (flat), and Nature (external)—its historical expressions are found in the family of processes through which capitalists and state-machineries make human and extra-human natures legible to capital accumulation" (193–94).

141. See Endnotes, "Communisation," 89–90.

142. See Merchant, *Death of Nature*, especially 42–68.

143. Rigby, in *Topographies of the Sacred*, 9–10, 20–21, also signals connections between ecofeminism and critical theory.

144. Sohn-Rethel, *Intellectual and Manual Labour*, 7.

145. Sohn-Rethel, *Intellectual and Manual Labour*, 17.

146. Sohn-Rethel, "Intellectual and Manual Labour," 34. For "negative allegory," see Levinson, *Wordsworth's Great Period Poems*, 8. For "denied positivism," see Liu, *Wordsworth*, 24. Both of these formulas are notably nondialectical as regards historical causation.

147. Sohn-Rethel, *Intellectual and Manual Labour*, 15.

148. Sohn-Rethel, "Intellectual and Manual Labour," 34.

149. Abrams, *Mirror and the Lamp*, 58.

150. On class consciousness in the early nineteenth century, see Thompson, *Making of the English Working Class*. My sense of the periodization of capitalism derives from K. Marx, *Results*. Thanks to Jensen Suther for conversation on these topics.

151. Wordsworth, *Excursion*, VIII.203–6; in what follows, I cite the poem parenthetically by book and line number.

152. For the classic formulation—"From each according to his abilities, to each according to his needs!"—see K. Marx, *Critique*, 347.

153. Wordsworth, "A slumber did my spirit seal," 7.

154. On time's remaking in early modern Europe, see Thompson, "Time, Work-Discipline." Thompson's focus is the time of production. On the relations among natural measures of space and time, and the abstract measure of circulation time, see K. Marx, *Capital*, 2:327.

155. Wordsworth, *Prelude* (1805), VI.622–24; in what follows, I cite the poem parenthetically by book and line number.

156. For "the tyranny of mind," see Galperin, *Return of the Visible*, 212–13.

Chapter 2

1. As Kant puts it in the 1787 "Preface" to the first *Critique*, "Reason must . . . compel nature to answer reason's own questions" (B xiii). On the understanding as "legislative for nature," see A126–27. Following scholarly convention, I cite the first *Critique* using A and B page numbers, which refer respectively to the 1781 and 1787 editions. I cite the text parenthetically.

2. Hegel, *Faith and Knowledge*, 74.

3. Hegel, *Faith and Knowledge*, 74.

4. On Hegel's rejection of "the instrument view of cognition," see Ng, *Hegel's Concept of Life*, 70.

5. Hegel's reading of Kant exerts a powerful influence on later critical theory. See Lukács, *History and Class Consciousness*, as well as Horkheimer and Adorno, *Dialectic of Enlightenment*. In a recent essay, "Racial Grammar," Terada presents Kantian cognition in a similar manner, arguing that Kant's "architectonic offering to the analytics of race is to create, for society's already present real abstractions of universal equivalence, spatiotemporal conditions that ensure that there is nothing else that can count as known" (275). According to Terada, Kant's theory of time, as elaborated in the first *Critique*'s "Analogies of Experience," structurally recapitulates, and lends conceptual coherence to, an emergent racial capitalist order.

6. I borrow the phrase "remaining time" from the work of Agamben, for whom it refers primarily to the messianic time of Pauline theology. See *Time That Remains*, as well as the earlier discussion in "Time and History." Kant himself uses a similar phrase, with a rather different inflection, in his response to J. H. Lambert's notion of absolute time; see the discussion below. On wild nature in the third *Critique*, see Gasché, *Idea of Form*.

7. Of course, Kant is a familiar figure in romantic studies, known mostly for his contributions to aesthetics. Since at least the 1960s, his theory of the sublime has been central to romanticist debate; the key contribution remains Ferguson, *Solitude and the*

Sublime. In this chapter, I turn instead to Kant's natural history writings, which I see as pivotal for romanticism.

8. See Kant, *Critique of Judgment,* 21–22, on the law of continuity as a maxim for "how we ought to judge" nature; in what follows, I cite the text parenthetically. For an overview of Kant's earlier treatment of the law of continuity, see Friedman, *Kant,* 31–32, and Watkins's note in *Natural Science,* 696–97n49.

9. For the "world spirit," see Kant's 1754 essay "Question," especially 180–81.

10. Kant, *Inaugural Dissertation,* III.14.3–4.

11. On the "primordial time" of the imagination in the first *Critique,* see Heidegger, *Kant.* Other major treatments of the role of time in Kant's philosophy include Deleuze, *Kant's Critical Philosophy;* Zuckert, *Kant on Beauty;* and Malabou, *Before Tomorrow.*

12. Here, I pass over the important issue of the relation between the forms of intuition and the a priori synthesis of the transcendental imagination (itself an apparently temporal process). This is a central concern in Kant's "Deduction of the Pure Concepts of the Understanding." See the disparate accounts in Heidegger, *Kant;* Malabou, *Before Tomorrow,* 7–9 and 111–19; and Rosefeldt, "Kant on Imagination."

13. Much contemporary Kant scholarship holds that "the theory of time as presented in the Transcendental Aesthetic was 'derivative' on a more fundamental theory of space" (Shabel, "Transcendental Aesthetic," 93–94n3). Given Kant's argument at A34/B50, as well as his emphasis on time throughout the first *Critique,* I see no compelling reason to privilege space. See Heidegger, *Kant,* 48–55, for a reading of the "Transcendental Aesthetic" closer to my own.

14. Kant, *Philosophical Correspondence,* 63–64.

15. Kant makes the same point about absolute space. For further discussion of change, see the "Analogies of Experience" in the first *Critique.*

16. In *Kant's Theory of Time,* al-Azm gives one standard account: Kant's trajectory is defined by the Leibniz-Newton debate over the relativity of space and time. The "Transcendental Aesthetic" mediates between Leibnizian relativism and Newtonian absolutism by defining time as transcendentally ideal (relative to a subject) and empirically real (absolute condition of all possible experience). See 1–28.

17. Grant, *Philosophies of Nature,* 128.

18. On these early natural history writings, see Schönfeld, *Philosophy;* Shell, *Kant,* 17–38; Regier, *Fracture and Fragmentation,* 88–94; and Passannante, *Catastrophizing,* 192–235.

19. Kant, *Inaugural Dissertation,* III.14.4. In the first *Critique,* see the "Anticipations of Perception" and the "Analogies of Experience" for further discussion of the law of continuity.

20. "Arithmetic attains its concepts of numbers by the successive addition of units in time, and pure mechanics especially can attain its concepts of motion *only by employing the representation of time*" (Kant, *Prolegomena,* 27; my emphasis). See Friedman, *Kant,* on Kant's construction of "space-time" as the foundation of the physical sciences.

21. For a discussion of Kantian time that also addresses the "tension between the transcendental idealism of the first *Critique* (1781), which locates human subjectivity as the source of any representation of the world, and a precritical work, the *Universal Natural History and Theory of the Heavens* (1755), in which we find a history of the universe the greater part of which precedes the appearance of man," see Bouton, "Dealing with Deep Time," especially 40–43.

22. On the textual history, see Louden, "Last Frontier," as well as Watkins's notes to the translation by Reinhardt.

23. Cooper, "Living Natural Products," 2; Cooper's focus is the difficulty presented by living beings for Kant's concept of a universal natural history.

24. Friedman, *Kant*, 5–14. See also Grant, *Philosophies of Nature*, 73–75.

25. For "the history of the atmosphere," see Kant, *Physical Geography*, 547; in what follows, I cite the English text parenthetically. (I refer intermittently to the 1802 German edition.)

26. See Zuckert, *Kant on Beauty*, 138n13, 140–41.

27. Sloan, "Kant," 635; on the fraught relation between physical geography and natural history, see especially 628n2 and 643n54. On this topic, see also Cooper, "Living Natural Products," whose account is closer to my own.

28. Grant, *Philosophies of Nature*, 128.

29. Zuckert, *Kant on Beauty*, 127.

30. Grant, *Philosophies of Nature*, 123.

31. Sloan, "Kant," 629. On the broader context for these debates, see also Rajan, "Spirit's Psychoanalysis," and Ellermann, "Late Coleridge."

32. I recognize that mathematical ratios are a form of analogy. For Kant's distinction between the mathematical and philosophical use of analogy, see Nassar, "Analogy," especially 244. On Kant's qualitative and analogical Newtonianism, see Schönfeld, *Philosophy*, 73–95.

33. "Nature is a temple wherein living pillars / Sometimes let slip some muddled words; / Man passes there through forests of symbols / Which observe him with familiar gazes" (Baudelaire, "Correspondences," 1–4). On analogy as a "research tool," see Breitenbach, "Biological Purposiveness," 137; Breitenbach herself does not entirely endorse this interpretation of Kant's analogies.

34. Kant's final understanding of analogy differs considerably from that of his contemporaries. On this complex topic, see again Nassar, "Analogy," as well as Beiser, *Romantic Imperative*, 153–70; Grant, *Philosophies of Nature*, 119–57; Halmi, *Genealogy*; and Förster, *Twenty-Five Years*, 250–76.

35. Friedman, *Kant's Construction of Nature*, 195. Friedman's focus is the *Metaphysical Foundations of Natural Science* (1786), but he addresses a wide range of writings on atmosphere by Kant and his contemporaries. For more on atmosphere in its scientific and poetic senses, see chapter 6 below, as well as Ford, *Wordsworth*, especially 62–71 and 127–48 (on Kant's "atmospheric aesthetics").

36. Kant, "New Notes," 376.

37. On Kant's debts to Leonhard Euler, who advocated for a pulsation theory of light, see Friedman, *Kant* and *Kant's Construction of Nature*, as well as Förster, *Kant's Final Synthesis*, 24–47.

38. For Kant's mature definition of matter as "the movable in space"—predicated on the union of space and time—see again Friedman, *Kant's Construction of Nature*. On the "contested" status of geography as a science of space, see Louden, "Last Frontier."

39. Leibniz, *Monadology*, 80, 69.

40. I read "liquid" (*flüssig* in German) as denoting the subtlety and changeability of matter. Cf. Milton: "God made / The firmament, expanse of liquid, pure, / Transparent, elemental air" (*Paradise Lost*, VII.263–65).

41. Grant, *Philosophies of Nature*, 128. While Grant addresses the relation between Kantian natural history and the law of continuity, his primary concern is Schelling's philosophy of nature.

42. Friedrich Hölderlin, "Preface to the Penultimate Draft of *Hyperion*," in *Sämtliche Werke, Kritische Textausgabe*, edited by D. E. Sattler (Darmstadt: Luchterhand, 1982), 10:162 ff., as quoted in Frank, *Philosophical Foundations*, 116.

43. Werner Pluhar translates Kant's "*Natur überhaupt*" as "nature as such." I amend the translation in accord with scholarly consensus.

44. Bouton, "Dealing with Deep Time," 42.

45. See al-Azm, *Kant's Theory of Time*, 71–84.

46. Zuckert, *Kant on Beauty*, 138.

47. See Terada, *Looking Away*, on appearance and illusion in the first *Critique*.

48. Agamben, "Time and History," 102: "Western man's incapacity to master time, and his consequent obsession with gaining it and passing it, have their origins in this Greek concept of time as a quantified and infinite *continuum* of precise fleeting instants." See also Kant, *Anthropology*, 126: "We are led along irresistibly in the stream of time . . . for time drags us from the present to the future (not the reverse)."

49. Kant, *Prolegomena*, 36.

50. Immanuel Kant, "On the Use of Teleological Principles in Philosophy," in *Kant's gesammelte Schriften* (Berlin: De Gruyter, 1912), 8:162, as quoted in Sloan, "Kant," 639–40.

51. Sloan, "Kant," 629n5. For a suggestive comparison of geological upheaval with Hume's challenge to the law of causation, see Passannante, *Catastrophizing*, 216–17.

52. Gasché, *Idea of Form*, 2. For Gasché, wild nature is the domain of aesthetic judgments about phenomena for which no determinate concept can be found. Teleological judgments, on the other hand, do employ the concept of a purpose. Given the stringent limits Kant imposes on the concept's use, I do not see teleological judgments as domesticating.

53. On the problem of underdetermination, see Gasché, *Idea of Form*; Zuckert, *Kant on Beauty*; and Ng, *Hegel's Concept of Life*, among others.

54. Ng, *Hegel's Concept of Life*, 33; see the entire discussion at 32–36.

55. On "wild and apparently ruleless [natural] beauty," see, in the third *Critique*, the "General Comment" to the "Analytic of the Beautiful," especially 93–95.

56. These are Kant's examples; see *Critique of Judgment*, 76, 84n60, and 236.

57. Others have noted that determinative judgment also involves reflection on the particular, and thus that the relation between these modes of judgment is closer than Kant implies. See Deleuze, *Kant's Critical Philosophy*, 58–61, as well as Steigerwald, "Natural Purposes."

58. Even sympathetic readers have questioned the philosophical legitimacy of the principle of purposiveness. For two recent discussions, see Ng, *Hegel's Concept of Life*, 43–50, on Kant's suggestion that the intelligibility of nature depends on the (indeterminate) idea of a supersensible intelligence, as well as Nathan Brown, *Rationalist Empiricism*, 24–27, on the subjective dogmatism underpinning Kant's claims about how empirical nature must be thought.

59. See Cooper, "Living Natural Products." Strictly speaking, Kant distinguishes organization from life. See the discussion in the third *Critique* at 254.

60. See Zuckert, *Kant on Beauty*, 14–17, 61–63.

61. Steigerwald, "Natural Purposes," 295.

62. See Zuckert, *Kant on Beauty*, 135–46.

63. Breitenbach's "Biological Purposiveness" is the key contribution to this debate. See also Nassar, "Analogy."

64. Breitenbach, "Biological Purposiveness," 136.

65. On analogy as enabling the "symbolic exhibition" of "a concept which only reason can think," see the *Critique of Judgment*, 225–28 and 356–59.

66. Breitenbach, "Biological Purposiveness," 143.

67. Schelling, "Introduction to the Outline," 194. For more on the analogy between the organism and the power of reason, see Beiser, *Romantic Imperative*, as well as Nassar, "Analogy," 250. Ng similarly understands Kant's analogy as crucial for the development of later romantic philosophy.

68. In the *Metaphysical Foundations*, Kant distinguishes between mechanistic and dynamic physics—a distinction that seems to be elided here. On Kant's criticisms of mechanism, his dynamic theory of matter, and the principle of purposiveness, see Friedman, *Kant's Construction of Nature*, especially the "Conclusion."

69. See Sloan, "Kant," and Nassar, "Analogy," for useful overviews of Kant's debate with Herder as the immediate context for this argument. On evolutionary thinking in Kant and his contemporaries, see Richards, *Meaning of Evolution*; Cohen, *Kant*; and Malabou, *Before Tomorrow*.

70. Of course, Kant is aware of the basic problem, which he deems unsolvable. See the discussion in section 78 of the "Critique of Teleological Judgment": "If we are to have a principle that makes it possible to reconcile the mechanical and teleological principles by which we judge nature, then . . . we must posit it in the supersensible" (297).

71. For an excellent overview, see Förster, *Kant's Final Synthesis*. Förster's English edition of the *Opus postumum* includes, in addition to these notes, a set of

writings from the late 1780s that he sees as the germ of the project; I cite this edition parenthetically.

72. See Förster's note to Kant, *Opus postumum*, 264–65n43. See also Grant, *Philosophies of Nature*, 128, as well as the broader discussion of planetary upheaval in Fenves, *Late Kant*.

Chapter 3

1. Hyppolite, *Studies*, 78.

2. As sympathetic a reader as Harris calls them "dreary." See Harris, *Hegel's Development*, xxxix.

3. See Lukács, *Young Hegel*. Lukács's 1948 book remains the most comprehensive study of the role played by economics in Hegel's intellectual formation. Its central claim is that Hegel "was the *only* philosopher of the age to have made a *serious* attempt to get to grips with the economic structure of capitalist society" and that "the *specific* form of dialectics evolved by him grew out of his preoccupation with the problems of capitalism and of economics" (565).

4. For historians, the origin of capitalism is a moving target. Max Weber argues that only in the mid-nineteenth century did "the provision of everyday wants by capitalistic methods" become the norm for western Europe (*General Economic History*, 207–9). Fernand Braudel, departing from Weber's emphasis on full-scale economic rationalization, tells a story more amenable to Hegel's reality; for Braudel, already by the fifteenth century, capital goods and a protoindustrial *Verlagssystem* of manufacture coexist with traditional *Grundherrschaft*. See *Wheels of Commerce*, 231ff.

5. I return to Hegel's concept of the "system of need" below. On the bare minimum, see Jarvis, *Wordsworth's Philosophic Song*, 91–92.

6. See Cole, *Birth of Theory*. Jameson, in *Hegel Variations*, argues that the 1807 *Phenomenology* clings to "a handicraft ideology" that "betrays no anticipation of the originalities of industrial production or the factory system" (68). Given Hegel's own earlier writing on the factory system, in the several versions of the Jena *Realphilosophie*, I am inclined to disagree.

7. Comay, *Mourning Sickness*, 2. See also Comay, "Hegel's Last Words," on the melancholic residues of the past in the pure present of absolute knowing.

8. Hyppolite, *Studies*, 73.

9. See Johnston, "Voiding of Weak Nature."

10. Hegel, *System of Ethical Life*, 247. In his translation, Harris felicitously chooses "evaporates" to render Hegel's *entflieht*.

11. See Malm, "Origins of Fossil Capitalism." Malm's history of "fossil capitalism" begins in the romantic period, with the transition from water to steam power. His claim is that this seemingly necessary development was anything but: "The term 'business-as-usual' is commonly employed as a stand-in for the fossil economy. As usual as this business now appears, it is not a fact of nature, nor the product of geological or biological history. . . . No piece of coal or drop of oil has yet turned itself

into fuel. No humans have yet engaged in systematic large-scale extraction of either to satisfy subsistence needs. Rather, fossil fuels necessitate commodity production and waged or forced labour as components of their very existence" (17). For the full presentation of the argument, see Malm, *Fossil Capital*.

12. Galperin, "'Describing What Never Happened,'" 363.

13. See Nathan Brown, *Rationalist Empiricism*, 73–89, on the relations among contingency and necessity, possibility and actuality in Hegel's *Logic*.

14. Žižek, *In Defense*, 459–60. On unsolvable problems in Hegel, see Jameson, *Hegel Variations*, 78–80.

15. In addition to Lukács and Hyppolite, see Avineri, *Hegel's Theory*, on Hegel's career-long investigation of civil society and the state, and his seeming "quietism" about alienation, inequality, and poverty.

16. Hegel, *Faith and Knowledge*, 53. In Hegel's later writings—including the *Encyclopaedia* of 1830—the overcoming of reflection retains its urgency.

17. F. H. Jacobi, letter to Karl Leonhard Reinhold, in *Hegel in Berichten seiner Zeitgenossen*, ed. Günther Nicolin (Hamburg: Felix Meiner, 1970), report 65, as quoted in Harris, *Hegel's Development*, xxiv. See Harris, *Hegel's Development*, "Processional Prelude," xix–lxx, for its useful account of Hegel's work on the *Critical Journal* and his precarious circumstances during the Jena period.

18. As one reviewer put it: "The reader is therefore requested to take the name *Hegel* as used in the following discussion, to refer simply to an individuality belonging to the system of Schelling" (quoted in Harris, *Hegel's Development*, xlviii).

19. Hegel, *Difference*, 94.

20. Hegel, *Difference*, 92, 89.

21. Hegel, *Faith and Knowledge*, 64; in what follows, I cite the text parenthetically.

22. See Gasché, *Tain of the Mirror*, 23–34.

23. Hegel, *Phenomenology of Spirit*, 32.

24. The *Phenomenology* returns to many of these intellectual-spiritual formations, and its treatment of the "Unhappy Consciousness" (126–38) and "The struggle of the Enlightenment with Superstition" (329–49) resonates strongly with the earlier text. On Hegel's first attempts to plot the dialectics of disenchantment, in texts like "The Spirit of Christianity and Its Fate," see Forster, *Hegel's Idea*, 22–60.

25. See Comay, *Mourning Sickness*, 182–83.

26. Hegel, *Early Theological Writings*, 310. On the young Hegel's philosophy of life, see Harris, *Hegel's Development*, 80.

27. On the "speculative identity" between life and self-consciousness, see Ng, *Hegel's Concept of Life*. According to Ng, "Hegel's positive thesis concerning speculative identity" develops from his critique of reflection and suggests "that there is a reciprocal and constitutive connection between the unity of self-conscious judgment on the one hand, and the unity of internal purposiveness or life on the other" (71).

28. Hegel alludes to Goethe's 1795 *Das Märchen*.

29. Hegel, "Philosophical Dissertation," 294.

30. See Ng, *Hegel's Concept of Life*, 70: "Hegel eventually calls this the instrument view of cognition, where mind as an instrument or tool (*Werkzeug*) is both distinct from the self (a tool at the self's disposal) and comes to filter, distort, reshape, or be a mere copy of that which it purports to know."

31. Gasché, *Tain of the Mirror*, 14.

32. For this argument, I follow Gabriel, *Transcendental Ontology*, 37–45. See, at 40–41, his different reading of the "iron king" passage.

33. On Hegel's own "developmental deduction" of human freedom from the life of nature, see Suther, "Hegel's Logic of Freedom."

34. Hegel, *Aesthetics*, 1:79–81.

35. One cannot overstate the importance of a concept of the infinite to Hegel. In *Faith and Knowledge*, it serves several functions. First, in Jacobi and Fichte in particular, it appears in inauthentic form, either as the empirical infinity of mere sensations (Jacobi) or as the purely formal, negative infinity of the subject striving to transcend nature (Fichte). See 112–14. But Hegel also invokes the "night" or withdrawal of the true infinite as a necessary stage in the resurrection of speculative knowledge: "Out of this nothing and pure night of infinity, as out of the secret abyss that is its birthplace, the truth lifts itself upward" (190).

36. Forster traces the philosopher's changing perspective on this problem of causation. In Forster's words, "It had been very characteristic of Hegel's *pre*phenomenological writings from the mid-1790s on to treat the types of thought that had arisen over the course of history as explicable in terms of the specific socio-economico-political contexts within which they had arisen" (*Hegel's Idea*, 461).

37. K. Marx and Engels, *German Ideology*, 414–15. Recent commentary gives a less antagonistic view of the Hegel-Marx relation. See, for one example among many, Nicholas Brown, "Work of Art." Meanwhile, Jarvis (in *Wordsworth's Philosophic Song*) maintains that *The German Ideology* is not a rejection of Hegel at all, but rather a rejection of the dogmas of Young Hegelianism.

38. Hegel, "Introduction on the Essence."

39. Hegel, "Introduction on the Essence." On the opposition between common sense (often claimed as "British") and theory (either "French" or "German"), see Simpson, *Romanticism, Nationalism*. For Hegel, common sense is nebulous enough to include certain types of theory—in particular, those that reassert the norms and practices they purport to explain.

40. Jameson, *Hegel Variations*, 127–28. See also the classic account of culture as a "whole way of life," from industry to art and politics, in R. Williams, *Culture and Society*.

41. Gabriel, *Transcendental Ontology*, 36. Like Wollstonecraft, Wordsworth, and Shelley, Hegel thus anticipates the *Dialectic of Enlightenment*, which also contests "the domination of the concept" over nature. For a very different reading of Hegel, see Kaufman, "Red Kant." Kaufman charges Hegel with the precise forms of conceptual domination critiqued in *Faith and Knowledge*.

42. See Avineri, *Hegel's Theory*, 1–2.

43. Adorno, "*Kultur* and Culture," 146.

44. Cf. Horkheimer and Adorno: "Bourgeois society is ruled by equivalence. It makes dissimilar things comparable by reducing them to abstract quantities. For the Enlightenment, anything which cannot be resolved into numbers . . . is illusion" (*Dialectic of Enlightenment*, 4).

45. See Lukács, *Young Hegel*, 168–78. Harris, in "Social Ideal," argues that Hegel's economics derive from Steuart more than Smith in their opposition to endless growth.

46. Of course, as Hegel points out, capitalism actually ensures that no one's needs will be definitively satisfied. As he explains in the 1802 *System of Ethical Life*, drafted contemporaneously with *Faith and Knowledge*, "The system of need . . . [is] a system of universal physical dependence on one another. For the totality of his need no one is independent. His labour, or whatever capacity he has for satisfying his need, does not secure its satisfaction for him. Whether the surplus that he possesses gives him a totality of satisfaction depends on an alien power over which he has no control" (167). In this text, Hegel argues that strong state regulation can overcome the arbitrariness of the market. He is not always so sanguine. See Avineri, *Hegel's Theory*, 87–109, 141–54.

47. Cf. Coleridge, in the first part of *Biographia Literaria* (1817), on Fichte's "boastful and hyperstoic hostility to NATURE" (1:159).

48. For a brief history of such images, from Hobbes to Benjamin, see Menely, "Anthropocene Air."

49. "An empty money-bag is a bag with respect to which money is already posited, to be sure, though with the *minus* sign; money can be immediately deduced from it because, as lacking, money is immediately posited" (*Faith and Knowledge*, 159).

50. On early nineteenth-century senses of the "speculative," see Esterhammer, "1824."

51. Ng outlines the problem well: "Hegel seems to be suggesting that conceiving of nature essentially in terms of oppositedness [as Fichte does]—at once a 'check' on and 'impetus' for our activity—leaves theoretical consciousness with two options: either the activity of consciousness is simply determined and caused by the object, or consciousness overcomes this determination by the object by 'dominating' it, where domination refers to merely negating an external limitation or opposition, rather than genuine synthesis or even genuine reciprocal determination" (*Hegel's Concept of Life*, 89). Of course, as Ng also notes, Hegel does not reject Fichte's thought entirely; see the discussion at 91–95. Thanks to Nathan Brown for conversation on this topic.

52. On Hegelian abstraction as "a *mode of social production*," see Mascat, "Hegel."

53. See Žižek, *Less Than Nothing*, 244ff., on the limits of ideology critique and the reality of abstraction in Hegel.

54. Hegel, *System of Ethical Life*, 228–31.

55. K. Marx, *Capital*, 1:255. Compare, too, the "general formula for capital [M-C-M]" (*Capital* 1:247–57) with Fichte's own formalization of the "reciprocal determination" of I and not-I (*Science of Knowledge*, 93–119). For a related discussion, see Endnotes,

"Moving Contradiction," on the "structural homology between Marx's *Capital* and Hegel's *Logic*" (115).

56. On "systemic amplification" in fossil capitalism, see Menely, "Anthropocene Air," 98. As Hegel puts it in his lectures of 1805–6, "Like every mass wealth becomes a force. The increase of wealth takes place partly by chance, partly through its universality, through distribution. It is a focus of attraction which casts its net widely and collects everything in its vicinity, just as a great mass attracts a lesser. To him that hath, more is given" (*Jenenser Realphilosophie*, ed. Johannes Hoffmeister [Leipzig: Felix Meiner, 1931–32], 2:232ff., as quoted in Lukács, *Young Hegel*, 334).

57. See Cerf and Harris's notes to their edition of *Faith and Knowledge*, 57, 58.

58. See Verene, "Hegel's Nature," and Pinkard, *Hegel*.

59. See, in order, M. Williams, *Deforesting the Earth*, 273–75; Braudel, *Wheels of Commerce*, 241; Lord, *Capital and Steam Power*, 215–17; Henderson, *Studies*, 123–65.

60. In the *System of Ethical Life*, 117–18, Hegel directly addresses the industrial use of steam power. See also Menely, "Anthropocene Air," 98: "The first technology that harnessed steam to produce mechanical force, the Newcomen engine of 1712, was used primarily to pump water from coal mines, utilizing coal energy to produce more coal energy. If capital is self-expanding value [and if, as I think Hegel might add, the idealist subject is self-expanding freedom], fossil fuels are self-generating energy."

61. See Lukács, *Young Hegel*, 330: "Through the use of tools the activity of man becomes formal and universal, but it remains 'his activity.' Not until the arrival of the machine is there any qualitative change." Cf. Cole, who argues (all discussion of machine technology aside) that Hegel is primarily concerned with precapitalist forms of alienated labor, which are only metaphorically mechanical. See *Birth of Theory*, 73–74.

62. Hegel, *System of Ethical Life*, 247.

63. See Hyppolite's lucid discussion of value and machine labor in *Studies*, 79–80. For the "iron law of wages," see K. Marx, *Critique*, 351–53. Marx himself is skeptical about this so-called law, as it implies that poverty can never be eliminated.

64. Hegel, *System of Ethical Life*, 248.

65. Thus, Hegel is no "economic romanticist" in Lenin's sense of the term. See *Characterization of Economic Romanticism*.

66. Hegel, *Philosophy of Right*, 270.

67. Hegel, *System of Ethical Life*, 249.

68. On Hegel's gothicism, see Comay, *Mourning Sickness*, 139–42.

69. Babbage, *On the Economy*, 17. Malm, in "Origins of Fossil Capitalism," also quotes Babbage at 15–16.

70. Babbage is quick to conclude that the machine is "only producing on a small scale compositions or decompositions which nature is incessantly at work in reversing, for the restoration of that equilibrium which we cannot doubt is constantly maintained throughout even the remotest limits of our system" (*On the Economy*, 17). In other words, he assures us, there is no way for humanity to disrupt the equilibrium of nature.

Chapter 4

1. Wollstonecraft, *Letters*, 29, 57, 99; in what follows, I cite the text parenthetically.

2. Commerce is a central category in eighteenth- and nineteenth-century political economy. In Adam Smith, it is basically synonymous with exchange. Money, for example, is described by Smith as "the universal instrument of commerce" (*Wealth of Nations*, 31). For Marx, however, commerce is a (logical) derivative of production. Thus, money is a "mode of commerce" within the capitalist mode of production, though the former is not inessential to the latter (*Capital*, 2:195–96). This is how Wollstonecraft (and Shelley) will use the term: to describe the forms of exchange that characterize a particular mode of production.

3. See Rigby, *Topographies of the Sacred*, 8, which presents language itself as anthropomorphizing: "If we are not to fall prey to ecopoetic hubris, we must ask of the literary work . . . how it alerts us to the inevitable loss entailed in the translation into merely human words of an experience of the givenness of more-than-human nature."

4. Bate, *Song of the Earth*, 61. See Garrard, *Ecocriticism*, 152–70, for an overview of the debate, with special attention given to the representation of animals.

5. De Man's essay hints at a broader definitional uncertainty, which I basically gloss over here. I register, however, that anthropomorphism's precise meaning has never been obvious. Aligned with devices such as personification and prosopopoeia—both of which are the subjects of a voluminous critical literature—anthropomorphism barely even appears in the *Princeton Encyclopedia of Poetry and Poetics*. Neat distinctions between these related terms are not easy to draw. Thus, in the later eighteenth century, personification and prosopopoeia were regarded as synonyms for "that Figure by which we attribute life and action to inanimate objects" (Blair, *Lectures*, 173). On the postclassical identification of these "rhetorical kinds," see Keenleyside, "Personification for the People," 448–49, 468n12.

6. De Man, "Anthropomorphism and Trope," 241.

7. De Man, "Anthropomorphism and Trope," 241.

8. De Man, "Anthropomorphism and Trope," 241. See Chase, *Decomposing Figures*, 107, on anthropomorphism as the "mystification" of prosopopoeia.

9. De Man, "Anthropomorphism and Trope," 241, 262.

10. Guyer, *Reading with John Clare*, 5.

11. Guyer, *Romanticism after Auschwitz*, 65.

12. De Man, "Anthropomorphism and Trope," 262.

13. On this problem of representation, see Goodman, "Conjectures on Beachy Head," 986: "How can a [historical] totality that cannot be directly represented nonetheless assert or insinuate its presence at the level of figure, or in 'the very syntax of poetic language itself?'" De Man's sense of history is not identical to Goodman's or to mine, but I do not think I stretch the terms of the analysis beyond recognition.

14. Methodologically speaking, my wager is that rhetorical reading can contribute to the work of critical theory. For a related approach to the use of anthropomorphism in contemporary poetry, see Ronda, "Anthropogenic Poetics" and *Remainders*. On the

affinities between de Manian deconstruction and critical theory, see Balfour, "History against Historicism."

15. On Godwin's titles and Wollstonecraft's "Hints," see Jump, *Mary Wollstone-craft*. Jump situates these fragments in the context of a late-century "fashion for apho-rism" (146–47).

16. Blair, *Lectures*, 173. On Wollstonecraft's study of Blair, see her *Collected Letters*, 138.

17. Blair, *Lectures*, 61.

18. Blair, *Lectures*, 173.

19. Blair, *Lectures*, 174, 62. J. G. Herder's 1772 *Treatise on the Origins of Language* tells a related story about personification, poetry, and the progressive development of human languages and cultures. Wollstonecraft may have been familiar with Herder's thought. Her onetime friend and lover, the artist Henry Fuseli, likely assisted with a Herder translation (published by Joseph Johnson in 1800, after Wollstonecraft's death). Review articles on Herder and his philosophy of language had appeared in English by 1796. See Angerson, "'Friend to Rational Piety.'" For a broad overview of theories of anthropomorphism in the eighteenth century, touching on Blair and Herder, see Regier, *Fracture and Fragmentation*, 52–74.

20. Wollstonecraft's skepticism about progress is determined, in complex ways, by the trajectory of the French Revolution. See Keach, *Arbitrary Power*, 104–11. She also responds to broader debates about the shape of human history. See Garret, "Anthro-pology," and Savarese, *Romanticism's Other Minds*, especially 17–40.

21. Among the many treatments of this topic, see Favret, *Romantic Correspon-dence*, 104–7; Jump, *Mary Wollstonecraft*, 74; Yousef, "Wollstonecraft, Rousseau"; and Pop, *Antiquity, Theatre*, 154–66.

22. Rousseau, *Discourse on Inequality*, 91.

23. Rousseau, *Discourse on Inequality*, 92–93.

24. Rousseau, *Essay on the Origin*, 305.

25. Rousseau, *Essay on the Origin*, 314.

26. Rousseau, *Essay on the Origin*, 318.

27. Rousseau, *Essay on the Origin*, 310.

28. Rousseau, *Essay on the Origin*, 310.

29. Horkheimer and Adorno, *Dialectic of Enlightenment*, 1.

30. See Jump, *Mary Wollstonecraft*, 147, on the influence of Blair. See also Jump, "'Kind of Witchcraft.'"

31. On Wollstonecraft and Wordsworth, see Jump, *Mary Wollstonecraft*, 152–54: it is "certain," Jump argues, "that both Coleridge . . . and Wordsworth read the Essay." For Wollstonecraft's influence on Shelley, see Keach, *Arbitrary Power*, 95–121.

32. Jump, "'Kind of Witchcraft,'" 244.

33. Wollstonecraft, "On Poetry," 11; in what follows, I cite the text parenthetically.

34. Wordsworth, "Preface to *Lyrical Ballads*," 599.

35. See Abrams, *Mirror and the Lamp*, "Orientation of Critical Theories."

36. Wollstonecraft, *Wrongs of Woman*, 169.

37. Wollstonecraft, "Hints," 274.

38. Lynch, "'Young Ladies,'" 699.

39. Lynch, "'Young Ladies,'" 708. In the *Vindication*, Wollstonecraft imagines a new system of education, which might cultivate without corrupting. She writes, "Only that education deserves emphatically to be termed cultivation of mind, which teaches young people how to begin to think" (163).

40. Lynch, "'Young Ladies,'" 699; Wollstonecraft, *Vindication*, 69.

41. Lynch, "'Young Ladies,'" 709. On greenhouses "as switch points in the networks of plant transfer that facilitated this era's global redistribution of flora," see Lynch, "'Young Ladies,'" 692. On imperial "uprooting," see Weil, *Venice Saved*.

42. On the painter Angelica Kauffman—a member of Wollstonecraft's extended circle, criticized for her reliance on sculptural models—see Roworth, "Anatomy Is Destiny." For a wide-ranging consideration of eighteenth-century ideas about gendered spectatorship, see Calè, *Fuseli's Milton Gallery*, especially the chapter "The Plot of Adam and Eve."

43. Lynch, "'Young Ladies,'" 699.

44. The language of effeminacy recalls Adam Ferguson's influential critique of civilization. Thanks to John Savarese for the observation. On the human body and its representation in antiquity, see Wollstonecraft, *Vindication*. Insisting that the ancients did not imitate individual bodies or artworks, Wollstonecraft says that "only insipid lifeless beauty is produced by a servile copy of even beautiful nature. Yet, independent of these observations, I believe that the human form must have been far more beautiful than it is at present, because extreme indolence, barbarous ligatures, and many causes, which forcibly act on it, in our luxurious state of society, did not retard its expansion, or render it deformed" (171).

45. Siegel, *Desire and Excess*, 36.

46. Siegel, *Desire and Excess*, 28.

47. Much has been said about romantic ruins—both as theme and as form. I have found the following studies helpful: Lacoue-Labarthe and Nancy, *Literary Absolute*, especially 4–5, 39–58; Terada, "Living a Ruined Life"; and Sachs, *Poetics of Decline*.

48. Wollstonecraft, *Wrongs of Woman*, 76.

49. Wollstonecraft, *Wrongs of Woman*, 76.

50. Wollstonecraft, *Wrongs of Woman*, 67.

51. Robert Southey, as quoted in Brekke and Mee, "Introduction," xxv.

52. See, in Brekke and Mee's edition of the *Letters*, the note at 188n89, where Richard Holmes is credited with the point about "Kubla Khan." It is clear that Wollstonecraft's description of a cascade near Fredericstadt (in Letter XV) influenced Shelley's poem too; Percy and Mary Shelley both admired the *Letters*. On the presence of lyric in the Scandinavian *Letters* itself, see Favret, *Romantic Correspondence*, 100.

53. See Lacoue-Labarthe and Nancy, *Literary Absolute*, 126–27.

54. Wollstonecraft shares with the theorists and artists of the picturesque an interest in wild nature. She opposes, however, the generalizing tendencies of picturesque landscape art. On Wollstonecraft's criticism of landscape aesthetics—as related to

her ideas about landed property—see Bohls, *Women Travel Writers*, 145–46. On the picturesque as a "redaction of phenomenal properties to general shapes," see Pfau, *Wordsworth's Profession*, 72.

55. For the political and economic background, see Nyström, *Mary Wollstonecraft's Scandinavian Journey*, and Packham, "Mary Wollstonecraft's Cottage Economics."

56. On the "temporal instabilities" of commerce and the aesthetics of ruin, see Sachs, *Poetics of Decline*, 7: "In a society moving with apparent speed into an unknown commercial future, ruins join time past and time present and thus serve both as a discursive counterweight to and sentimental icon of decline." On Wollstonecraft's sense of "historical untimeliness" as well as her intuitions of "disaster to come," see Juengel, "Mary Wollstonecraft's Perpetual Disaster," paras. 6–7.

57. Pfau, *Wordsworth's Profession*, 61, 112; but see also the entire discussion at 17–139.

58. For "philosophical daydreaming," see Juengel, "Mary Wollstonecraft's Perpetual Disaster," para. 1.

59. On the politics of improvement, see Galperin, "'Describing What Never Happened.'"

60. On formal subsumption as a phase of capitalist development, see K. Marx, *Results*, 1021: in formal, as opposed to real, subsumption, "capital subsumes the labour process as it finds it, that is to say, it takes over an *existing labour process*, developed by different and more archaic modes of production." On capital goods, see Braudel, *Wheels of Commerce*.

61. For more on the history and significance of alum mining, see Rowney, "Reframing Romantic Nature," chap. 1.

62. For Yousef, these failed personifications are a way of acknowledging that nature cannot be a substitute for human sociality: "A *rock face* does not smile; the personification is impossible because nothing, perhaps, is so gratifying and irreplaceable in the intersubjective encounter than the eliciting of a smile" ("Wollstonecraft, Rousseau," 552–53).

63. Cf. Marx: "If money . . . 'comes into the world with a congenital blood-stain on one cheek,' capital comes dripping from head to toe, from every pore, with blood and dirt" (*Capital*, 1:925–26). On Wollstonecraft's abolitionism and its limits, see Thomas, *Romanticism and Slave Narratives*, 86–89.

Chapter 5

1. Following scholarly tradition, I focus on the version of "There was a Boy" embedded in *The Prelude* (1805) at V.389–422. For "concourse wild," see 403. In what follows, I cite the poem parenthetically by book and line number.

2. Chase, *Decomposing Figures*, 13.

3. The essential readings of "There was a Boy," pursued in close relation to one another, remain those of Hartman (in *Wordsworth's Poetry*); de Man (in "Time and History"); and Ferguson (in *Wordsworth*). I draw on all three in what follows.

4. In other words, my Wordsworth is the unremarkable, not the apocalyptic, Wordsworth. See the discussion of apocalypse in chapter 1, as well as Hartman's 1987 collection *Unremarkable Wordsworth*, especially "The Unremarkable Poet," 207–19. See also François on Wordsworth's "lyric of inconsequence" (*Open Secrets*, 154). For De Quincey's phrase, to which I return below, see *Recollections*, 164. I cite the *Recollections* parenthetically throughout.

5. See the "Prospectus to 'The Recluse,'" which opens 1814's *Excursion*. Here Wordsworth describes "the individual Mind" and "the external World" as "exquisitely . . . fitted" to one another (63–71). These well-known lines hardly capture the complexity of Wordsworth's thinking about nature. For a relevant rereading of the "Prospectus," which adduces a certain historical materialism from its figurative language, see Galperin, *History of Missed Opportunities*, 45.

6. François, *Open Secrets*, 161; Gurton-Wachter, *Watchwords*, 86. See also the very recent discussion in Bate, *Radical Wordsworth*, 56–57.

7. Wordsworth notoriously claimed that "'he had never read a word of German metaphysics, thank Heaven!'" (quoted in Jarvis, *Wordsworth's Philosophic Song*, 153). For a reformulation of the question of "Wordsworth and philosophy" rooted in the specificity of poetic thinking, see Jarvis.

8. This is not so different from Kant's sense of things; according to the first *Critique*, all cognition requires spontaneous mental activity and "receptivity for impressions." Yet for Kant the former takes precedence (see, e.g., A50/B74, A120–21). See again Jarvis, who locates in Wordsworth's poetry "a capacity to receive and depend upon the non-human" (*Wordsworth's Philosophic Song*, 50). Similarly, François reads "There was a Boy" as a poem of "quiet intrusion, a stealing into that is also a coming to rest, as the boy is suspended in the exercise of a power to receive that puts him beyond all seeking" (*Open Secrets*, 162).

9. Kant, *Anthropology*, 56. See also *Oxford English Dictionary*, s.v. "impressive," especially definitions 2 and 4.

10. Galperin, *History of Missed Opportunities*, 52. Galperin also remarks, significantly, that the double take ends in "divestiture, in which the claim to ownership [of the material world] is relinquished" (56).

11. Wordsworth, "Lines written," 89.

12. On "stray gifts" as "the logic, or the absence of logic, of nature itself," see Jarvis, *Wordsworth's Philosophic Song*, 105. On Wordsworth's relation to nature "as a relation of Grace," see Hartman, *Wordsworth's Poetry*, 9. My argument is additionally informed by François's account of the literature of "*natural revelation*," which she defines in terms of "a gift of revelation so transmuted it's taken for granted—absorbed into the ground of the ordinary—before being perceived as such, buried as part of its reception rather than repression" (*Open Secrets*, 9–10). Reflecting on the theological background, François presents the "image of the buried talent," from the parable of the talents, as "a violation of the project of enlightenment itself" (24; see Matt. 25:14–30 [NRSV]). The unspent coin, she argues, when read as a "surprising vindication not simply of secrecy but of 'unknowingness,'" comes to resemble the gift of grace (26).

Crucially, François's argument goes one step further and identifies a (romantic) ethics of grace that is also "a relaxation or a suspension of the law, an exemption, a remission or release from obligation" (62). The parable of the workers in the vineyard (Matt. 20 [NRSV])—especially in John Ruskin's famous socialist interpretation—might also be considered here, though François does not discuss it. Neither does she address De Quincey on accidental revelation.

13. The Solitary, says Hartman, "is forced to suffer a vision of glory" (*Wordsworth's Poetry*, 308). Below, I draw on his reading of this episode; see *Wordsworth's Poetry*, 306–12.

14. Thanks to Naomi Levine for first pointing this out to me. For a suggestive phonological and grammatical analysis of Wordsworth's poetry, see Prynne, "Mental Ears." Commenting on the language of gift and blessing in Wordsworth, Prynne observes that the poet's "passive-mood construction[s]" are a "warran[t]" for the "passive-recipient aspect of 'gift'; in each case the question of initiating agency is occluded" (150n29).

15. In what follows, I cite the poem parenthetically by book and line number.

16. Abrams, "English Romanticism," 66.

17. Here I depart from Chase's important study of "accidents of disfiguration" in Wordsworth. For Chase, focusing on book V of *The Prelude*, Wordsworth's poetry is marked by a "peculiar [argumentative] slide" whereby "a defense of benign chance turns into a defense of chance disasters" (14). I concur with Chase's careful explication of the drowned man episode and its traumatic structure (25–26, 211n10). Still, a nearly unnarratable accident is not always a trauma. As I argue, nature's accidental revelation remains irreducible to trauma's (negative) narrative form.

18. See Galperin, *Return of the Visible*, 213–14.

19. Wordsworth, "By their floating Mill," 27–28. See Jarvis, *Wordsworth's Philosophic Song*, 104–7.

20. Terada, *Looking Away*, 3.

21. Terada, *Looking Away*, 3, 4.

22. Terada, *Looking Away*, 4.

23. Wordsworth, "Preface to *Lyrical Ballads*," 599; *Excursion*, VIII.203.

24. I cite the poem parenthetically by line number.

25. Hartman, *Wordsworth's Poetry*, 98. Hartman is discussing *An Evening Walk*, published in 1793 and significantly revised just before the writing of "Incipient Madness."

26. On the metaphysics and ethics of life in Wordsworth, see Potkay, *Wordsworth's Ethics*, 23–24, 80–89. For a related discussion of Spinoza's influence on Wordsworth, see Levinson, "Motion and a Spirit."

27. *Being* is Wordsworth's term. Capitalized (and thereby hypostatized) in *The Excursion*, it appears as follows in a relevant passage from the 1797–98 "Ruined Cottage": "'what we feel of sorrow and despair / From ruin and from change, and all the grief / The passing shews of being leave behind, / Appeared an idle dream that could not live / Where meditation was'" (520–24). The lines are spoken by the Pedlar, who seeks

consolation for Margaret's death. For a less consolatory account of Wordsworthian being, see Fry, "Green to the Very Door?"

28. On the relations among imagination, consciousness, and perception—in Wordsworth and his critics—see chapter 1.

29. On Wordsworth's classification of his poems, see Ferguson, *Wordsworth*, 35–95. For Ferguson, the "Poems of the Imagination" "represent a hard-won dialectical synthesis into asceticism: they are spiritual exercises, acts of the mind repeatedly in the process of finding exactly how little must suffice" (70). In "There was a Boy," I would add, the mind also finds how little it must demand.

30. Wordsworth, "Preface to *Poems*," 635.

31. Wordsworth, "Preface to *Poems*," 635; my emphasis.

32. Timothy Morton reads "There was a Boy" as refusing the "immediacy . . . 'Romantic ecology' wants to hear in the echoes of the owls across the lake" (*Ecology without Nature*, 76). Morton aligns the "sense of immediacy" with "ecomimesis," or the ideological mystification that supposedly defines all "environmental writing" (76). I understand mimesis differently, as a form of mediation.

33. By contrast, in 1798's MS JJ the passage reads as follows: "he [would] stand alone / Beneath the trees or by the glimmering lake / And through his fingers woven in one close knot / Blow mimic hootings to the silent owls / And bid them answer him."

34. Hartman, *Wordsworth's Poetry*, 21; de Man, "Time and History," 6.

35. Wordsworth, "Preface to *Lyrical Ballads*," 606. De Man cites this passage as "a good commentary on the opening scene of the poem" ("Time and History," 7). On the problem of reflection in romantic philosophy, see chapter 3. On the literary critical afterlives of romantic reflection, see Wasser, *Work of Difference*.

36. Horkheimer and Adorno, *Dialectic of Enlightenment*, 148. On the transformations of mimesis in Adorno's thought, see Hammer, *Adorno's Modernism*, 59–64.

37. Horkheimer and Adorno, *Dialectic of Enlightenment*, 148.

38. For a fuller account of the relationship between the prodigy and the Winander boy, see Galperin, *Return of the Visible*, 103–7. Galperin also discusses the Winander boy's "'engines' of mediation and power": "These engines may . . . be nothing more than his hands and mouth and his human brain; yet the orchestration they perform, and the response they conspire to evoke, make the Winander boy even more successful [than the prodigy] . . . in controlling the world he inhabits" (105).

39. Horkheimer and Adorno, *Dialectic of Enlightenment*, 9, 148.

40. Hartman, *Wordsworth's Poetry*, 20.

41. Hartman, *Wordsworth's Poetry*, 21.

42. For two important accounts of romantic narrative and its discontents, see François, *Open Secrets*, 136, on "poems that record only to set aside narrative gain"; and Galperin, *History of Missed Opportunities*, 20, on historical narrative as "a retrospect of the possible." Thanks to Sean Barry for conversation on this topic.

43. On hanging as an image of anxiety and "a prefiguration of [the boy's] death," see de Man, "Time and History," 7–8. On the poem's use of enjambment as a way

of "underscoring how an anticipatory listening is built into verse form," see Gurton-Wachter, *Watchwords*, 90.

44. Cf. de Man's account of "the moment when the analogical correspondence with nature no longer asserts itself": "The experience hits as a sudden feeling of dizziness, a falling or a threat of falling, a *vertige* of which there are many examples in Wordsworth" ("Time and History," 7). I would say that the "correspondence" between the Winander boy and nature is never as secure as de Man makes it out to be. Thus, the dizziness of its withdrawal is also somewhat milder.

45. Wordsworth, "Nutting," 43, 53–54.

46. Here the 1798 version differs significantly. It ends with "the bosom of the steady lake" (MS JJ).

47. Hartman, *Wordsworth's Poetry*, 21.

48. Hartman, *Wordsworth's Poetry*, 22. To Hartman's great credit, he also shows how Wordsworth returns from the sight of death—from imagination, as Hartman understands it—to stay with nature. On this, see chapter 1.

49. Simpson, *Wordsworth, Commodification*, 212–13.

50. For "the shrunken lives of the coming proletariat," see Simpson, *Wordsworth, Commodification*, 213.

51. Liu, *Wordsworth*, 18.

52. Liu, *Wordsworth*, 20.

53. Nersessian, *Calamity Form*, 80.

54. Nersessian, *Calamity Form*, 89.

55. Wordsworth, "A slumber did my spirit seal," 8.

56. See M. Brown, *Preromanticism*, for a related discussion of Thomas Gray and William Collins—two likely influences on the ending of Wordsworth's poem.

57. Gray, "Elegy," 36.

Chapter 6

1. Symonds, *Shelley*, 25–26.

2. For the modern history of ether theory, see Schofield, *Mechanism and Materialism*, Milutis, *Ether*, and Ford, *Wordsworth*, as well as the discussion in chapter 2. Grabo, *Newton among Poets*, provides an exhaustive catalog of Shelley's allusions to these ideas.

3. Shelley, "Ode to the West Wind," 27, 19. See Leavis, *Revaluation*, especially 204–5. For a related account of Leavis on Shelley's atmospheric imagery, see Wang, *Romantic Sobriety*, 166–67, 171–72.

4. See Newton, "Hypothesis." On ether and eighteenth-century philosophy of mind, see Wroe, "Shelley's Good Vibrations."

5. The best recent criticism has explored how Shelley's poetry pursues "an experiential undoing of any effort to draw lines between the mind and the things outside it" (Jager, *Unquiet Things*, 239). For helpful, if widely divergent, accounts of Shelley's

philosophy—variously characterized as skeptical, idealist, materialist, and "skeptical idealist"—see Wasserman, *Shelley*; Roberts, *Shelley*; Hamilton, *Metaromanticism*, 139–55; and Michael, *British Romanticism*, 203–29.

6. Prynne, letter, 620.

7. Prynne, letter, 620.

8. I first learned about Prynne's letter from Wilson, *Shelley*. See especially 23–29 on the relation between poetic thinking and the theory of life. I share Wilson's skepticism about any approach to Shelley's poetry in which "the process of 'lyricising' science has no significant effect on the thinking that science is always already taken to have set forth" (27). In general, my reading of Shelley (and of Prynne's letter) aligns with Wilson's; it differs in its emphasis on metaphor and in specifying Shelley's style as ethereal.

9. Shelley, *Defence of Poetry*, 512, 530–31.

10. The body of scholarship on Shelley's figurative language is extensive. In addition to the work of Leavis and Prynne, the following studies have been particularly illuminating for me: Empson, *Seven Types of Ambiguity*, 155–61; de Man, "Shelley Disfigured"; Armstrong, *Language as Living Form*, especially 32–34 and 113–40; Ulmer, *Shelleyan Eros*, especially 3–24; Pyle, "'Frail Spells'"; White, *Romantic Returns*, 101–28; Wang, *Romantic Sobriety*, 163–89; and Carlson, "Like Love."

11. Leavis, *Revaluation*, 210. As discussed in chapter 1, such resistance to romanticism powerfully conditions Abrams's intervention in *Mirror and the Lamp*.

12. Shelley, *Queen Mab*, VIII.238; in what follows, I cite the poem parenthetically by canto and line number.

13. Shelley, *Prometheus Unbound*, II.v.40; in what follows, I cite the poem parenthetically by act, scene, and line number.

14. Newton, *Philosophical Writings*, 136.

15. Newton, *Philosophical Writings*, 136.

16. Newton, *Philosophical Writings*, 114.

17. Newton, *Philosophical Writings*, 114.

18. See Schofield, *Mechanism and Materialism*, 101–3, 106.

19. Newton, "Hypothesis."

20. Newton, "Hypothesis."

21. On the multiple "fluid matters" of eighteenth-century materialism, see Schofield, *Mechanism and Materialism*, 16. For the "holism" of Newtonian ether theory, see Milutis, *Ether*, 8.

22. *Community* is Kant's term, adapted from Newton's natural philosophy, for the form of relation between substances. See, e.g., the first *Critique*, B111.

23. Newton, "Hypothesis."

24. Hölderlin, "In my boyhood days," 125. Today, the ether reminds us that old and new materialisms are not so clearly opposed. On the relations between "romantic aerography" and new materialism, see Speitz, "Affect and Air."

25. See Grabo, *Newton among Poets*, as well as Reisner, "Some Scientific Models," and Curran, *Shelley's Annus Mirabilis*.

26. Shelley, *Refutation of Deism*, 133.

27. Shelley, *Refutation of Deism*, 133. On the "mechanist," see the *Defence of Poetry*, 529, where Shelley also describes imagination as the "principle" of quality, or "value" (510). For a canonical account of qualities in bodies, with which Shelley was intimately familiar, see Locke, *Essay Concerning Human Understanding* (1689), book II, chap. 8. See also book III, chap. 10, §15, on the idea of matter. Like Locke, Shelley aligns sensible qualities (color, sound, heat, taste, and so on) with the feeling of pleasure or pain in a perceiver. Unlike Locke, Shelley definitively attributes the capacity for sensation to nature as a whole.

28. Shelley, *A Refutation of Deism*, 133.

29. Shelley, *Refutation of Deism*, 131.

30. Wilson, *Shelley*, 6–7; here, Wilson draws on the thought of Michel Henry.

31. Hogg, *Shelley at Oxford*, 15. On "the chemical revolution" and the development of ether theory in the romantic period, see Friedman, *Kant*, 264–90.

32. Hogg, *Shelley at Oxford*, 17–18, 20.

33. For more on the *Defence* and the mastery of nature, see chapter 1. In general, my reading of Shelley differs from those that find in his early thought "more an extension than a repudiation of technological domination and self-destructive exploitation" (Gidal, "'O Happy Earth!'" 75). See also Bewell, *Romanticism and Colonial Disease*, 205–20.

34. Beiser, *Romantic Imperative*, 15.

35. Shelley, *Letters*, 114–15.

36. Shelley, *Letters*, 115.

37. Shelley, *Defence of Poetry*, 512. For more on Shelley's phantoms as ambivalent figures of the aesthetic, see Pyle, "'Frail Spells.'"

38. Shelley, *Defence of Poetry*, 532.

39. Shelley, *Defence of Poetry*, 513. On the dissolution of the self in Shelley, see Khalip, *Anonymous Life*, especially 115–32.

40. Shelley, *Defence of Poetry*, 532.

41. Shelley, *Defence of Poetry*, 533.

42. Shelley, *Laon and Cythna, or The Revolt of Islam*, as quoted in Jager, *Unquiet Things*, 220. For Jager's reading of the "subtler language" as a language of hope "wrought" from the "wreckage" of modernity, see 219–23.

43. Horkheimer and Adorno, *Dialectic of Enlightenment*, 4–5.

44. See Wilson, *Shelley*, 13, on "the apprehension of life" as "a possessive phrase" signaling life's "own ability to apprehend rather than, conversely, to be apprehended" intellectually. For a comparison between Kantian and Shelleyan apprehension in the context of the sublime, see Wang, *Romantic Sobriety*, 172.

45. See Reiman and Fraistat's note in *Shelley's Poetry and Prose*, 15. Wasserman, for instance, in *Shelley*, begins his comprehensive reading of Shelley's poetry with "Alastor" (1816).

46. Thompson, *Making of the English Working Class*, 98: "Godwin's philosophical anarchism reached a working-class public only after the [Napoleonic] Wars; and

then mainly through the Notes to Shelley's *Queen Mab*, in Richard Carlile's pirated editions." Miller has explored the significance of Shelley's poem for later nineteenth-century socialist organizations; see *Slow Print*, 149–58.

47. The Engels anecdotes are frequently repeated; for one source, see his letters of 1839–40 in *Engels: 1838–1842*, vol. 2 of K. Marx and Engels, *Collected Works*. See also E. Marx and Aveling, "Shelley and Socialism."

48. This important aspect of Shelley's writing was observed already by E. Marx and Aveling in "Shelley and Socialism." In a classic 1957 essay, Matthews explores the "inviting analogy between social upheaval and the highly topical science of geology" recurrent in the poet's work ("Volcano's Voice in Shelley," 564). See also Curran, *Shelley's Annus Mirabilis*, and Bewell, *Romanticism and Colonial Disease*, on the conjuncture of natural philosophy and politics.

49. Such claims resonate with the rationalist tradition as well as with Newtonian etherealism. For Shelley's immanent critique of the Spinozist "radical enlightenment," see Jager, *Unquiet Things*, 224–43.

50. Shelley, "On Life," 508.

51. In his discussion of *Laon and Cythna*, Keach observes that Shelley's "subtler language" is etymologically bound to the image of weaving: "*sub-tela*" is derived "from *texere*, to weave," as he explains, and it suggests something "woven fine, woven under as well as '"within"' [in this case] the web or *textus* of language" (*Arbitrary Power*, 118). Clearly, Newton too was aware of the association.

52. Empson, *Seven Types of Ambiguity*, 160.

53. Horkheimer and Adorno, *Dialectic of Enlightenment*, 9.

54. For a fuller account of Canto V in *Queen Mab*, see Wilson, *Shelley*, 66–85.

55. See Grabo, who cites Newton's claim that "'nature may be nothing but ether condensed by a fermental principle'" (*Newton among Poets*, 97).

56. Adorno, *Minima Moralia*, "Sur l'eau." While Adorno's aphorism later invokes Guy de Maupassant, I have been unable to locate a direct source for the French. I read it as alluding to the famous "Fifth Walk" in *Reveries*, where Rousseau describes his pleasure in idleness as he lies in a boat off the shore of Saint-Pierre. See Khalip, *Anonymous Life*, 13–14, on Adorno's aphorism and the romantic ethics of impersonality.

57. Cf. Spinoza, *Ethics* (1677), on the "third kind of knowledge"—the knowledge of our participation in "God or nature." As is well known, Percy and Mary Shelley were devoted readers of Spinoza.

58. Here, Shelley's thought resonates with a long tradition of antiwork politics. On this history, see Dauvé and Nesic, "Love of Labour?" See also Merchant, *Death of Nature*, 29–41, on the "normative constraints" against natural-resource extraction that had to be overcome in the transition to capitalism. Simply put, Shelley seeks to rearticulate such constraints.

59. Shelley, "Additional Notes," 339.

60. Shelley, "Additional Notes," 340.

61. Shelley, "Additional Notes," 340. Meanwhile, in a poem like "Mont Blanc" (1816), Shelley presents natural history as catastrophic. For more on competing visions of natural history in Shelley's writing, see Higgins, *British Romanticism*, 55–108.

62. J. D. Michaelis, as quoted in Lowth, *Lectures*, 207–8n.

63. Shelley, *Declaration of Rights*, 71.

64. K. Marx, *Critique*, 351–52. In answer to the so-called socialism of generalized poverty, Marx offers the following (Shelleyan) thought: "From each according to his abilities, to each according to his needs!" (347). For a reading of Marx's ethic grounded in absolute dispossession—as opposed to "the possession of ability and the possession of need"—see Harney and Moten, *Undercommons*, 99. Shelley himself proposes that community need not begin with humanity (conceived as a determinate set of abilities and needs).

65. Symonds, *Shelley*, 166.

66. Benjamin, "Critique of Violence," 251–52. "False dialectics" is Agamben's rendering of Benjamin's phrase. See "For a Theory."

67. On Shelley's typological reading of the French Revolution, see Wasserman, *Shelley*, 305. On his sense of the Revolution's "failure," see Jager, "Translating Love," especially 244.

68. Shelley, *Defence of Poetry*, 530.

69. Hegel, *System of Ethical Life*, 247.

70. I allude to Keats's *Hyperion* (1819), which Shelley praises in the "Preface" to *Adonais* (1821) "as second to nothing that was ever produced by a writer of the same years" (409).

71. Weil, *Intimations of Christianity*, 44–45. "Force" is the usual rendering of Weil's "*force*"; I amend the Routledge translation (which uses "might") accordingly. For two related discussions of a romantic Weil, see François, *Open Secrets*, 39–46; and Gurton-Wachter, *Watchwords*, 154–56, 180–87.

72. Weil, *Gravity and Grace*, 101.

73. Invisible Committee, *To Our Friends*, 77.

74. Consider Mary Shelley's *Frankenstein; or, The Modern Prometheus* (1818).

75. Weil, *Intimations of Christianity*, 67.

76. Weil, *Intimations of Christianity*, 70. Shelley, too, sees parallels between Prometheus and Jesus. On this lesser-known interpretive tradition, see Meaney, *Simone Weil's Apologetic Use*, 148–52.

77. Weil, *Intimations of Christianity*, 65.

78. On the earth's song as "approach[ing] a non-representational sense experience of pure sound and the animation of all things," see Jager, "Translating Love," 248. See also Michael, *British Romanticism*, 218–29, on atmospheric imagery in *Prometheus Unbound*. While Michael, among many others, finds these "high-pitched effusions on Love . . . unsatisfying" (228), I see them as a considerable aesthetic and political achievement.

79. Jager, "Translating Love," 247.

80. Jager, "Translating Love," 247–48.

81. Shelley, "On Love," 504, 503. In this 1818 essay, Shelley develops a Platonic notion of longing rather different from his later depiction of love. I do not read either one as involving "a metaphorical imperialism founded on the repression of difference" (Ulmer, *Shelleyan Eros*, 9).

82. For "love *in* and *of* the world," see Jager, "Translating Love," 247.

83. Weil, *Gravity and Grace*, 65.

Works Cited

Abrams, M. H. "The Correspondent Breeze: A Romantic Metaphor." In *The Correspondent Breeze: Essays on English Romanticism*, 25–43. New York: Norton, 1984.

———. "English Romanticism: The Spirit of the Age." In *The Correspondent Breeze: Essays on English Romanticism*, 44–75. New York: Norton, 1984.

———. *The Mirror and the Lamp: Romantic Theory and the Critical Tradition*. Oxford: Oxford University Press, 1971.

———. *Natural Supernaturalism: Tradition and Revolution in Romantic Literature*. New York: Norton, 1971.

Adorno, Theodor. *Aesthetics*. Translated by Wieland Hoban. Cambridge: Polity Press, 2017.

———. *Aesthetic Theory*. Translated by Robert Hullot-Kentor. Minneapolis: University of Minnesota Press, 1997.

———. *Hegel: Three Studies*. Translated by Shierry Weber Nicholsen. Cambridge, MA: MIT Press, 1993.

———. "Husserl and the Problem of Idealism." *Journal of Philosophy* 37.1 (1940): 5–18.

———. *Kant's "Critique of Pure Reason."* Translated by Rodney Livingstone. Stanford, CA: Stanford University Press, 2001.

———. "*Kultur* and Culture." *Social Text* 27.2 (2009): 145–58.

———. *Minima Moralia: Reflections on a Damaged Life*. 1951. Translated by Dennis Redmond. Marxists Internet Archive, 2005. https://www.marxists.org/reference/archive/adorno/1951/mm/index.htm.

———. "On Lyric Poetry and Society." In *Notes to Literature*, translated by Shierry Weber Nicholsen, 1:37–54. New York: Columbia University Press, 1991.

———. "Parataxis: On Hölderlin's Late Poetry." In *Notes to Literature*, translated by Shierry Weber Nicholsen, 2:109–49. New York: Columbia University Press, 1992.

———. *Philosophical Elements of a Theory of Society*. Edited by Tobias ten Brink and Marc Phillip Nogueira. Translated by Wieland Hoban. Cambridge: Polity Press, 2019.

Agamben, Giorgio. "For a Theory of Destituent Power." *Chronos*, February 2014. http://www.chronosmag.eu/index.php/g-agamben-for-a-theory-of-destituent -power.html.

———. "Time and History: Critique of the Instant and the Continuum." In *Infancy and History: On the Destruction of Experience*, translated by Liz Heron, 97–116. New York: Verso, 1993.

———. *The Time That Remains: A Commentary on the Letter to the Romans*. Translated by Patricia Dailey. Stanford, CA: Stanford University Press, 2005.

al-Azm, Sadiq Jalal. *Kant's Theory of Time*. New York: Philosophical Library, 1967.

Angerson, Catherine. "'A Friend to Rational Piety': The Early Reception of Herder by Protestant Dissenters in Britain." *German Life and Letters* 69.1 (2016): 1–21.

Armstrong, Isobel. *Language as Living Form in Nineteenth-Century Poetry*. Sussex: Harvester, 1982.

Avineri, Shlomo. *Hegel's Theory of the Modern State*. Cambridge: Cambridge University Press, 1972.

Babbage, Charles. *On the Economy of Machinery and Manufactures*. London: Charles Knight, 1832.

Balfour, Ian. "History against Historicism, Formal Matters, and the Event of the Text: De Man with Benjamin." In *Legacies of Paul de Man*, edited by Marc Redfield, 49–61. New York: Fordham University Press, 2007.

Bate, Jonathan. *Radical Wordsworth: The Poet Who Changed the World*. New Haven, CT: Yale University Press, 2020.

———. *The Song of the Earth*. Cambridge, MA: Harvard University Press, 2000.

Baudelaire, Charles. "Correspondences." In *The Flowers of Evil*, translated by Nathan Brown. Montreal: Anteism Books, 2022.

Beiser, Frederick. *The Romantic Imperative: The Concept of Early German Romanticism*. Cambridge, MA: Harvard University Press, 2006.

Benjamin, Walter. *The Concept of Criticism in German Romanticism*. In *Selected Writings*, edited by Marcus Bullock and Michael W. Jennings, 1:116–200. Cambridge, MA: Harvard University Press, 2004.

———. "Critique of Violence." In *Selected Writings*, edited by Marcus Bullock and Michael W. Jennings, 1:236–52. Cambridge, MA: Harvard University Press, 2004.

Bewell, Alan. *Romanticism and Colonial Disease*. Baltimore: Johns Hopkins University Press, 1999.

Blair, Hugh. *Lectures on Rhetoric and Belles Lettres*. Edited by Linda Ferreira-Buckley and S. Michael Halloran. Carbondale: Southern Illinois University Press, 2005.

Bloom, Harold. *Shelley's Mythmaking*. New Haven, CT: Yale University Press, 1959.

———. *The Visionary Company: A Reading of English Romantic Poetry*. Ithaca, NY: Cornell University Press, 1971.

Bohls, Elizabeth A. *Women Travel Writers and the Language of Aesthetics, 1716–1818.* Cambridge: Cambridge University Press, 1995.

Bouton, Christophe. "Dealing with Deep Time: The Issue of Ancestrality from Kant to Hegel." *Res: Anthropology and Aesthetics* 69–70 (Spring-Autumn 2018): 38–51.

Braudel, Fernand. *The Wheels of Commerce.* Vol. 2 of *Civilization and Capitalism, 15th-18th Century.* Translated by Siân Reynolds. New York: Harper and Row, 1982.

Breitenbach, Angela. "Biological Purposiveness and Analogical Reflection." In *Kant's Theory of Biology,* edited by Ina Goy and Eric Watkins, 131–48. Berlin: Walter de Gruyter, 2014.

Brekke, Tone, and Jon Mee. "Introduction." In *Letters Written in Sweden, Norway, and Denmark,* by Mary Wollstonecraft, ix–xxviii. Oxford: Oxford University Press, 2009.

———, eds. *Letters Written in Sweden, Norway, and Denmark.* By Mary Wollstonecraft. Oxford: Oxford University Press, 2009.

Brown, Marshall. *Preromanticism.* Stanford, CA: Stanford University Press, 1991.

Brown, Nathan. *The Limits of Fabrication: Materials Science, Materialist Poetics.* New York: Fordham University Press, 2017.

———. *Rationalist Empiricism: A Theory of Speculative Critique.* New York: Fordham University Press, 2021.

Brown, Nicholas. "The Work of Art in the Age of Its Real Subsumption under Capital." *nonsite,* March 2012. https://nonsite.org/the-work-of-art-in-the-age-of-its-real-subsumption-under-capital/.

Buck-Morss, Susan. *Hegel, Haiti, and Universal History.* Pittsburgh, PA: University of Pittsburgh Press, 2009.

Calè, Luisa. *Fuseli's Milton Gallery: "Turning Readers into Spectators."* Oxford: Clarendon Press, 2014.

Carlson, Julie. "Like Love: The Feel of Shelley's Similes." In *Romanticism and the Emotions,* edited by Joel Faflak and Richard C. Sha, 76–97. Cambridge: Cambridge University Press, 2014.

Cerf, Walter, and H. S. Harris, eds. *Faith and Knowledge.* By G. W. F. Hegel. Albany: State University of New York Press, 1977.

Chai, Leon. *Romantic Theory: Forms of Reflexivity in the Revolutionary Era.* Baltimore: Johns Hopkins University Press, 2006.

Chakrabarty, Dipesh. "The Climate of History: Four Theses." *Critical Inquiry* 35 (Winter 2009): 197–222.

Chase, Cynthia. *Decomposing Figures: Rhetorical Readings in the Romantic Tradition.* Baltimore: Johns Hopkins University Press, 1986.

Cicero. *On Academic Scepticism.* Translated by Charles Brittain. Indianapolis, IN: Hackett, 2006.

Clark, David Lee, ed. *Shelley's Prose.* By Percy Shelley. New York: New Amsterdam, 1988.

Cohen, Alix. *Kant and the Human Sciences: Biology, Anthropology, and History.* New York: Palgrave Macmillan, 2009.

Cole, Andrew. *The Birth of Theory*. Chicago: University of Chicago Press, 2014.

Coleridge, S. T. *Biographia Literaria*. Edited by Walter Jackson Bate and James Engell. Vol. 7 of *Collected Works*, edited by Kathleen Coburn. Princeton, NJ: Princeton University Press, 1983.

Comay, Rebecca. "Hegel's Last Words: Mourning and Melancholia at the End of the *Phenomenology*." In *The Ends of History: Questioning the Stakes of Historical Reason*, edited by Amy Swiffen and Joshua Nichols, 141–60. London: Routledge, 2013.

———. *Mourning Sickness: Hegel and the French Revolution*. Stanford, CA: Stanford University Press, 2011.

Cooper, Andrew. "Living Natural Products in Kant's Physical Geography." *Studies in History and Philosophy of Biological and Biomedical Sciences* 78 (2019): 1–10.

Cronon, William. "The Trouble with Wilderness; or, Getting Back to the Wrong Nature." In *Uncommon Ground: Rethinking the Human Place in Nature*, edited by William Cronon, 69–90. New York: Norton, 1995.

Culler, Jonathan. "The Mirror Stage." In *High Romantic Argument: Essays for M. H. Abrams*, edited by Lawrence Lipking, 149–63. Ithaca, NY: Cornell University Press, 1981.

Cunningham, David. "Capitalist Epics: Abstraction, Totality, and the Theory of the Novel." *Radical Philosophy* 163 (September/October 2010): 11–23.

Curran, Stuart. *Shelley's Annus Mirabilis: The Maturing of an Epic Vision*. San Marino, CA: Huntington Library, 1975.

Dauvé, Gilles, and Karl Nesic. "Love of Labour? Love of Labour Lost . . ." *Endnotes* 1 (October 2008): 104–52.

Deleuze, Gilles. *Kant's Critical Philosophy: The Doctrine of the Faculties*. Translated by Hugh Tomlinson and Barbara Habberjam. Minneapolis: University of Minnesota Press, 1985.

de Man, Paul. *Aesthetic Ideology*. Edited by Andrzej Warminski. Minneapolis: University of Minnesota Press, 1996.

———. "Anthropomorphism and Trope in the Lyric." In *Rhetoric of Romanticism*, 239–62.

———. *Blindness and Insight: Essays in the Rhetoric of Contemporary Criticism*. Minneapolis: University of Minnesota Press, 1983.

———. "Criticism and Crisis." In *Blindness and Insight*, 3–19.

———. "Foreword to Revised, Second Edition." In *Blindness and Insight*, xi–xii.

———. "Intentional Structure of the Romantic Image." In *Rhetoric of Romanticism*, 1–17.

———. *The Post-romantic Predicament*. Edited by Martin McQuillan. Edinburgh: Edinburgh University Press, 2012.

———. "Preface." In *Rhetoric of Romanticism*, vii–ix.

———. "Process and Poetry." In *Critical Writings, 1953–1978*, edited by Lindsay Waters, 64–75. Minneapolis: University of Minnesota Press, 1989.

———. *The Rhetoric of Romanticism*. New York: Columbia University Press, 1984.

———. "The Rhetoric of Temporality." In *Blindness and Insight*, 187–228.

———. "Shelley Disfigured." In *Rhetoric of Romanticism*, 93–123.

———. "Time and History in Wordsworth." *Diacritics* 17.4 (1987): 4–17.

De Quincey, Thomas. *Recollections of the Lakes and the Lake Poets.* Edited by David Wright. Harmondsworth: Penguin, 1970.

Ellermann, Greg. "Late Coleridge and the Life of Idealism." *Studies in Romanticism* 54.1 (2015): 33–55.

Empson, William. *Seven Types of Ambiguity.* London: Chatto and Windus, 1949.

Endnotes. "Communisation and Value-Form Theory." *Endnotes* 2 (April 2010): 68–105.

———. "The Moving Contradiction: The Systematic Dialectic of Capital as a Dialectic of Class Struggle." *Endnotes* 2 (April 2010): 106–28.

Engels, Friedrich. *Engels: 1838–1842.* Vol. 2 of *Karl Marx and Friedrich Engels: Collected Works.* New York: International Publishers, 1975.

Esterhammer, Angela. "1824: Improvisation, Speculation, and Identity-Construction." BRANCH: Britain, Representation, and Nineteenth-Century History, extension of the site Romanticism and Victorianism on the Net, edited by Dino Franco Felluga. July 2012. http://www.branchcollective.org/?ps_articles=angela-esterhammer -1824-improvisation-speculation-and-identity-construction.

Favret, Mary. *Romantic Correspondence: Women, Politics, and the Fiction of Letters.* Cambridge: Cambridge University Press, 1993.

Federici, Silvia. *Caliban and the Witch: Women, the Body, and Primitive Accumulation.* Brooklyn, NY: Autonomedia, 2004.

Fenves, Peter. *Late Kant: Towards Another Law of the Earth.* New York: Routledge, 2003.

Ferguson, Frances. *Solitude and the Sublime: The Romantic Aesthetics of Individuation.* New York: Routledge, 1992.

———. *Wordsworth: Language as Counter-spirit.* New Haven, CT: Yale University Press, 1977.

Fichte, J. G. *Science of Knowledge (Wissenschaftslehre), with First and Second Introductions.* Translated by Peter Heath and John Lachs. New York: Appleton-Century-Crofts, 1970.

Ford, Thomas H. *Wordsworth and the Poetics of Air.* Cambridge: Cambridge University Press, 2018.

Förster, Eckart. *Kant's Final Synthesis: An Essay on the "Opus postumum."* Cambridge, MA: Harvard University Press, 2000.

———. *The Twenty-Five Years of Philosophy: A Systematic Reconstruction.* Translated by Brady Bowman. Cambridge, MA: Harvard University Press, 2017.

Forster, Michael N. *Hegel's Idea of a Phenomenology of Spirit.* Chicago: University of Chicago Press, 1998.

François, Anne-Lise. "'A Little While' More: Further Thoughts on Hartman's Nature as Paraclete." *Essays in Romanticism* 22.2 (2015): 133–49.

———. *Open Secrets: The Literature of Uncounted Experience.* Stanford, CA: Stanford University Press, 2007.

Frank, Manfred. *The Philosophical Foundations of Early German Romanticism*. Translated by Elizabeth Millán. Albany: State University of New York Press, 2003.

Friedman, Michael. *Kant and the Exact Sciences*. Cambridge, MA: Harvard University Press, 1992.

———. *Kant's Construction of Nature: A Reading of the "Metaphysical Foundations of Natural Science."* Cambridge: Cambridge University Press, 2013.

Fry, Paul H. "Green to the Very Door? The Natural Wordsworth." *Studies in Romanticism* 35.4 (1996): 535–51.

Gabriel, Markus. *Transcendental Ontology: Essays in German Idealism*. London: Bloomsbury, 2013.

Galperin, William. "'Describing What Never Happened': Jane Austen and the History of Missed Opportunities." *ELH* 73.2 (2006): 355–82.

———. *The History of Missed Opportunities: British Romanticism and the Emergence of the Everyday*. Stanford, CA: Stanford University Press, 2017.

———. *The Return of the Visible in British Romanticism*. Baltimore: Johns Hopkins University Press, 1993.

Garrard, Greg. *Ecocriticism*. New York: Routledge, 2004.

Garrett, Aaron. "Anthropology: The 'Original' of Human Nature." In *The Cambridge Companion to the Scottish Enlightenment*, edited by Alexander Broadie, 79–93. Cambridge: Cambridge University Press, 2003.

Gasché, Rodolphe. *The Idea of Form: Rethinking Kant's Aesthetics*. Stanford, CA: Stanford University Press, 2002.

———. *The Tain of the Mirror: Derrida and the Philosophy of Reflection*. Cambridge, MA: Harvard University Press, 1986.

Geulen, Eva. "Adorno's *Aesthetic Theory*." In *A Companion to Adorno*, edited by Peter E. Gordon, Espen Hammer, and Max Pensky, 397–411. Hoboken, NJ: Wiley, 2020.

Gidal, Eric. "'O Happy Earth! Reality of Heaven!': Melancholy and Utopia in Romantic Climatology." *Journal for Early Modern Cultural Studies* 8.2 (2008): 74–101.

Gill, Stephen, ed. *William Wordsworth*. By William Wordsworth. Oxford: Oxford University Press, 1989.

Goodman, Kevis. "Conjectures on Beachy Head: Charlotte Smith's Geological Poetics and the Grounds of the Present." *ELH* 81 (2014): 983–1006.

Gordon, Peter E. *Adorno and Existence*. Cambridge, MA: Harvard University Press, 2016.

Grabo, Carl. *A Newton among Poets: Shelley's Use of Science in "Prometheus Unbound."* Chapel Hill: University of North Carolina Press, 1930.

Grant, Iain Hamilton. *Philosophies of Nature after Schelling*. London: Bloomsbury, 2006.

Gray, Thomas. "Elegy Written in a Country Churchyard." Thomas Gray Archive, edited by Alexander Huber, 2018. https://www.thomasgray.org/cgi-bin/display.cgi?text=elcc.

Gurton-Wachter, Lily. *Watchwords: Romanticism and the Poetics of Attention*. Stanford, CA: Stanford University Press, 2016.

Guyer, Sara. *Reading with John Clare: Biopolitics, Sovereignty, Romanticism.* New York: Fordham University Press, 2015.

———. *Romanticism after Auschwitz.* Stanford, CA: Stanford University Press, 2007.

Halmi, Nicholas. *The Genealogy of the Romantic Symbol.* Oxford: Oxford University Press, 2007.

Hamilton, Paul. *Metaromanticism: Aesthetics, Literature, Theory.* Chicago: University of Chicago Press, 2003.

Hammer, Espen. *Adorno's Modernism: Art, Experience, and Catastrophe.* Cambridge: Cambridge University Press, 2015.

Harney, Stefano, and Fred Moten. *The Undercommons: Fugitive Planning and Black Study.* Wivenhoe, UK: Minor Compositions, 2013.

Harris, H. S. *Hegel's Development: Night Thoughts (Jena 1801–6).* Oxford: Clarendon Press, 1983.

———. "The Social Ideal of Hegel's Economic Theory." In *Hegel's Philosophy of Action*, edited by Laurence Stepelevich and David Lamb, 49–74. Ann Arbor: University of Michigan Press, 1983.

Hartman, Geoffrey. "Romanticism and Anti-self-consciousness." In *Beyond Formalism: Literary Essays, 1958–1970*, 298–310. New Haven, CT: Yale University Press, 1970.

———. *A Scholar's Tale: Intellectual Journey of a Displaced Child of Europe.* New York: Fordham University Press, 2007.

———. *The Unmediated Vision: An Interpretation of Wordsworth, Hopkins, Rilke, and Valéry.* New York: Harcourt, Brace and World, 1966.

———. *The Unremarkable Wordsworth.* Minneapolis: University of Minnesota Press, 1987.

———. *Wordsworth's Poetry, 1787–1814.* Cambridge, MA: Harvard University Press, 1964.

Hegel, G. W. F. *Aesthetics: Lectures on Fine Art.* Translated by T. M. Knox. Oxford: Oxford University Press, 1975.

———. *The Difference between Fichte's and Schelling's System of Philosophy.* Translated by H. S. Harris and Walter Cerf. Albany: State University of New York Press, 1977.

———. *Early Theological Writings.* Translated by T. M. Knox and Richard Kroner. Philadelphia: University of Pennsylvania Press, 1971.

———. *Faith and Knowledge.* Translated by Walter Cerf and H. S. Harris. Albany: State University of New York Press, 1977.

———. "Introduction on the Essence of Philosophical Criticism Generally, and Its Relationship to the Present State of Philosophy in Particular." *Kritisches Journal der Philosophie* 1.1 (1802): iii–xxiv. Translated by H. S. Harris. Marxists Internet Archive. https://www.marxists.org /reference/archive/hegel/works/cj/introduction .htm.

———. *La phénoménologie de l'esprit.* Translated by Jean Hyppolite. Paris: Aubier, 1939–41.

———. *Phenomenology of Spirit*. Translated by A. V. Miller. Oxford: Oxford University Press, 1977.

———. "Philosophical Dissertation on the Orbits of the Planets." Translated by Pierre Adler. *Graduate Faculty Philosophy Journal* 12.1 and 2 (1987): 269–309.

———. *Philosophy of Right*. Translated by T. M. Knox. Oxford: Oxford University Press, 1967.

———. *System of Ethical Life and First Philosophy of Spirit*. Translated by H. S. Harris and T. M. Knox. Albany: State University of New York Press, 1979.

Heidegger, Martin. *Kant and the Problem of Metaphysics*. Translated by James S. Churchill. Bloomington: Indiana University Press, 1962.

Henderson, W. O. *Studies in the Economic Policy of Frederick the Great*. London: Routledge, 1963.

Herder, J. G. *Treatise on the Origin of Language*. In *Philosophical Writings*, translated by Michael N. Forster, 65–164. Cambridge: Cambridge University Press, 2002.

Higgins, David. *British Romanticism, Climate Change, and the Anthropocene: Writing Tambora*. Basingstoke: Palgrave Macmillan, 2017.

Hogg, Thomas Jefferson. *Shelley at Oxford*. London: Methuen, 1904.

Hölderlin, Friedrich. "Being Judgement Possibility." In *Classic and Romantic German Aesthetics*, edited by J. M. Bernstein, 191–92. Cambridge: Cambridge University Press, 2003.

———. "In my boyhood days." In *Poems and Fragments*, translated by Michael Hamburger, 122–25. London: Anvil, 2004.

Horkheimer, Max, and Theodor Adorno. *Dialectic of Enlightenment: Philosophical Fragments*. Translated by Edmund Jephcott. Stanford, CA: Stanford University Press, 2002.

Husserl, Edmund. "Philosophy as Rigorous Science." In *Phenomenology and the Crisis of Philosophy*, translated by Quentin Lauer, 71–147. New York: Harper and Row, 1965.

Hyppolite, Jean. *Genesis and Structure of Hegel's "Phenomenology of Spirit."* Translated by Samuel Cherniak and John Heckman. Evanston, IL: Northwestern University Press, 1979.

———. *Studies on Marx and Hegel*. Translated by John O'Neill. New York: Basic Books, 1969.

Invisible Committee. *To Our Friends*. Translated by Robert Hurley. South Pasadena, CA: Semiotext(e), 2015.

Jager, Colin. "Translating Love in *Prometheus Unbound*." In *Imagining Religious Toleration: A Literary History of an Idea, 1600–1830*, edited by Alison Conway and David Alvarez, 234–58. Toronto: University of Toronto Press, 2019.

———. *Unquiet Things: Secularism in the Romantic Age*. Philadelphia: University of Pennsylvania Press, 2014.

Jameson, Fredric. *The Hegel Variations: On the "Phenomenology of Spirit."* New York: Verso, 2010.

Jarvis, Simon. *Wordsworth's Philosophic Song*. Cambridge: Cambridge University Press, 2007.

Johnston, Adrian. "The Voiding of Weak Nature: The Transcendental Materialist Kernels of Hegel's *Naturphilosophie*." *Graduate Faculty Philosophy Journal* 33.1 (2012): 103–57.

Juengel, Scott J. "Mary Wollstonecraft's Perpetual Disaster." Romantic Circles Praxis, January 2012. https://romantic-circles.org/praxis/disaster/HTML/praxis.2012 .juengel.html.

Jump, Harriet Devine. "'A Kind of Witchcraft': Mary Wollstonecraft and the Poetic Imagination." *Women's Writing* 4.2 (1997): 235–45.

———. *Mary Wollstonecraft: Writer*. London: Harvester, 1994.

Kant, Immanuel. *Anthropology from a Pragmatic Point of View*. Translated by Robert B. Louden. Cambridge: Cambridge University Press, 2006.

———. *Critique of Judgment*. Translated by Werner S. Pluhar. Indianapolis, IN: Hackett, 1987.

———. *Critique of Pure Reason*. Translated by Werner S. Pluhar. Indianapolis, IN: Hackett, 1996.

———. *Inaugural Dissertation*. Translated by William J. Eckoff. New York: Columbia College, 1894.

———. "New Notes to Explain the Theory of the Winds." Translated by Olaf Reinhardt. In Watkins, *Natural Science*, 374–85.

———. *Opus postumum*. Translated by Eckart Förster. Cambridge: Cambridge University Press, 1995.

———. *Philosophical Correspondence, 1759–99*. Translated by Arnulf Zweig. Chicago: University of Chicago Press, 1967.

———. *Physical Geography*. Translated by Olaf Reinhardt. In Watkins, *Natural Science*, 434–678.

———. *Physische Geographie*. Königsberg: Göbbels und Unzer, 1802.

———. *Prolegomena to Any Future Metaphysics*. Translated by James W. Ellington. Indianapolis, IN: Hackett, 1977.

———. "The Question, Whether the Earth Is Ageing, Considered from a Physical Point of View." Translated by Olaf Reinhardt. In Watkins, *Natural Science*, 165–81.

Kaufman, Robert. "Intervention & Commitment Forever! Shelley in 1819, Shelley in Brecht, Shelley in Adorno, Shelley in Benjamin." Romantic Circles Praxis, May 2001. https://romantic-circles.org/praxis/interventionist/kaufman/kaufman.html.

———. "Legislators of the Post-everything World: Shelley's *Defence* of Adorno." *ELH* 63 (1996): 707–33.

———. "Red Kant, or The Persistence of the Third *Critique* in Adorno and Jameson." *Critical Inquiry* 26 (Summer 2000): 682–724.

Keach, William. *Arbitrary Power: Romanticism, Language, Politics*. Princeton, NJ: Princeton University Press, 2004.

Keenleyside, Heather. "Personification for the People: On James Thomson's *The Seasons*." *ELH* 76.2 (2009): 447–72.

Khalip, Jacques. *Anonymous Life: Romanticism and Dispossession*. Stanford, CA: Stanford University Press, 2008.

Kojève, Alexandre. *Introduction to the Reading of Hegel: Lectures on the "Phenomenology of Spirit."* Translated by James H. Nichols Jr. Ithaca, NY: Cornell University Press, 1980.

Lacoue-Labarthe, Philippe, and Jean-Luc Nancy. *The Literary Absolute: The Theory of Literature in German Romanticism.* Translated by Philip Barnard and Cheryl Lester. Albany: State University of New York Press, 1988.

Latour, Bruno. *We Have Never Been Modern.* Translated by Catherine Porter. Cambridge, MA: Harvard University Press, 1993.

Leavis, F. R. *Revaluation: Tradition and Development in English Poetry.* New York: George W. Stewart, 1947.

Lehman, Robert S. "Formalism, Mere Form, and Judgment." *New Literary History* 48 (2017): 245–63.

Leibniz, Gottfried Wilhelm. *Monadology.* In *Discourse on Metaphysics and the Monadology*, translated by George R. Montgomery. Amherst, NY: Prometheus Books, 1992.

Lenin, V. I. *A Characterization of Economic Romanticism: Sismondi and Our Native Sismondists.* Moscow: Foreign Languages Publishing House, 1951.

Levinson, Marjorie. "A Motion and a Spirit: Romancing Spinoza." *Studies in Romanticism* 46.4 (2007): 367–408.

———. *Wordsworth's Great Period Poems.* Cambridge: Cambridge University Press, 1986.

Liu, Alan. *Wordsworth: The Sense of History.* Stanford, CA: Stanford University Press, 1989.

Locke, John. *An Essay Concerning Human Understanding.* Edited by Peter H. Nidditch. Oxford: Clarendon Press, 1975.

Lord, John. *Capital and Steam Power, 1750–1800.* London: P. S. King and Son, 1923.

Louden, Robert B. "The Last Frontier: The Importance of Kant's *Geography.*" *Society and Space* 32 (2014): 450–65.

Lowth, Robert. *Lectures on the Sacred Poetry of the Hebrews.* Translated by George Gregory. Boston: Joseph T. Buckingham, 1815.

Löwy, Michael, and Robert Sayre. *Romanticism against the Tide of Modernity.* Translated by Catherine Porter. Durham, NC: Duke University Press, 2001.

Lukács, Georg. *History and Class Consciousness: Studies in Marxist Dialectics.* Translated by Rodney Livingstone. Cambridge, MA: MIT Press, 1971.

———. *The Young Hegel: Studies in the Relations between Dialectics and Economics.* Translated by Rodney Livingstone. Cambridge, MA: MIT Press, 1976.

Lynch, Deidre Shauna. "'Young Ladies Are Delicate Plants': Jane Austen and Greenhouse Romanticism." *ELH* 77 (2010): 689–729.

Macksey, Richard, and Eugenio Donato, eds. *The Structuralist Controversy.* Baltimore: Johns Hopkins University Press, 1972.

Malabou, Catherine. *Before Tomorrow: Epigenesis and Rationality.* Translated by Carolyn Shread. Cambridge: Polity Press, 2016.

———. *What Should We Do with Our Brain?* Translated by Sebastian Rand. New York: Fordham University Press, 2008.

Malm, Andreas. *Fossil Capital: The Rise of Steam Power and the Roots of Global Warming*. New York: Verso, 2016.

———. "In Defence of Metabolic Rift Theory." Verso Blog, March 2018. https://www.versobooks.com/blogs/3691-in-defence-of-metabolic-rift-theory.

———. "The Origins of Fossil Capitalism: From Water to Steam in the British Cotton Industry." *Historical Materialism* 21.1 (2013): 15–68.

Marcuse, Herbert. *One-Dimensional Man: Studies in the Ideology of Advanced Industrial Society*. Boston: Beacon, 1966.

Marriott, David S. "The Rites of Difficulty." *Fragmente* 7 (1997): 118–37.

Marx, Eleanor, and Edward Aveling. "Shelley and Socialism." *To-Day*, April 1888, 103–16. Marxists Internet Archive. https://www.marxists.org/archive/eleanor-marx/1888/04/shelley-socialism.htm.

Marx, Karl. *Capital*. Vol. 1. Translated by Ben Fowkes. New York: Penguin, 1992.

———. *Capital*. Vol. 2. Translated by David Fernbach. New York: Penguin, 1992.

———. *Critique of the Gotha Programme*. In *Political Writings*, vol. 3, translated by David Fernbach, 339–59. New York: Vintage, 1974.

———. *Grundrisse*. Translated by Martin Nicolaus. New York: Penguin, 1993.

———. *Results of the Immediate Process of Production*. In *Capital*, vol. 1, translated by Rodney Livingstone, 948–1084. New York: Penguin, 1992.

Marx, Karl, and Friedrich Engels. *The German Ideology*. In *Writings of the Young Marx on Philosophy and Society*, edited by Loyd D. Easton and Kurt H. Guddat, 403–73. Garden City, NY: Doubleday Anchor, 1967.

Mascat, Jamila M. H. "Hegel and the Advent of Modernity: A Social Ontology of Abstraction." *Radical Philosophy* 2.1 (February 2018): 29–46.

Matthews, G. M. "A Volcano's Voice in Shelley." In Reiman and Fraistat, *Shelley's Poetry and Prose*, 550–68.

Mbembe, Achille. *Critique of Black Reason*. Translated by Laurent Dubois. Durham, NC: Duke University Press, 2017.

McGann, Jerome. *The Romantic Ideology: A Critical Investigation*. Chicago: University of Chicago Press, 1983.

Meaney, Marie Cabaud. *Simone Weil's Apologetic Use of Literature: Her Christological Interpretation of Ancient Greek Texts*. Oxford: Oxford University Press, 2008.

Menely, Tobias. "Anthropocene Air." *minnesota review* 93 (2014): 93–101.

Merchant, Carolyn. *The Death of Nature: Women, Ecology, and the Scientific Revolution*. New York: Harper Collins, 1990.

Michael, Timothy. *British Romanticism and the Critique of Political Reason*. Baltimore: Johns Hopkins University Press, 2016.

Miller, Elizabeth Carolyn. *Slow Print: Literary Radicalism and Late Victorian Print Culture*. Stanford, CA: Stanford University Press, 2013.

Milton, John. *Paradise Lost*. Edited by David Scott Kastan. Indianapolis, IN: Hackett, 2005.

Milutis, Joe. *Ether: The Nothing That Connects Everything*. Minneapolis: University of Minnesota Press, 2006.

Moore, Jason. *Capitalism in the Web of Life: Ecology and the Accumulation of Capital.* New York: Verso, 2015.

Morton, Timothy. "Coexistence and Coexistents: Ecology without a World." In *Ecocritical Theory: New European Approaches,* edited by Axel Goodbody and Kate Rigby, 168–80. Charlottesville: University of Virginia Press, 2011.

———. "Conversation with Hans Ulrich Obrist." *Dis,* October 2014. http://www .dismagazine.com/disillusioned/discussion-disillusioned/68280/hans-ulrich -obrist-timothy-morton/.

———. *Ecology without Nature: Rethinking Environmental Aesthetics.* Cambridge, MA: Harvard University Press, 2007.

Nassar, Dalia. "Analogy, Natural History and the Philosophy of Nature: Kant, Herder and the Problem of Empirical Science." *Journal of the Philosophy of History* 9 (2015): 240–57.

———. "Romantic Empiricism after the 'End of Nature.'" In *The Relevance of Romanticism: Essays on German Romantic Philosophy,* edited by Dalia Nassar, 296–313. Oxford: Oxford University Press, 2014.

Nersessian, Anahid. *The Calamity Form: On Poetry and Social Life.* Chicago: University of Chicago Press, 2020.

———. "Romantic Difficulty." *New Literary History* 49 (2018): 451–66.

Newton, Isaac. "Hypothesis Explaining the Properties of Light." The Newton Project, edited by Rob Iliffe and Scott Mandelbrote, University of Oxford, 2003. http:// www.newtonproject.ox.ac.uk/view/texts/normalized/NATP00002.

———. *Philosophical Writings.* Rev. ed. Edited by Andrew Janiak. Cambridge: Cambridge University Press, 2014.

Ng, Karen. *Hegel's Concept of Life: Self-Consciousness, Freedom, Logic.* Oxford: Oxford University Press, 2020.

Ngai, Sianne. "Visceral Abstractions." *GLQ* 21.1 (2015): 33–63.

Nyström, Per. *Mary Wollstonecraft's Scandinavian Journey.* Translated by George Otter. Göteborg: Küngliga Vetenskaps och Vitterhets Samhället, 1980.

Packham, Catherine. "Mary Wollstonecraft's Cottage Economics: Property, Political Economy, and the European Future." *ELH* 84 (2017): 453–74.

Passannante, Gerard. *Catastrophizing: Materialism and the Making of Disaster.* Chicago: University of Chicago Press, 2019.

Pfau, Thomas. *Wordsworth's Profession: Form, Class, and the Logic of Early Romantic Cultural Production.* Stanford, CA: Stanford University Press, 1997.

Pinkard, Terry. *Hegel: A Biography.* Cambridge: Cambridge University Press, 2000.

Pop, Andrei. *Antiquity, Theatre, and the Painting of Henry Fuseli.* Oxford: Oxford University Press, 2015.

Postone, Moishe. *Time, Labor, and Social Domination: A Reinterpretation of Marx's Critical Theory.* Cambridge: Cambridge University Press, 1993.

Potkay, Adam. *Wordsworth's Ethics.* Baltimore: Johns Hopkins University Press, 2012.

Prynne, J. H. Letter. *Times Literary Supplement,* May 28, 1971, 620.

———. "Mental Ears and Poetic Work." *Chicago Review* 55.1 (2010): 126–57.

Pyle, Forest. "'Frail Spells': Shelley and the Ironies of Exile." In Reiman and Fraistat, *Shelley's Poetry and Prose*, 663–69.

Rajan, Tilottama. "Displacing Post-structuralism: Romantic Studies after Paul de Man." *Studies in Romanticism* 24.4 (1985): 451–74.

———. "Spirit's Psychoanalysis: Natural History, the History of Nature, and Romantic Historiography." *European Romantic Review* 14.2 (2003): 187–96.

Redfield, Marc. *Theory at Yale: The Strange Case of Deconstruction in America*. New York: Fordham University Press, 2015.

Regier, Alexander. *Fracture and Fragmentation in British Romanticism*. Cambridge: Cambridge University Press, 2010.

Reiman, Donald, and Neil Fraistat, eds. *Shelley's Poetry and Prose*. By Percy Shelley. New York: Norton, 2002.

Reisner, Thomas A. "Some Scientific Models for Shelley's Multitudinous Orb." *Keats-Shelley Journal* 23 (1974): 52–59.

Richards, Robert J. *The Meaning of Evolution: The Morphological Construction and Ideological Reconstruction of Darwin's Theory*. Chicago: University of Chicago Press, 1992.

Rigby, Kate. *Reclaiming Romanticism: Towards an Ecopoetics of Decolonization*. London: Bloomsbury, 2020.

———. *Topographies of the Sacred: The Poetics of Place in European Romanticism*. Charlottesville: University of Virginia Press, 2004.

Roberts, Hugh. *Shelley and the Chaos of History: A New Politics of Poetry*. University Park: Penn State University Press, 1997.

Robinson, Josh. *Adorno's Poetics of Form*. Albany: State University of New York Press, 2018.

Ronda, Margaret. "Anthropogenic Poetics." *minnesota review* 83 (2014): 102–11.

———. "Mourning and Melancholia in the Anthropocene." *Post45*, June 2013. https://post45.org/2013/06/mourning-and-melancholia-in-the-anthropocene/.

———. *Remainders: American Poetry at Nature's End*. Stanford, CA: Stanford University Press, 2018.

Rosefeldt, Tobias. "Kant on Imagination and the Intuition of Time." In *The Imagination in German Idealism and Romanticism*, edited by Gerad Gentry and Konstantin Pollok, 48–65. Cambridge: Cambridge University Press, 2019.

Rousseau, Jean-Jacques. *A Discourse on Inequality*. Translated by Maurice Cranston. New York: Penguin, 1984.

———. *Essay on the Origin of Languages*. In *Essay on the Origin of Languages and Writing Related to Music*, translated by John T. Scott, 289–332. Hanover, NH: Dartmouth College Press, 2000.

———. *Reveries of the Solitary Walker*. Translated by Peter France. New York: Penguin, 1979.

Rowney, Matthew. "Reframing Romantic Nature." PhD diss., City University of New York, 2015.

Roworth, Wendy Wassyng. "Anatomy Is Destiny: Regarding the Body in the Art of Angelica Kauffman." In *Femininity and Masculinity in Eighteenth-Century Art and Culture*, edited by Gillian Perry and Michael Rossington, 41–62. Manchester: Manchester University Press, 1994.

Sachs, Jonathan. *The Poetics of Decline in British Romanticism*. Cambridge: Cambridge University Press, 2018.

Savarese, John. *Romanticism's Other Minds: Poetry, Cognition, and the Science of Sociability*. Columbus: Ohio State University Press, 2020.

Schelling, F. W. J. "Introduction to the Outline of a System of the Philosophy of Nature." In *First Outline of a System of the Philosophy of Nature*, translated by Keith R. Peterson, 193–232. Albany: State University of New York Press, 2004.

Schmidt, Alfred. *The Concept of Nature in Marx*. Translated by Ben Fowkes. New York: Verso, 2014.

Schmitt, Carl. *Political Theology: Four Chapters on the Concept of Sovereignty*. Translated by George Schwab. Chicago: University of Chicago Press, 2005.

Schofield, Robert. *Mechanism and Materialism: British Natural Philosophy in an Age of Reason*. Princeton, NJ: Princeton University Press, 1970.

Schönfeld, Martin. *The Philosophy of the Young Kant: The Precritical Project*. Oxford: Oxford University Press, 2000.

Shabel, Lisa. "The Transcendental Aesthetic." In *The Cambridge Companion to Kant's "Critique of Pure Reason,"* edited by Paul Guyer, 93–117. Cambridge: Cambridge University Press, 2010.

Shell, Susan Meld. *Kant and the Limits of Autonomy*. Cambridge, MA: Harvard University Press, 2009.

Shelley, Percy. "Additional Notes on *Queen Mab*." In Clark, *Shelley's Prose*, 338–41.

———. *Adonais*. In Reiman and Fraistat, *Shelley's Poetry and Prose*, 407–27.

———. *A Declaration of Rights*. In Clark, *Shelley's Prose*, 70–72.

———. *A Defence of Poetry*. In Reiman and Fraistat, *Shelley's Poetry and Prose*, 509–35.

———. *The Letters of Percy Bysshe Shelley*. Edited by Roger Ingpen. London: Sir Isaac Pitman and Sons, 1912.

———. "Ode to the West Wind." In Reiman and Fraistat, *Shelley's Poetry and Prose*, 297–301.

———. "On Life." In Reiman and Fraistat, *Shelley's Poetry and Prose*, 505–9.

———. "On Love." In Reiman and Fraistat, *Shelley's Poetry and Prose*, 503–4.

———. *Prometheus Unbound*. In Reiman and Fraistat, *Shelley's Poetry and Prose*, 202–86.

———. *Queen Mab*. In Reiman and Fraistat, *Shelley's Poetry and Prose*, 15–71.

———. *A Refutation of Deism*. In Clark, *Shelley's Prose*, 118–37.

Siegel, Jonah. *Desire and Excess: The Nineteenth-Century Culture of Art*. Princeton, NJ: Princeton University Press, 2000.

Siewert, Charles. "Consciousness and Intentionality." In *The Stanford Encyclopedia of Philosophy*, edited by Edward N. Zalta. Stanford University, Spring 2017. https://plato.stanford.edu.

Simpson, David. *Romanticism, Nationalism, and the Revolt against Theory*. Chicago: University of Chicago Press, 1993.

———. *Wordsworth, Commodification, and Social Concern: The Poetics of Modernity*. Cambridge: Cambridge University Press, 2009.

Sloan, Philip R. "Kant on the History of Nature: The Ambiguous Heritage of the Critical Philosophy for Natural History." *Studies in History and Philosophy of Biological and Biomedical Sciences* 37 (2006): 627–48.

Smith, Adam. *The Wealth of Nations*. New York: Modern Library, 2000.

Sohn-Rethel, Alfred. *Intellectual and Manual Labour: A Critique of Epistemology*. Translated by Martin Sohn-Rethel. Atlantic Highlands, NJ: Humanities Press, 1978.

———. "Intellectual and Manual Labour: An Attempt at a Materialistic Theory." *Radical Philosophy* 6 (Winter 1973): 30–37.

Speitz, Michele. "Affect and Air: The Speculative Spirit of the Age." In *Romanticism and Speculative Realism*, edited by Chris Washington and Anne McCarthy, 37–55. London: Bloomsbury, 2019.

———. "Conceptualization of Wilderness." In *Encyclopedia of the World's Biomes*, edited by Michael I. Goldstein and Dominick A. DellaSala. Amsterdam: Elsevier, 2020.

Spinoza, Baruch. *Ethics, Treatise on the Emendation of the Intellect, and Selected Letters*. Indianapolis, IN: Hackett, 1992.

Steigerwald, Joan. "Natural Purposes and the Reflecting Power of Judgment: The Problem of the Organism in Kant's Critical Philosophy." *European Romantic Review* 21.3 (2010): 291–308.

Suther, Jensen. "Hegel's Logic of Freedom: Towards a 'Logical Constitutivism.'" *Review of Metaphysics* 73.4 (2020): 771–814.

Symonds, John Addington. *Shelley*. London: Macmillan, 1922.

Terada, Rei. "Living a Ruined Life: De Quincey's Damage." In *Romanticism and the Emotions*, edited by Joel Faflak and Richard C. Sha, 215–40. Cambridge: Cambridge University Press, 2014.

———. *Looking Away: Phenomenality and Dissatisfaction, Kant to Adorno*. Cambridge, MA: Harvard University Press, 2009.

———. "The Racial Grammar of Kantian Time." *European Romantic Review* 28.3 (2017): 267–78.

Thomas, Helen. *Romanticism and Slave Narratives: Transatlantic Testimonies*. Cambridge: Cambridge University Press, 2000.

Thompson, E. P. *The Making of the English Working Class*. New York: Vintage, 1966.

———. "Time, Work-Discipline, and Industrial Capitalism." *Past and Present* 38 (December 1967): 56–97.

Toscano, Alberto. "The Open Secret of Real Abstraction." *Rethinking Marxism* 20.2 (April 2008): 273–87.

Ulmer, William A. *Shelleyan Eros: The Rhetoric of Romantic Love*. Princeton, NJ: Princeton University Press, 1990.

Verene, Donald Phillip. "Hegel's Nature." In *Hegel and the Philosophy of Nature*, edited by Stephen Houlgate, 209–26. Albany: State University of New York Press, 1998.

Vermeulen, Pieter. *Geoffrey Hartman: Romanticism after the Holocaust*. London: Continuum, 2010.

Vishmidt, Marina. *Speculation as a Mode of Production: Forms of Value Subjectivity in Art and Capital*. Leiden: Brill, 2018.

Wahl, Jean. *Le malheur de la conscience dans la philosophie de Hegel*. Paris: Rieder, 1929.

Wang, Orrin N. C. *Romantic Sobriety: Sensation, Revolution, Commodification, History*. Baltimore: Johns Hopkins University Press, 2011.

Wasser, Audrey. *The Work of Difference: Modernism, Romanticism, and the Production of Literary Form*. New York: Fordham University Press, 2016.

Wasserman, Earl. *Shelley: A Critical Reading*. Baltimore: Johns Hopkins University Press, 1971.

Waters, Lindsay. "Paul de Man: Life and Works." In de Man, *Critical Writings, 1953–1978*, edited by Lindsay Waters, ix–lxxiv. Minneapolis: University of Minnesota Press, 1989.

Watkins, Eric, ed. *Natural Science*. By Immanuel Kant. Cambridge: Cambridge University Press, 2012.

Weber, Max. *General Economic History*. Translated by Frank H. Knight. New York: Collier Books, 1961.

Weil, Simone. *Gravity and Grace*. Translated by Emma Crawford and Mario von der Ruhr. New York: Routledge, 2002.

———. *Intimations of Christianity among the Ancient Greeks*. New York: Ark/Routledge, 1987.

———. *Venice Saved*. Translated by Silvia Panizza and Philip Wilson. London: Bloomsbury, 2019.

White, Deborah Elise. *Romantic Returns: Superstition, Imagination, History*. Stanford, CA: Stanford University Press, 2000.

Williams, Michael. *Deforesting the Earth: From Prehistory to Global Crisis*. Chicago: University of Chicago Press, 2003.

Williams, Raymond. *Culture and Society, 1780–1950*. New York: Harper and Row, 1966.

Wilner, Joshua. "Pitching Apocalypse." *Essays in Romanticism* 22.2 (2015): 215–33.

Wilson, Ross. *Shelley and the Apprehension of Life*. Cambridge: Cambridge University Press, 2013.

Wimsatt, W. K. "The Structure of Romantic Nature Imagery." In *The Verbal Icon: Studies in the Meaning of Poetry*, 103–16. Lexington: University of Kentucky Press, 1954.

Wollstonecraft, Mary. *Collected Letters*. Edited by Ralph M. Wardle. Ithaca, NY: Cornell University Press, 1979.

———. "Hints." In *The Works of Mary Wollstonecraft*, edited by Janet Todd and Marilyn Butler, 5:268–76. London: Pickering and Chatto, 1989.

———. *Letters Written in Sweden, Norway, and Denmark*. Edited by Tone Brekke and Jon Mee. Oxford: Oxford University Press, 2009.

———. "On Poetry." In *The Works of Mary Wollstonecraft*, edited by Janet Todd and Marilyn Butler, 7:3–11. London: Pickering and Chatto, 1989.

———. *A Vindication of the Rights of Woman.* Edited by Carol H. Poston. New York: Norton, 1975.

———. *The Wrongs of Woman.* In *"Mary" and "The Wrongs of Woman,"* edited by Gary Kelly, 63–178. Oxford: Oxford University Press, 2007.

Wordsworth, William. "By their floating Mill." In Gill, *William Wordsworth*, 325–26.

———. *The Excursion.* Edited by Sally Bushell, James A. Butler, and Michael C. Jaye. The Cornell Wordsworth. Ithaca, NY: Cornell University Press, 2007.

———. "Incipient Madness." In *Poems Written in Youth; Poems Referring to the Period of Childhood*, vol. 1 of *The Poetical Works of William Wordsworth*, edited by Ernest De Selincourt and Helen Darbishire, 314–16. Oxford: Oxford University Press, 1952.

———. "Lines written a few miles above Tintern Abbey." In Gill, *William Wordsworth*, 131–35.

———. MS JJ. Edited by Helen Darbishire. From Goslar to Grasmere, edited by Sally Bushell and Jeff Cowton, Lancaster University and the Wordsworth Trust, 2008. http://collections.wordsworth.org.uk/GtoG/home.asp?page=MSJJTheEarly Prelude.

———. "Nutting." In Gill, *William Wordsworth*, 153–54.

———. "Preface to *Lyrical Ballads*." In Gill, *William Wordsworth*, 595–615.

———. "Preface to *Poems*." In Gill, *William Wordsworth*, 626–39.

———. *The Prelude* (1805). In Gill, *William Wordsworth*, 375–590.

———. *The Prelude* (1850). In *Complete Poetical Works*, edited by Thomas Hutchinson and Ernest De Selincourt, 494–588. Oxford: Oxford University Press, 1936.

———. "The Ruined Cottage." In Gill, *William Wordsworth*, 31–44.

———. "A slumber did my spirit seal." In *Complete Poetical Works*, edited by Thomas Hutchinson and Ernest De Selincourt, 149. Oxford: Oxford University Press, 1936.

Wroe, Ann. "Shelley's Good Vibrations: His Marginal Notes to Hartley's *Observations on Man*." *Wordsworth Circle* 41 (2010): 36–41.

Yousef, Nancy. "Wollstonecraft, Rousseau, and the Revision of Romantic Subjectivity." *Studies in Romanticism* 38.4 (1999): 537–57.

Žižek, Slavoj. *In Defense of Lost Causes.* New York: Verso, 2009.

———. *Less Than Nothing: Hegel and the Shadow of Dialectical Materialism.* New York: Verso, 2013.

Zuckert, Rachel. *Kant on Beauty and Biology: An Interpretation of the "Critique of Judgment."* Cambridge: Cambridge University Press, 2007.

Index

Abrams, M. H.: on anthropomorphism, 71; biblical apocalypse, romantic reconception of, 90; on expression, 75; on Kant, 29; Marxist critical theory/romantic studies and, 2, 4, 7, 8–10, 29–30; *The Mirror and the Lamp* (1953), 8, 9, 13, 20, 122n11, 148n11; modernity, humanist narrative of, 25, 27, 124n52; on nature and imagination, 13–15, 17, 20, 23; Wordsworth's *Prelude* and, 33

Adonais (Shelley, 1821), 151n70

Adorno, Gretel, 123n24

Adorno, Theodor: on abstraction, 24–26, 27, 28, 127n113; de Man and, 19, 22; on education and civilization, 95; on form, 7, 12–13, 121n1, 123n37; Hartman and, 17; Hegel anticipating, 63; Marxist critical theory/romanticism and, 2–4, 7–13, 22–23, 127n113; on mimesis, 95; nature in thought of, 11–13, 25, 120n12; on phenomenology, 19, 126n84; Shelley and, 106, 111–12; Wordsworth and, 30–31, 33

Adorno, Theodor, works: *Aesthetic Theory* (1961–69/1970), 11–13, 123n35, 123n41, 123–24n43; *Dialectic of Enlightenment* (with Horkheimer, 1944/1969), 8, 24–26, 28, 30, 95, 123n24, 137n41, 138n44; "On Lyric Poetry and Society" (1957–58), 11, 123n43; "Parataxis: On Hölderlin's Late Poetry" (1963–65), 11, 123n38

Aeschylus, 116

Aesthetic Theory (Adorno, 1961–69/1970), 11–13, 123n35, 123n41, 123–24n43

Aesthetics (Hegel, 1835), 61

Agamben, Giorgio, 130n6, 133n48, 151n66

al-Azm, Sadiq Jalal, 131n16

Allison, Henry, 47

Alum Mine at Egeberg (Edy, 1820), 84

analogy, Kant on, 41–42, 45–47, 49–53, 132n34

Analytical Review, 73

anthropomorphism: de Man on, 71–72, 140n5; Wollstonecraft on, 5, 70–73, 76–78, 81–85

9 781503 628489